ICONS 2020

The Fifteenth International Conference on Systems

February 23 - 27, 2020

Lisbon, Portugal

ICONS 2020 Editors

Christoph Knieke, Technische Universität Clausthal, Institute for Software and Systems Engineering, Germany

Mo Mansouri University of South-Eastern Norway USA

Giulio Telleschi, MBDA, Italy

Printed from e-media with permission by:

Curran Associates, Inc.
57 Morehouse Lane
Red Hook, NY 12571

Some format issues inherent in the e-media version may also appear in this print version.

Printed with permission by Curran Associates, Inc. (2020)

International Academy, Research, and Industry Association (IARIA)
412 Derby Way
Wilmington, DE 19810

Phone: (408) 893-6407
Fax: (408) 527-6351

petre@iaria.org

Additional copies of this publication are available from:

Curran Associates, Inc.
57 Morehouse Lane
Red Hook, NY 12571 USA
Phone: 845-758-0400
Fax: 845-758-2633
Email: curran@proceedings.com
Web: www.proceedings.com

Table of Contents

ICONS 2020

Forward

The Fifteenth International Conference on Systems (ICONS 2020), held between February 23-27, 2020 in Lisbon, Portugal, continued a series of events covering a broad spectrum of topics, including fundamentals on designing, implementing, testing, validating and maintaining various kinds of software and hardware systems.

In the last years, new system concepts have been promoted and partially embedded in new deployments. Anticipative systems, autonomic and autonomous systems, self-adapting systems, or on-demand systems are systems exposing advanced features. These features demand special requirements specification mechanisms, advanced behavioral design patterns, special interaction protocols, and flexible implementation platforms. Additionally, they require new monitoring and management paradigms, as self-protection, self-diagnosing, self-maintenance become core design features.

The design of application-oriented systems is driven by application-specific requirements that have a very large spectrum. Despite the adoption of uniform frameworks and system design methodologies supported by appropriate models and system specification languages, the deployment of application-oriented systems raises critical problems. Specific requirements in terms of scalability, real-time, security, performance, accuracy, distribution, and user interaction drive the design decisions and implementations.

This leads to the need for gathering application-specific knowledge and develop particular design and implementation skills that can be reused in developing similar systems.
Validation and verification of safety requirements for complex systems containing hardware, software and human subsystems must be considered from early design phases. There is a need for rigorous analysis on the role of people and process causing hazards within safety-related systems; however, these claims are often made without a rigorous analysis of the human factors involved. Accurate identification and implementation of safety requirements for all elements of a system, including people and procedures become crucial in complex and critical systems, especially in safety-related projects from the civil aviation, defense health, and transport sectors.

Fundamentals on safety-related systems concern both positive (desired properties) and negative (undesired properties) aspects. Safety requirements are expressed at the individual equipment level and at the operational-environment level. However, ambiguity in safety requirements may lead to reliable unsafe systems. Additionally, the distribution of safety requirements between people and machines makes difficult automated proofs of system safety. This is somehow obscured by the difficulty of applying formal techniques (usually used for equipment-related safety requirements) to derivation and satisfaction of human-related safety requirements (usually, human factors techniques are used).

We welcomed academic, research and industry contributions. The conference had the following tracks:

- Complex and specialized systems
- Embedded systems and applications/services
- Computer vision and computer graphics
- Application-oriented systems

We take here the opportunity to warmly thank all the members of the ICONS 2020 technical program committee, as well as all the reviewers. The creation of such a high quality conference program would not have been possible without their involvement. We also kindly thank all the authors who dedicated much of their time and effort to contribute to ICONS 2020. We truly believe that, thanks to all these efforts, the final conference program consisted of top quality contributions.

We also thank the members of the ICONS 2020 organizing committee for their help in handling the logistics and for their work that made this professional meeting a success.

We hope that ICONS 2020 was a successful international forum for the exchange of ideas and results between academia and industry and to promote further progress in the area of systems. We also hope that Lisbon, Portugal provided a pleasant environment during the conference and everyone saved some time to enjoy the historic charm of the city.

ICONS 2020 Chairs

ICONS Steering Committee

Marko Jäntti, University of Eastern Finland, Finland
Zoubir Mammeri, IRIT - Paul Sabatier University, France
Raimund Ege, Northern Illinois University, USA
Mark Austin, University of Maryland at College Park, USA

ICONS 2020

Committee

ICONS Steering Committee

Marko Jäntti, University of Eastern Finland, Finland
Zoubir Mammeri, IRIT - Paul Sabatier University, France
Raimund Ege, Northern Illinois University, USA
Marc Austin, University Of Maryland, USA

ICONS 2020 Technical Program Committee

Qammer H. Abbasi, University of Glasgow, Scotland, UK
Witold Abramowicz, Poznan University of Economics, Poland
Abdelouhab Aitouche, YNCREA/HEI | University of Lille, France
Ali Al-Humairi, German University of Technology (GUtech), Oman
Mohammed Al-Khafajiy, Liverpool John Moores University, UK
Marc Austin, University Of Maryland, USA
Snježana Babić, Juraj DobrilaUniversityofPula, Croatia
Lubomir Bakule, Institute of Information Theory and Automation, Czech Republic
Suvadip Batabyal, BITS Pilani, Hyderabad Campus, India
Alejandro J. Bianchi, LIVEWARE S.A. / Universidad Catolica Argentina, Argentina
Francesco Bianconi, Università degli Studi di Perugia, Italy
Birthe Boehm, Siemens AG, Germany
Frédéric Bousefsaf, Université de Lorraine, France
Eugenio Brusa, Politecnico di Torino, Italy
Miriam A. Carlos Mancilla, Centro de investigación, Innovación y Desarrollo Tecnológico CIIDETEC- UVM, Mexico
Rachid Chelouah, Ecole Internationale des Sciences du Traitement de l'Information (EISTI), France
Dejiu Chen, KTH, Sweden
Albert M. K. Cheng, University of Houston, USA
François Coallier, École de technologie supérieure, Montreal, Canada
David Cordeau, XLIM UMR CNRS 7252 | University of Poitiers, France
Jacques Demongeot, University J. Fourier of Grenoble, France
Raimund Ege, Northern Illinois University, USA
Miguel Franklin, Universidade Federal do Ceará, Brazil
Marta Franova, CNRS & LRI & INRIA, France
Christos Gatzidis, Bournemouth University, UK
Mahadev Gawas, Vellore Institute of Technology (VIT), India
Laxmi Gewali, University of Nevada - Las Vegas (UNLV), USA
Ghayoor Gillani, University of Twente, Netherlands
Michael Grant, Johns Hopkins University School of Medicine, USA
Jan Haase, University of Lübeck, Germany
Marius Heinrichsmeyer, University of Wuppertal, Germany
Maryline Helard, INSA Rennes, France

Copyright Information

For your reference, this is the text governing the copyright release for material published by IARIA.

The copyright release is a transfer of publication rights, which allows IARIA and its partners to drive the dissemination of the published material. This allows IARIA to give articles increased visibility via distribution, inclusion in libraries, and arrangements for submission to indexes.

I, the undersigned, declare that the article is original, and that I represent the authors of this article in the copyright release matters. If this work has been done as work-for-hire, I have obtained all necessary clearances to execute a copyright release. I hereby irrevocably transfer exclusive copyright for this material to IARIA. I give IARIA permission or reproduce the work in any media format such as, but not limited to, print, digital, or electronic. I give IARIA permission to distribute the materials without restriction to any institutions or individuals. I give IARIA permission to submit the work for inclusion in article repositories as IARIA sees fit.

I, the undersigned, declare that to the best of my knowledge, the article is does not contain libelous or otherwise unlawful contents or invading the right of privacy or infringing on a proprietary right.

Following the copyright release, any circulated version of the article must bear the copyright notice and any header and footer information that IARIA applies to the published article.

IARIA grants royalty-free permission to the authors to disseminate the work, under the above provisions, for any academic, commercial, or industrial use. IARIA grants royalty-free permission to any individuals or institutions to make the article available electronically, online, or in print.

IARIA acknowledges that rights to any algorithm, process, procedure, apparatus, or articles of manufacture remain with the authors and their employers.

I, the undersigned, understand that IARIA will not be liable, in contract, tort (including, without limitation, negligence), pre-contract or other representations (other than fraudulent misrepresentations) or otherwise in connection with the publication of my work.

Exception to the above is made for work-for-hire performed while employed by the government. In that case, copyright to the material remains with the said government. The rightful owners (authors and government entity) grant unlimited and unrestricted permission to IARIA, IARIA's contractors, and IARIA's partners to further distribute the work.

A Systemic Look at the Norwegian Health Care System with Focus on Gestational Diabetes Mellitus

Ellen Veronica Bjørkkjær
University of South-Eastern Norway
Kongsberg, Norway
e-mail: vero.bjorkkjar@hotmail.com

Mo Mansouri
University of South-Eastern Norway
Kongsberg, Norway
e-mail: momansouri@gmail.com

Abstract—**The human is a complex machine and the health care system is the mechanic hired to maintain and repair both the hardware and software. External forces are constantly pushing out ``software-updates'', ``bugs'' and ``viruses'' affecting the human being in different ways. Finding the best way to treat a patient is challenging without knowing the patients background story. That story is formed from the moment the patient is born and is pushed in different directions by various sources. Family, friends, teachers, strangers, media, and for the last 15 years or so, social media, are all contributors to shaping the mind of a young individual. This paper looks closer at the physiological and psychological causes and effects of diagnosing pregnant women with Gestational Diabetes Mellitus (GDM), and the authors reflect and discuss how the Norwegian health care system can treat the condition in a way that supports individuality and complexity. Diseases that are correlated with certain lifestyles are frequently mentioned in media, often as warnings or motivation for a healthy lifestyle. However, the reasons for getting these diseases are more complex than usually presented. The entire fault is put on the individual's ability to live healthy, which is an unfair burden that may again result in low self-esteem and poor lifestyle choices. Systems thinking tools such as the conceptagon and systemigram are utilized in an attempt to capture the complexity of the problem and the system most suitable for solving it.**

Keywords – Systems thinking; Health information management; Systems engineering; Clinical diagnosis, Psychology

I. INTRODUCTION

Gestational Diabetes Mellitus (GDM) is a diagnosis seen in between 6-11% of pregnant Norwegian women [1]. Hormones due to the pregnancy causes the insulin to have lower effect and if the body is not able to compensate for this, the blood sugar levels may rise above a defined limit. The reason why the body is not able to compensate for the increased need for insulin is not well documented, but factors such as genetics, lifestyle, obesity, age, ethnicity and environment are often mentioned [2], [3]. The combination of these factors determines the risk of developing this condition. Most of the literature focus on the technical causes and effects of being diagnosed with GDM [4]–[6], while the psychological effects are not considered to the same degree. It is reasonable to assume that receiving such a diagnose will have some effect on the wellbeing of the patient, in addition to the frequent need for blood sugar monitoring and potential medication. In today's society, a person diagnosed with any kind of diabetes will automatically be exposed to some degree of stigma. The word diabetes is often correlated with laziness, low self-discipline and unhealthy eating. Many people will choose not to share the diagnosis with their surroundings, which may influence how well they are able to manage the condition. When a pregnant woman is diagnosed with GDM without receiving sufficient information from the doctor she will probably try to acquire the information herself. The Internet is overflowing with relevant, irrelevant, correct and incorrect information, which can be challenging to filter, and the patient may end up being stressed and worried. The purpose of this paper is to illustrate the complexity of the GDM diagnosis. By using systems thinking tools, the authors can look at the current gestational diabetes research from a new perspective. The Norwegian health care system is treated as the System of Interest (SoI), while the patient is seen as a stakeholder. The authors have used system engineering tools, such as the conceptagon and systemigram to create the models that are presented in section II. A research study of causes and effects of being diagnosed with GDM has been performed by the authors in section III before adding own reflections in section IV, and conclusion and further work in section V.

II. MATERIALS AND METHODS

In order to analyze, synthesize and inquire the system of interest, a framework called conceptagon is utilized and described in the next subsections. A systemigram is developed and presented to identify the relationships and activities between the SoI and its stakeholders. Both the conceptagon and systemigram are included in the systems engineering toolkit and are helpful when striving to achieve a holistic view of a problem or system, according to the methodology done in other domains [7]–[10].

A. Conceptagon

The conceptagon [11] is a framework for applied systems thinking. Its purpose is to present different concepts in a common language that system experts with different backgrounds can understand. The conceptagon, consisting of the SoI in the center and seven triples distributed around it, is shown in Figure 1. The triples each include three concepts that are known as fundamental terms in several disciplines. During the next paragraphs, the authors describe the SoI through each of the concepts shown in the conceptagon.

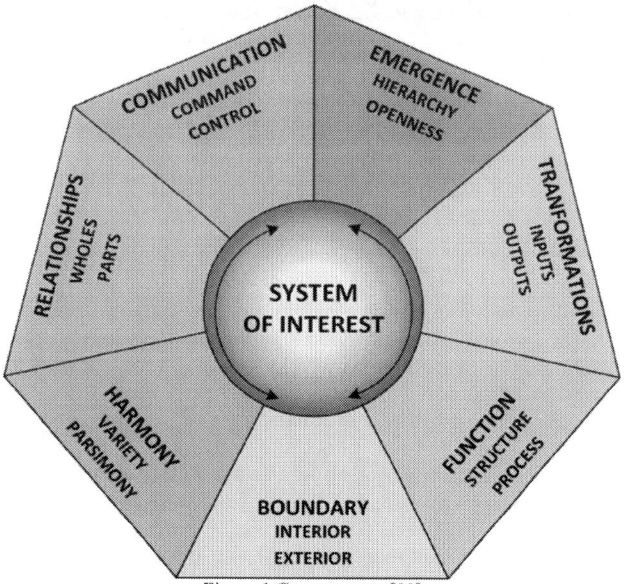

Figure 1 Conceptagon [11]

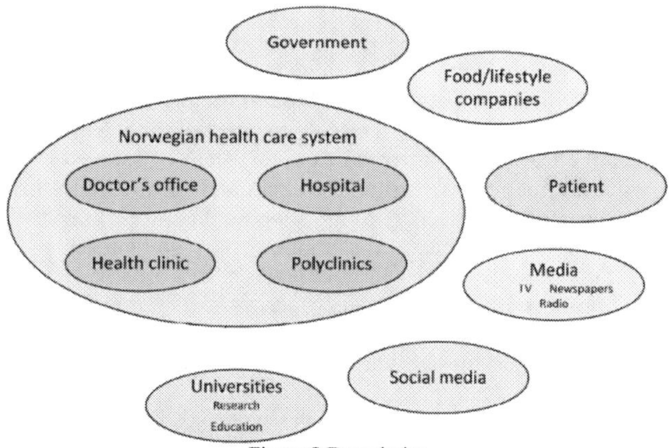

Figure 2 Boundaries

1) Boundary: The boundaries are defined by identifying the interior and the exterior of the SoI and are crucial for understanding what the SoI consists of. The interior includes factors that the SoI have control over and that is relevant to the problem presented in this paper, while the exterior identifies factors that must be taken into account. The SoI may be able to impact the external factors, but does not have control over them. Figure 2 presents the interior and exterior of the SoI. The Norwegian health care system is split into several divisions with different functions. The doctor's office is where the patient have their check ups and regular visits; the health clinic gives support to women during their pregnancy and follow up kids with check ups and vaccines; the hospitals treats serious and acute illness; and the polyclinics treat patients that are in need of specialists. The government is shown as part of the exterior of the SoI. The Norwegian health care system is funded by the government. Universities often collaborate with the Norwegian health care system to get support from specialists and to stay on top of what kind of research is needed. Food and lifestyle companies, such as food producers and gyms, are often driven by a need to make money. They have an indirect impact on the SoI by affecting the patients in one direction or the other. The patient is also seen as part of the exterior and giving the patient the best care possible is the main purpose of the SoI. Media and social media are, like the food/lifestyle companies indirectly affecting the SoI by pushing unfiltered information, commercials, research, opinions and warnings on the patient.

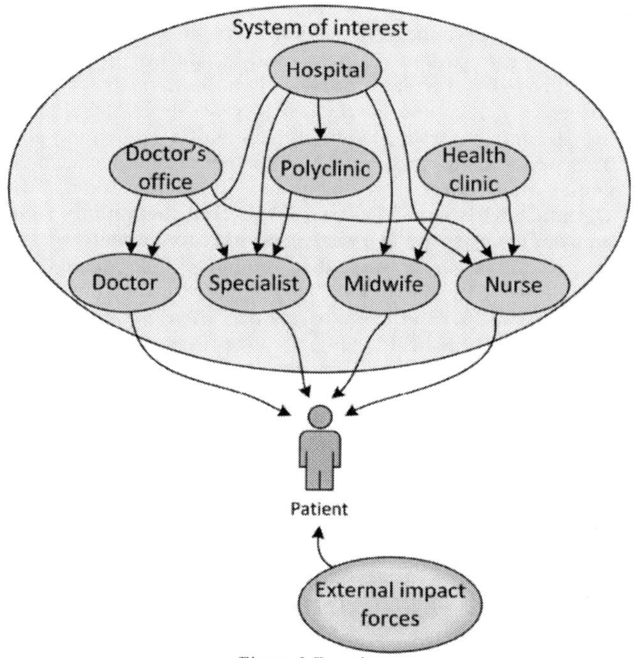

Figure 3 Functions

2) Function: As described in paragraph 1), the different divisions of the SoI have different functions. As illustrated in Figure 3, the patient will receive support and information from at least four different functions in the Norwegian health care system. The employees are stationed at different locations and use different computer systems. The patient needs to bring what is called a "health card" to each appointment, which is a piece of paper that the doctor, nurse, midwife or specialist fills out after each visit. Due to strict laws against sharing personal data, information cannot automatically be shared with other parts of the health care system in all cases.

3) Transformations: A system should always transform the given input to a desired output. Figure 4 shows that the patient gives input to the Norwegian health care system in form of body measurements (weight, height, etc.), test materials (blood, urin, saliva), personal history and reflections. The health care systems are tasked to use the given input to provide the patient a diagnose, suitable treatment, relevant information and necessary support.

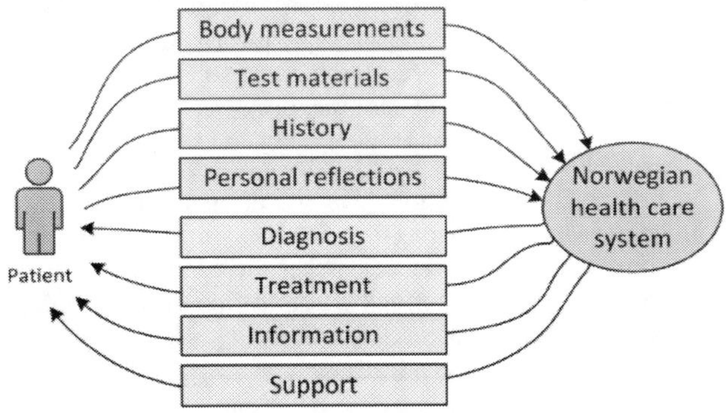

Figure 4 Transformations

4) Emergence: The Norwegian health care system is dependent on using reliable tools and cannot afford to be pioneers in using new technology. Machines, computer systems and medicine must all be certified to meet appropriate standards. The consequences of failure can be fatal. Introducing new medicine or treatment methods will therefore take time before it is approved and considered safe.

5) Communication: The divisions in the Norwegian health care system that is in focus during this paper are funded by the state or the county. Hospitals and polyclinics that are funded by the state will be able to offer more equal treatment throughout the country. The doctor's office and health clinics that are founded by each county might offer different services and level of support from county to county. Each facility has control over themselves, after complying with certain requirements, but the funding has an impact on the possibilities.

6) Relationships: To best support the patient, all parts of the system should work as a whole. The constantly increasing use of technology in todays society introduces a world of opportunities to integrate systems and share information. Despite this, the different functions in the Norwegian health care system are not sharing information in an effective manner. Security and restrictions for sharing personal data sets limitations and slows down the "digitalization". Today the patient needs to bring a "health card" to each appointment. After being diagnosed with GDM at the doctors office, she needs to bring her "health card" to the health center and the ultrasound appointments and describe to them what the status is.

7) Harmony: The Norwegian health care system offers a large variety of services. As shown in Figure 5, the different functions are funded by different parts of the Norwegian government. The allocated resources for the different functions may therefore vary. The functions that are covered by the county are often low on resources, while the functions covered by the state have stricter requirements for resource allocation.

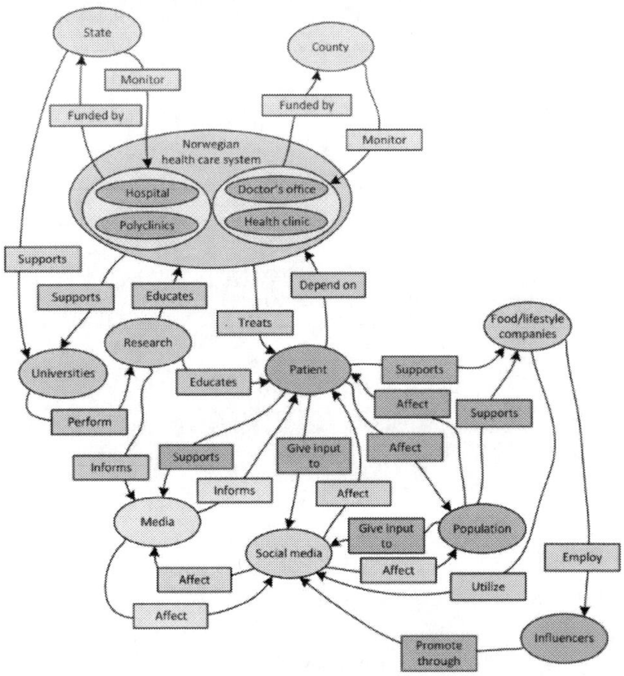

Figure 5 Systemigram

B. Systemigram

Identifying stakeholders and the relationship between them is useful to obtain a holistic view. Figure 5 presents a systemigram where the system of interest, its stakeholders and the relationships are identified. As illustrated, the patient is affected by a number of other stakeholders that cannot be controlled by the system of interest (SoI). It is important to identify these and acknowledge their presence. In that way, the health care system can develop means to reduce the negative effects these external factors may have on the patients.

III. RESEARCH STUDY

While gathering research, the authors aimed to answer the following three questions:

- What are the risk factors for being diagnosed with GDM?
- What are the potential physiological effects for the woman and baby?
- What are the potential psychological effects for the woman and what can these result in?

A. Developing GDM

6-11% of pregnant Norwegian women are diagnosed with GDM [1]. The reasons for developing the condition are complex and not fully documented. What is known is that during a pregnancy, the hormones released in the body reduces the effectiveness of the insulin. In most cases the body is able to increase the insulin production sufficiently, but in other cases not. Factors that increases the risk of developing GDM are [12]:

- Glucosuria
- Family history of type 2 diabetes or GDM
- History of unexplained fetal demise
- High age
- Obesity

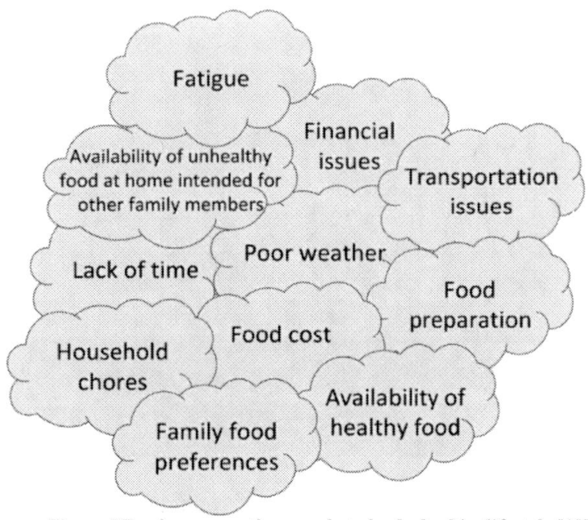

Figure 6 Barriers preventing people to lead a healthy lifestyle [13]

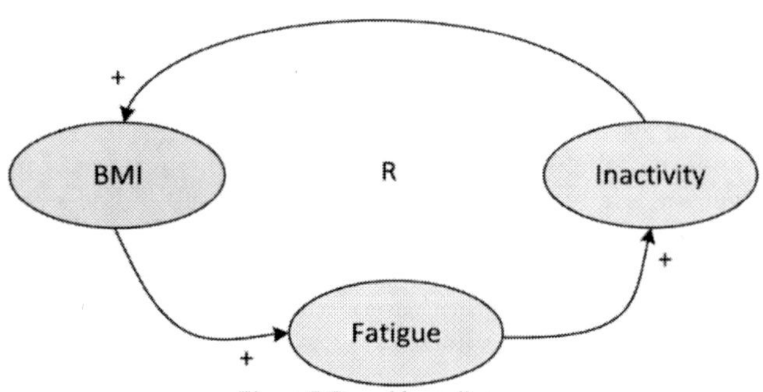

Figure 7 Causal loop diagram

If we look at the last point, obesity, which is the factor that is often in focus, the causes for this are again complex. Three commonly known factors for developing a high BMI are:

- Lifestyle
- Genetics
- Environment

When eating too much and/or unhealthy food and performing little exercise, the body will gain weight. How much and in what rate may depend on genetics. How to stop the obesity epidemic, that is frequently mentioned in the news these days, is not a question with a straightforward answer. The media's focus and the "black and white" attitude of some people may be a contributing factor to the problem rather than the solution. Devsam et al. [13] mentions some barriers preventing people to lead a healthy lifestyle. These are illustrated in Figure 6. Barriers such as fatigue may also be observed as an effect of unhealthy lifestyle choices, resulting in a downward spiral that is hard to come out of. The reinforcing causal loop diagram in Figure 7 illustrates this phenomenon.

B. Physiological effects of GDM

GDM is a condition that is usually limited to the pregnancy. A well-managed condition will not contribute to any dangerous consequences, but if the condition is not well managed the risk of serious complications for the baby, as listed below, may increase significantly [14]:

- High gestational birth weight
- Overall metabolic complications
- Stillbirth
- Shoulder dystocia

Similarly, if the condition is poorly managed, consequences for the mother may be [15]:

- Hypertension
- Cesarean delivery
- Risk of developing diabetes type 2 later in life

A positive outcome of receiving the diagnosis is actually that many women are able to change their lifestyle during pregnancy and able to maintain the new lifestyle after giving birth [16].

C. Psychological effects of GDM

Evans and O'Brien say in their paper [17]:

> *"The implication that impending motherhood is a condition of risk or peril that requires 'surveillance, control, and intervention at any sign of deviation from normal' might undermine one's self-identity and desired level of autonomy as a pregnant woman."*

Even a normal pregnancy introduces new thoughts, worries and changes to the body that in themselves can be overwhelming. Being informed about abnormalities can add unnecessary stress and worry. Several studies have been conducted on this topic and a common conclusion of most of these studies are that the women diagnosed with GDM have more negative emotions attached to their pregnancy and health than women without the diagnosis. Devsam et al. [13] conducted a study where they gathered the initial responses from women who was diagnosed with GDM, before proposing a framework to enhance midwifery assessment. The initial responses are presented in Figure 8. The guilt could be related to not taking better care of themselves, staying in a stressful job or having the baby late in life. The women repeatedly asked questions about the causes of their condition and often blamed themselves for it [13], [18]. They also had negative reactions as to how to control the condition, as shown in Figure 9.

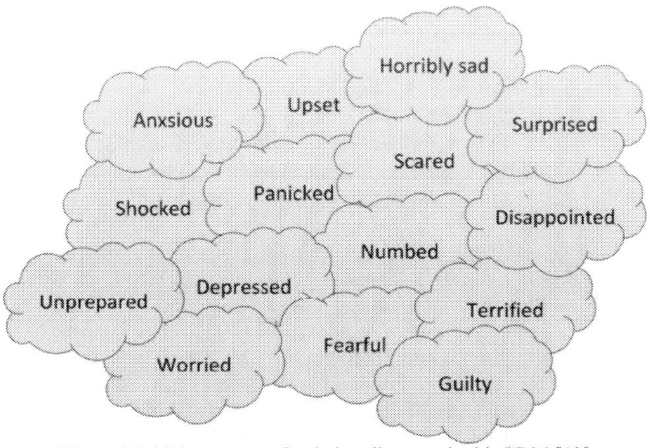

Figure 8 Initial response after being diagnosed with GDM [13]

Figure 9 Reactions on how to manage GDM [13]

IV. Reflection and Discussion

Is the benefits of testing, diagnosing and treating pregnant women with GDM outweighing the negative psychological implications the diagnosis may have on the individuals? Jarrett [19] writes in his paper that:

> *"The association between blood glucose concentrations and fetal weight is lost when adjustment is made for maternal weight and age."*

He also states that:

> *"The women with gestational diabetes in the original Boston studies had higher perinatal mortality, though the difference was not statistically significant, and the published analyses did not sufficiently examine the potential confounding variables, of which age and obesity were the most obvious."*

This implicates that the GDM diagnosis itself is not causing the complications, and may only introduce extra stress to the patient. There is however reason to believe that receiving the diagnosis may have positive impact on the patient's ability to change their lifestyle. According to Sjøgren et al. [16] 34% of the women included in their study that was diagnosed with GDM were able to stick to a healthy diet also after pregnancy. Egeland et al. [20] states that GDM does introduce higher risk of adverse perinatal outcomes. Detection and control of the diagnosis will help reduce these risks, but how can the health care system best treat and support the women receiving the diagnosis? As several studies show, the psychological impact on the patient is significant and should not be underestimated. Lawson et al. [18] states that women experience fear, depression and anxiety. It is important that the patient receives relevant and correct information immediately after the diagnosis has been set, to outweigh the often "one-sided" information introduced by the media. As described by Devsam et al. [13], Swedish women experienced a two weeks gap between receiving the diagnosis and having the first appointment at the specialized diabetes clinic where they had to seek information from books and the Internet in between. During the appointment with the specialist, their concerns were reduced. This implies that it is beneficial to reserve some time after the glucose intolerance test to properly inform and support the women that is diagnosed with GDM.

V. Conclusion

The first part of the paper presents the health care system as the system of interest by using different systems thinking tools. The purpose of using these tools is to illustrate the complexity of the system of interest and the gestational diabetes diagnosis in an understandable way. The last part of the paper discusses the physiological and psychological aspects of the diagnosis before discussing the positive and negative effects of being diagnosed. Even though the research is pointing in different directions regarding the potential consequences of GDM, the diagnosis can be a wakeup call that motivates the patient to adopt a healthier lifestyle. The psychological implications should not be underestimated, but considered to a greater extent in the health care system. Giving thorough information as close to the diagnosing as possible should be prioritized to avoid a long period where the patient seeks information that may turn out irrelevant or incorrect. Some future work could be a research study investigating if rapid and thorough information reduces the negative psychological effects on the patient. Such a study may give the health care system motivation to prioritize giving the information earlier. Another interesting case for future work would be using systems thinking methods, such as the conceptagon and systemigram, to identify which factors have the most positive and negative impact on the psychology of the patient. This may contribute to finding focus areas for information flow.

REFERENCES

[1] D. N. Legeforeningen, "New guidelines for gestational diabetes mellitus - https://legeforeningen.no/Fagmed/Norsk-gynekologisk-forening/Nyheter/20171/Endelig-nye-retningslinjer-for-svangerskapsdiabetes/."

[2] X. Xiong, L. D. Saunders, F. L. Wang, and N. N. Demianczuk, "Gestational diabetes mellitus: prevalence, risk factors, maternal and infant outcomes," *Int. J. Gynecol. Obstet.*, vol. 75, no. 3, pp. 221–228, Dec. 2001, doi: 10.1016/S0020-7292(01)00496-9.

[3] C. J. Petry, "Gestational diabetes: risk factors and recent advances in its genetics and treatment," *Br. J. Nutr.*, vol. 104, no. 6, pp. 775–787, Sep. 2010, doi: 10.1017/S0007114510001741.

[4] E. A. Reece, "The fetal and maternal consequences of gestational diabetes mellitus," *J. Matern. Neonatal Med.*, vol. 23, no. 3, pp. 199–203, Mar. 2010, doi: 10.3109/14767050903550659.

[5] R. Kaaja and T. Rönnemaa, "Gestational Diabetes: Pathogenesis and Consequences to Mother and Offspring," *Rev. Diabet. Stud.*, vol. 5, no. 4, pp. 194–202, 2008, doi: 10.1900/RDS.2008.5.194.

[6] P. Damm, A. Houshmand-Oeregaard, L. Kelstrup, J. Lauenborg, E. R. Mathiesen, and T. D. Clausen, "Gestational diabetes mellitus and long-term consequences for mother and offspring: a view from Denmark," *Diabetologia*, vol. 59, no. 7, pp. 1396–1399, Jul. 2016, doi: 10.1007/s00125-016-3985-5.

[7] M. Mansouri, A. Gorod, T. H. Wakeman, and B. Sauser, "Maritime Transportation System of Systems management framework: a System of Systems Engineering approach," *Int. J. Ocean Syst. Manag.*, vol. 1, no. 2, p. 200, 2009, doi: 10.1504/IJOSM.2009.030185.

[8] N. Khansari, M. Mansouri, and A. Mostashari, "The conceptual models of energy behavior and energy behavioral change," in *2015 IEEE Conference on Technologies for Sustainability (SusTech)*, 2015, pp. 109–112, doi: 10.1109/SusTech.2015.7314331.

[9] B. A. Normann and M. Mansouri, "School Shootings in the U.S. – Where to Begin," in *Complex Systems Design & Management*, Cham: Springer International Publishing, 2020, pp. 103–116.

[10] C. Caches and M. Mansouri, "Applications of Systems Thinking for Scooter Sharing Transportation System," in *Complex Systems Design & Management*, Cham: Springer International Publishing, 2020, pp. 192–192.

[11] J. Boardman, B. Sauser, L. John, and R. Edson, "The conceptagon: A framework for systems thinking and systems practice," in *2009 IEEE International Conference on Systems, Man and Cybernetics*, 2009, pp. 3299–3304, doi: 10.1109/ICSMC.2009.5346211.

[12] E. A. Reece, G. Leguizamón, and A. Wiznitzer, "Gestational diabetes: the need for a common ground," *Lancet*, vol. 373, no. 9677, pp. 1789–1797, May 2009, doi: 10.1016/S0140-6736(09)60515-8.

[13] B. U. Devsam, F. E. Bogossian, and A. S. Peacock, "An interpretive review of women's experiences of gestational diabetes mellitus: Proposing a framework to enhance midwifery assessment," *Women and Birth*, vol. 26, no. 2, pp. e69–e76, Jun. 2013, doi: 10.1016/j.wombi.2012.12.003.

[14] O. Langer, Y. Yogev, O. Most, and E. M. J. Xenakis, "Gestational diabetes: The consequences of not treating," *Am. J. Obstet. Gynecol.*, vol. 192, no. 4, pp. 989–997, Apr. 2005, doi: 10.1016/j.ajog.2004.11.039.

[15] B. Casey, "Pregnancy Outcomes in Women With Gestational Diabetes Compared With the General Obstetric Population," *Obstet. Gynecol.*, vol. 90, no. 6, pp. 869–873, Dec. 1997, doi: 10.1016/S0029-7844(97)00542-5.

[16] B. Sjögren, N. Robeus, and U. Hansson, "Gestational diabetes: A case-control study of women's experience of pregnancy, health and the child," *J. Psychosom. Res.*, vol. 38, no. 8, pp. 815–822, Nov. 1994, doi: 10.1016/0022-3999(94)90069-8.

[17] M. K. Evans and B. O'Brien, "Gestational Diabetes: The Meaning of an At-Risk Pregnancy," *Qual. Health Res.*, vol. 15, no. 1, pp. 66–81, Jan. 2005, doi: 10.1177/1049732304270825.

[18] E. J. Lawson and S. Rajaram, "A transformed pregnancy: the psychosocial consequences of gestational diabetes.," *Sociol. Heal. Illn.*, vol. 16, no. 4, pp. 536–562, Sep. 1994, doi: 10.1111/1467-9566.ep11347644.

[19] R. J. Jarrett, "Gestational diabetes: a non-entity?," *BMJ*, vol. 306, no. 6869, pp. 37–38, Jan. 1993, doi: 10.1136/bmj.306.6869.37.

[20] G. M. Egeland, R. Skjarven, and L. M. Irgens, "Birth characteristics of women who develop gestational diabetes: population based study," *BMJ*, vol. 321, no. 7260, pp. 546–547, Sep. 2000, doi: 10.1136/bmj.321.7260.546.

Validation of a Failure-Cause Searching and Solution-Finding Algorithm in Production based on Complaint Information from the Use Phase

Validation using an industrial example from the field of precision machining and cold forming

Nadine Schlüter
University of Wuppertal
Product Safety and Quality Engineering
Wuppertal, Germany
Email: schlueter@uni-wuppertal.de

Marius Heinrichsmeyer
University of Wuppertal
Product Safety and Quality Engineering
Wuppertal, Germany
Email: heinrichsmeyer@uni-wuppertal.de

Fynn Kösling
University of Wuppertal
Product Safety and Quality Engineering
Wuppertal, Germany
Email: fynn.koesling-hk@uni-wuppertal.de

Amirbabak Ansari
University of Wuppertal
Product Safety and Quality Engineering
Wuppertal, Germany
Email: aansari@uni-wuppertal.de

Abstract — **Nowadays, constantly increasing demands on products lead to great opportunities, but also major challenges. Complaint management, in particular, is also affected by this, as the high complexity of products and production systems can often lead to failures. In connection with digitalization, companies face the challenge of having to handle complex and extensive information. In the field of complaint management, not only the amount of information increase but also the number of sources, channels, formats, etc. While the companies act more and more globally and digitally, the complaint management in German mechanical engineering is still predominantly carried out manually. In order to improve the processing time and the analysis of complaints, as well as to implement the automated processing of complaint information, the fundamental research project FusLa [funding code: SCHL 2225/1-1] funded by the German Research Foundation (DFG) was launched. The aim is to develop an algorithm that automates the evaluation of relevant complaint information from different types of complaint texts. This paper evaluates the functionality of the algorithm in the context of a validation example from the field of precision machining and cold forming.**

Keywords-Algorithm; Complaint Management; Business Process Re-Engineering for Manufacturing; Decision Support

I. INTRODUCTION

Due to the increasing internationalization of our time, the complexity of products and their producing companies is constantly increasing. The need for a higher individualization of products inevitably leads to new challenges for the company's requirements management, as product requirements become more and more complex [1]. Although this increases the opportunities on the market, it also means that the failure risks increase significantly. Therefore, a direct relationship exists between the complexity of a product and the failures that occur. An increasing number of complaints automatically accompanies an increasing number of failures. Complaints mean additional costs for a company, which have to be minimized in the context of increasing complexity.

To eliminate failures and thus avoid complaints, companies rely on different approaches, including the software-supported 8D report. However, these approaches show numerous weaknesses when it comes to dealing with the complexity that prevails in production systems. There is no model integration that enables the traceability of causes of failure within the production system. To process the flow of information generated by complaints and master the complexity of the production system it is necessary to use a model approach. For this particular problem, the current approaches, as demonstrated in section II, reach their limits or do not yet focus on complaint management. In order to solve this problem, an algorithm based on the current state of the art was developed [2] and validated in the industry. In the following section II, this paper deals with the current state of the art and examines which findings have been gained in science as well as in industry with regard to failure-cause searching and solution-finding based on complaint information. Within the framework of this paper, future-oriented approaches will mainly be considered and examined for interfaces to the topic. Section III describes the developed algorithm with its functions and methods as well as the applied validation. Finally, the results of the validation carried out previously are being used for an evaluation in section IV. Moreover, it gives an outlook for upcoming research fields.

II. STATE OF THE ART

Considering the field of science, there are some research projects that focus on failure-cause searching and solution-finding in production systems. However, it turned out that these research projects either are not related to complaint management, do not function algorithm-based and thus are not automated, or just subjective evaluations take place. At this point, some of the already published works of the research group Product Safety and Quality Engineering can be referenced, which have already dealt with this topic and in which the current state of science and technology has been analyzed in detail. These include the ICONS 2019 Paper [3]. In addition, the state of the art was examined in detail in the

GQW Paper 2019 [4] for the probing as well as in the QMOD 2019 Papers [5] for the prioritization and in [6] for the failure cause localization of the algorithm. In this paper, the focus shall be on the future-oriented approaches and validation of the algorithm in the sense of an extension of the previous publications. These are explained and examined in the following. Especially at the present time, the relevance of Artificial Intelligence (AI) for the processing of large amounts of information is increasing. However, a distinction must be made between AI, big data, and Machine to Machine communications (M2M) [7]. AI has the goal to enable cognitive-like functions of a machine to analyze and interpret data and to solve problems on this basis. It is, therefore, a better fit for decision making [8]. The purpose of big data, however, is to process and analyze large amounts of data and a large variety of data in order to achieve a specific result. That means that the potential of AI in the area of complaint management is enormous in order to be able to react to failures and eliminate them. AI could develop the possibility to learn from known complaint information in order to be able to exert a preventive effect and prevent future complaints. In order to analyze how far the current future-oriented approaches are when dealing with the mentioned problem, some service platforms were examined and evaluated for this purpose. The investigated platforms are IBM Watson Compare & Comply [9], Apache Spark [10], Amazon Comprehend [11], Microsoft Analytics Platform System [12], Google BigQuery [13], PrediCX [14], CEMax [15], and Adobe Analytics [16]. All these platforms work based on machine learning. They are able to identify, structure, analyze, and evaluate information in text sources. This would also make them suitable for processing complaint texts if they were programmed for this purpose. However, the evaluation of the platforms showed that the analyzed platforms are currently not able to perform a comprehensive failure-cause search and solution-finding in production based on information from the use phase. However, it is necessary to develop such applications in order to deal with the ever-increasing complexity of production systems. In order to enable the use in complaint management, concepts are needed that define how the service platforms are to deal with complaints and which information is relevant. At the same time, such a concept can provide the procedure for failure-cause search and solution-finding for the platform.

III. Functionality And Validation Of The Algorithm

The algorithm for failure-cause search and solution-finding was developed after the acquisition of various requirements regarding the current state of science and technology. These requirements led to the fact that the algorithm had to consist of the following modules:

- information probing of complaint information [4]
- prioritization of complaint information [5]
- localization of failure-causes [6] and
- solution-finding for failure-causes.

A. *Functionality of the Algorithm*

As can be seen, the complaint information from the use phase of the product is accessed and filtered within the information probing, so that only the relevant information is being used further. Relevant information can be, e.g., product names, company name, technical drawing number, etc. That information is then being used by the algorithm to determine across several dimensions within the prioritization which complaint has the highest priority. Thereby necessary resources, such as time, personnel or costs can be used in the best possible way for the failure-cause localization. The basis for failure-cause localization is a previously developed model of the corresponding production system. Here, correlations between the essential views of the production systems are stored according to the eDeCoDe model (enhanced Demand Compliant Design) developed by Winzer [17] and Nicklas [18]. These views can be, e.g., components, functions, processes, persons or requirements. An example of such a model of a production system is shown in Figure 1 below. This Figure visualizes all relationships of R1.2, i.e., requirement 1.2 has relationships to the other requirements, functions, processes, persons, and components.

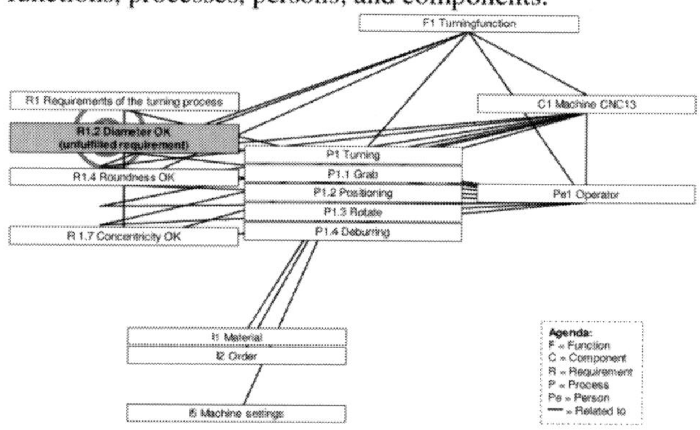

Figure 1. Example of a model of a production system according to [17].

With the help of this model, the algorithm is able to make assumptions based on probabilities about which part of the production system is responsible for the failure that led to the complaint. Once the cause of the failure has been localized, a possible solution will be found by pointing out the necessary measures. This is based on the STOP principle, whereby substitutional, technical, organizational and person-related measures can be offered [19]. Once the measure has been determined, it is up to the producing company to implement it, adapt it, or not use it at all. Due to the focus of the paper, a more detailed description of the algorithm is deliberately omitted. A detailed explanation of the theoretical concept of the algorithm can be found in the papers IEEE QR2MSE [2] and ICONS 2019 [3] published by the research group Product Safety and Quality. After the theoretical concept was completely developed, the algorithm was programmed with Microsoft Office - Visual Basic Application (VBA) and turned into a usable software. In section B of this chapter, the validation using an industrial example is described and evaluated in detail.

B. Validation in Industry

The validation in the industry is used to determine whether the algorithm provides meaningful information and assessments and how the different quality of the complaint information affects the results of the algorithm. At this point in the project, only the feasibility of the theoretical concept and also the effect of the quality of complaints on the result of the algorithm have been examined. A long-term study to measure the performance of the algorithm has not yet been carried out but is planned for the future. While the current validations were only carried out based on a requirement evaluation, the time, cost and personnel expenditure of the algorithm should also be measured and evaluated as parameters in the coming months. This should also contribute to the reproducibility of the results and transparency of the evaluation. Starting with the validation, the company of the industry example will be presented. In order to preserve the anonymity of the company and to protect internal know-how, all company-related information was deliberately concealed. The validation was carried out using the example of a company in the field of precision machining and cold forming. This area is used among other things for the production of strain-hardened and cold-formed parts, e.g., shafts or spindles, which are predominantly manufactured for the automotive industry. This industrial example is noteworthy because the complaint handling is subject to the high standards of the automotive industry. This demonstrates that the algorithm can meet such high standards. In order that the algorithm can carry useful results for the failure cause searching and solution-finding, it was first necessary to create the appropriate information basis. This means that first, all necessary customer information, product information, or order information had to be localized and then a model of the production system had to be created and also prepared for access as part of the evaluation. In this paper, this process is referred to as "preparation for validation". This is essential because it cannot be assumed that a company has all the necessary information in the required format.

1) Preparation for Validation

The preparation of the validation was divided into three steps. In the first step, all information systems of the company were examined for available information about customers, products, and orders. Since the company used very different systems for the respective information, the required information was prepared by the algorithm in Excel sheets and compiled for evaluation. This meant that it was not necessary to program the interfaces for each specific information system. However, at this point, it should be noted that for the practical implementation of the algorithm in industry, exactly such an interface to the existing information systems of the respective company must be programmed and set up by software developers. After the successful mapping of the information systems, in a second step, a model of the socio-technical production system with the eDeCoDe approach was developed. Besides the use of existing documents (e.g., technical drawings, test plans) and the discussion with the process managers of the company as well as the testing, this industrial example offered the possibility to go through all processes for the claimed product systematically with the production manager. It allowed to link the requirements, components, functions, and persons. This not only contributed to a better understanding of the connections within the company but also showed that the company was very interested in the implementation. The correlations between the elements were mapped using Design Structure and Domain Mapping matrices. The result of the collaboration was a production system that comprised 69 requirements for a product under complaint, 21 functions, 22 processes (25 inputs/11 outputs) as well as 11 components and 9 persons involved. With the acquisition of the production system and the associated system elements, the third step in the preparation of the validation could take place. This clearly defined the relationships between the type and importance of the failure and the previously collected requirements. This step is necessary in order to determine for the algorithm which type of failure is the non-fulfilled requirement and what significance this non-fulfillment has. In order not to manipulate the result of the algorithm with regard to the evaluation of a non-fulfilled requirement, the definition of the relationships was discussed based on documents (e.g., Failure Mode and Effects Analysis) and in conversation with the company's experts (e.g., production/complaint management). The result of this elaboration is two matrices for the correlations between the requirements to be fulfilled and the type of failure as well as the significance of the failure. After the three steps for the preparation of the validation had been completed, the actual validation of the algorithm could take place. The validation was based on a very detailed customer complaint relating to an unfulfilled requirement for the SGW product. The SGW product is usually installed in passenger cars and is a critical component of safety. In this case, the complaint text was available in digital form so that it was possible to transfer the complaint text to the intended surface within a few seconds (Figure 3).

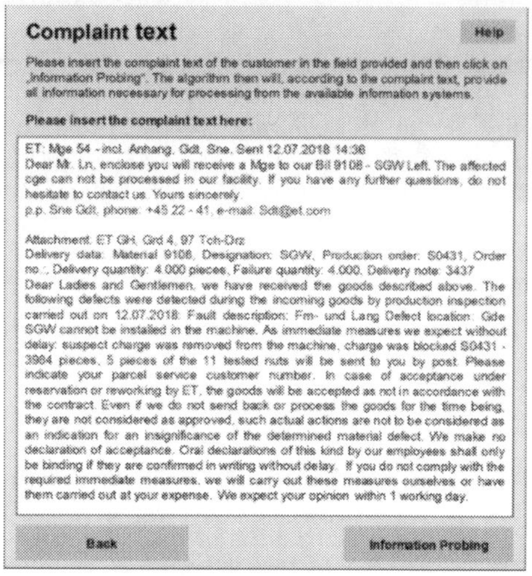

Figure 2. Complaint text of the product SGW according to [20]

2) Information probing of the complaints

Based on the present complaint text, the algorithm recognized the first and last name, organization, and address of the customer and transferred them, as shown in Figure 3, to the fields provided for this purpose in the surface of the information probing.

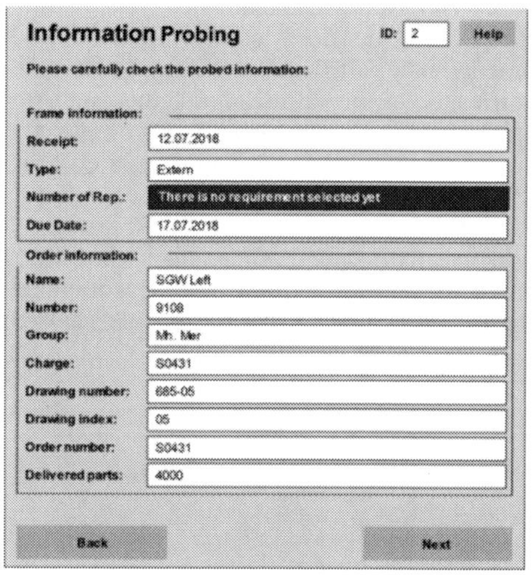

Figure 3. Information probing of the complaints of the product SGW according to [20]

With the help of this information, the algorithm filled in the other fields within the interface. In addition to collecting the date information, the algorithm was also able to identify relevant complaint information relating to the product. The algorithm not only correctly examined its name but also its number, group, and drawing details. The number of products delivered could also be determined via the interface to the ordering system and entered in the field provided for this purpose. Despite the more detailed failure description in the complaint text, this step showed that the algorithm could not assign exactly which unfulfilled requirement was actually involved. Although the algorithm recognizes the product and thus assigns all recorded product requirements to the unfulfilled requirement field as a selection, this is not an automated process. In addition, the user must manually select which requirement was actually not fulfilled. The background of this problem is the lack of standardization of the complaint texts. With the execution of the first step of the validation, the second step started.

3) Prioritization of the complaint

In order to check how the prioritization is influenced by the quality of the complaint text, two prioritizations were performed based on the previously prepared complaint information, as shown in Figure 4.

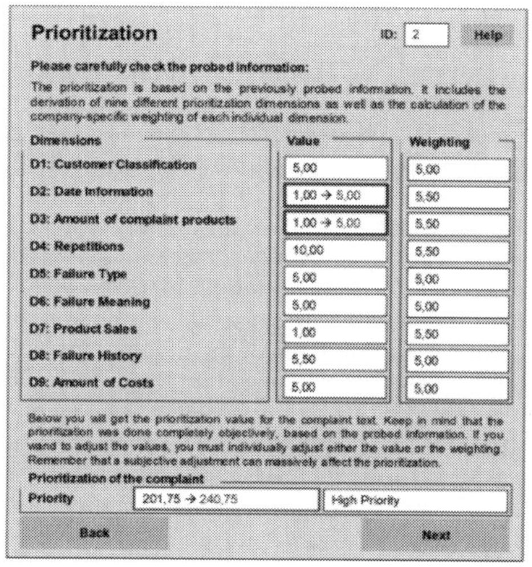

Figure 4. Prioritizing the complaint of the product SGW according to [20].

The gathered information was used to prioritize the complaint. For this, the algorithm calculates different dimensions. How this calculation is carried out is described in detail in [5]. In order to investigate how the quality of the complaint text affects the prioritization, dimension 2 and 3 were evaluated completely in the first step and incompletely in the second step. The second prioritization deliberately deleted information from the fields "ABC Classification", "Due Date" and "Amount of complaint products". The algorithm calculates and uses the reference value of 5.00 in Dimension 2 and Dimension 3 for missing information as you can see in Figure 4. This changes the dimension values and weightings. This has both advantages and disadvantages. On the one hand, it enables the algorithm to enter a dimension value and a weighting. This becomes critical when the influence of missing information becomes so great that an initially less relevant complaint becomes a complaint with high priority. In the worst case, this could lead to companies making incorrect decisions about the order in which complaints are to be processed and thus not using resources (personnel & time) in a targeted and meaningful manner. The solution to this problem also lies in the standardization of complaint texts.

4) Failure-cause localization of the complaint

Since the localization of the causes of the failure is carried out similarly to the prioritization on the basis of the collected, relevant complaint information, the phase was repeatedly reviewed on the basis of a complete and an incomplete information basis. In this case, the unfulfilled requirement was deliberately deleted from the corresponding field in Figure 5. The algorithm could not make a statement about which elements of the production system were related to the requirement because there was no information about the unfulfilled requirement. This means that without a reference to the unfulfilled requirement, it is not possible to locate the cause of the failure. It seems necessary to choose a more consistent procedure, such as [21] that is developed for networks or to standardize the specification of the unfulfilled requirement. Figure 5 illustrates the complete fault cause localization. The incomplete map, which was not inserted for space reasons, looks the same, but only with empty fields. The theoretical process of localization is described in [6] in detail.

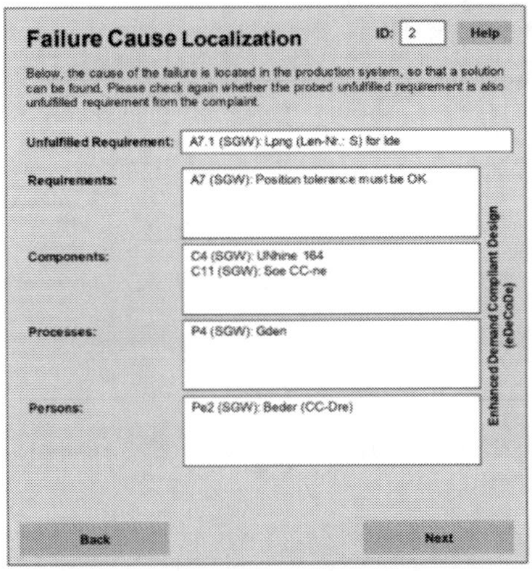

Figure 5. Failure-cause localization of the complaint of the product SGW - complete and unprocessed according to [20].

Once again, it makes sense to describe unfulfilled requirements in complaint texts, such as those stored in the technical drawing or specifications. In this case, the algorithm can identify the causes of the failure very well within the production system. This statement is because of the evaluation of the SGW product complaint included exactly those system elements that led to the cause of the failure. The company's statements about the actual cause of the defect also confirmed the statement that the algorithm could actually perform a targeted localization of the cause of the defect. At this point, it should be noted that the results of the algorithm depend not only on the quality of the complaint text but also on the quality of the production system. Only if the system elements and their interrelationships are completely captured, a targeted localization of the failure-causes is possible.

5) Solution-finding of the complaints

Validation of the solution-finding process showed that this process is completely independent of the quality of the complaint text or the information basis. By the given solutions in the form of measures, the algorithm can act also with a lower quality of the information. Figure 6 visualizes the measures proposed by the algorithm based on Organizational measures (O) for the failure-cause Component 4 (C4).

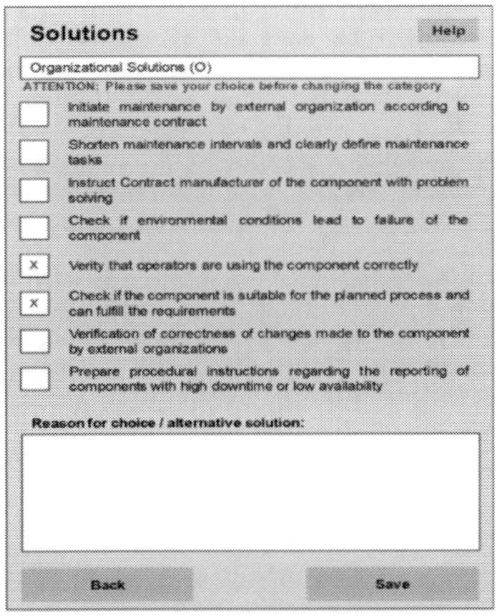

Figure 6. Measures proposed for the cause of the failure of C4 (SGW): UNhine 164 according to [20].

The result showed that it is possible to find a solution with the help of the measures, regardless of the quality of the information base or the complaint text.

IV. CONCLUSIONS

The validation using the industrial example in the field of precision machining and cold forming has shown that the performance of the algorithm is significantly influenced by the quality of the information in the input. In order to avoid a lack of information during the writing of the complaint, a standardization of the complaint text is strongly required. A lack of information would mean a high additional effort in the search for the cause of the failure and in finding a solution. This problem of probing of information could be solved by modifying the input mask of the complaint. Within the prioritization, the algorithm succeeded in compensating missing information by the formation of average values. Thereby set at least an estimated value for the prioritization of the complaint. In addition, here the impact was shown due to the quality of the complaint text, which can be improved by standardization. The validation has also shown that the quality of the complaint text has a strong effect on the localization of the cause of failure. On the other hand, it also turned out that the influence of the quality of the production system could be minimized. The reason lies in the self-developed user interface for checking the production system by the operator. A residual risk remains, however, as incorrect entries by the user are still possible. A solution for this would be the specification of the requirements in the complaint text according to the technical drawing or the specifications. With regard to finding a solution, the following findings could be gained from the validation. It has been shown that the quality of the complaint text has no technical effect on the solution-finding. However, it does affect the quality of the solution-finding. Therefore, measures can be derived at any time independently of the quality of the complaint text. The measures proposed by the algorithm led to the successful elimination of the failure-cause in the industry example. However, it was also noticed negatively that missing failure-cause information has strong effects on the probability calculation and therefore no adequate evaluation is possible without concrete information about failure rates or the competencies of persons. Furthermore, this information was not documented in the industry example. These findings follow the need for interfaces to Computer-Aided Quality (CAQ) systems in production in order to enable the algorithm to automatically access the necessary failure-cause information. Similarly, it should be examined whether alternative methods are more suitable for probability evaluation. The above-mentioned improvement potentials are now to be further investigated and implemented within the framework of future research projects.

ACKNOWLEDGMENTS

The authors thank the German Research Foundation (DFG) for the support of the Project FusLa [funding code: SCHL 2225/1-1].

REFERENCES

[1] S. Cook, "Complaint management excellence," Kogan Page, London, 2012.

[2] M. Heinrichsmeyer, N. Schlüter, A. Ansari, "Algorithm based handling of complaints data from the usage phase," in 2019 International Conference on Quality, Reliability, Risk, Maintenance, and Safety Engineering, IEEE QR2MSE, pp. 399–406, 2019.

[3] M. Heinrichsmeyer, N. Schlüter, A. Ansari, "Algorithm for Dealing with Complaints Data from the Use Phase," in Proceedings ICONS 2019, Sendra C., S. Valencia, Spanien, pp. 1–6, 2019.

[4] M. Heinrichsmeyer, N. Schlüter, A. Ansari, "Algorithmus zur automatisierten Abfrage relevanter Informationen aus Kundenreklamationen," in Bericht zur GQW-Jahrestagung, Schmitt, R., pp. Status: Accepted and will be published, 2019.

[5] M. Heinrichsmeyer, N. Schlüter, I. Lemke, "Development of an automated prioritization procedure for complaints," in Proceedings of Quality Management and Organisational Development/ an International Conference on Quality and Service Sciences, QMOD, 2019.

[6] M. Heinrichsmeyer, N. Schlüter, F. Kösling, "Localization of failure causes in production using complaint information by the means of an algorithm to achieve sustainable quality," in Proceedings of Quality Management and Organisational Development/ an International Conference on Quality and Service Sciences, QMOD, 2019.

[7] C.-G. Hong and C. Dietze, "Enabling Digital Excellence Through Business Process Management and Process Frameworks," in Future Telco, Krüssel, P. Springer International Publishing Cham, 2019.

[8] A. Holz, "Artificial Intelligence in Business. Reshaping work and organizations," GRIN Verlag, vol. 1, München, 2019.

[9] IBM Watson Compare & Comply, "*Extract data from contracts and governing documents to in-crease productivity, reduce costs and minimize exposure*," [Online]. Available from: https://www.ibm.com/cloud/compare-and-comply, 19.12.2019.

[10] Apache Spark, "*Framework for Cluster Computing*," [Online]. Available from: https://spark.apache.org/docs/latest/index.html, 10.09.2019.

[11] Amazon Comprehend, "*Natural Language Processing*," [Online]. Available from: https://aws.amazon.com/de/comprehend/, 10.09.2019.

[12] Microsoft Analytics Platform System, "*Microsoft Data Platform*," [Online]. Available from: https://www.microsoft.com/en-us/sql-server/default.aspx, 10.09.2019.

[13] Google BigQuery, "*A serverless, highly-scalable, and cost-effective cloud data warehouse*," [Online]. Available from: https://cloud.google.com/bigquery/, 10.09.2019.

[14] PrediCX, "*Complaint Handling*," [Online]. Available from: https://warwickanalytics.com/use-cases/complaint-handling/, 10.09.2019.

[15] CEMax, "*CEMax Complaint Management*," [Online]. Available from: https://www.c-m-x.com/sol-complaint-management/, 10.09.2019.

[16] Adobe Analytics, "*Digital Analysis Platform*," [Online]. Available from: https://www.adobe.com/analytics/adobe-analytics.html#, 10.09.2019.

[17] P. Winzer, "Generic Systems Engineering," Springer Vieweg, vol. 2. Auflage, Berlin, Heidelberg, 2016.

[18] J.-P. G. Nicklas, "Ansatz für ein modellbasiertes Anforderungsmanagement für Unternehmensnetzwerke," Shaker, vol. 1, Aachen, 2016.

[19] J. Brauweiler, A. Zenker-Hoffmann, M. Will, "Arbeitsschutzmanagementsysteme nach ISO 45001:2018," Springer Fachmedien Wiesbaden, vol. 2. Aufl. 2019, Wiesbaden, 2019.

[20] M. Heinrichsmeyer, N. Schlüter, H. Dransfeld, F. Kösling, "Validation of a Failure Cause Searching and Solution Finding Algorithm for Failures in Production; based on Complaints of a Company in the Field of Stamping and Metal Forming," in International Journal On Advances, IARIA 2019, International Academy, Research, and Industry Association, 2019 - Status: Accepted and will be published.

[21] Y. Shang, "*Localized recovery of complex networks against failure*," [Online]. Available from: https://www.nature.com/articles/srep30521#citeas, 10.09.2019.

Investigating the Feasibility to Acquire System Performance Information of a Complex System from Limited Maintenance Data

Tzu-Chia Kao[1] and Snow H. Tseng[1,2]*
[1]*Department of Electrical Engineering,*
[2]*Graduate Institute of Photonics and Optoelectronics,*
National Taiwan University, Taipei 10617, Taiwan
*Email: stseng@ntu.edu.tw

***Abstract*—We investigate the feasibility to extract system performance information based upon limited maintenance record of the Taipei Rapid Transit Corporation (TRTC). The maintenance record consists of malfunction incident rate per month of the Taipei metro system. It is desired to estimate the system lifetime from the maintenance record. However, whether such information is contained in the maintenance record, and furthermore, if the information can be extracted is to be determined. Moreover, the problem is further complicated by the regular maintenance, which further tampers the embedded information. The research goal is to assess the feasibility to acquire the desired information from the available dataset.**

Keywords-degradation; maintenance; metro; MRT; performance analysis.

I. Introduction

It is desirable to obtain system information from the maintenance data. In this research, we investigate the Mass Rapid Transit (MRT) system of Taipei Rapid Transit Corporation (TRTC), which began operation in 1996 for 23 years [1]. By analyzing the Taipei MRT maintenance records, we further explore the possibility to acquire information indicative of the system performance. The research objective is to determine whether it is possible to acquire reliable information of the system performance from the limited time-span maintenance records. If such information can be extracted, it may be helpful to diagnose the condition of the Taipei MRT system.

The performance and degradation of metropolitan metro systems play a crucial part in the civilians daily life and have attracted much attention of general public. The performance, malfunction, or maintenance all have huge impacts on the daily life of the passengers and civilians. Assessment and quantification of the system current status is essential to enhance performance. The performance of such complex system is commonly analyzed using the degradation curve model; analysis of the reliability is based on failure rate and maintenance records [2]. By assessing the condition of the system, improvement of the maintenance and performance can be recommended.

The performance record of various metropolitan metro systems in the world are studied. For example, the subway system in New York City, USA, has a long history. As reported in [3], train R36 serviced from 1964 to 2003, a total of 39 years. R160s were used to replace 45-year-old trains. In another news report about the old trains [4], the oldest trains for New York City Subway were planned to serve for 58 years, and now this type of trains are actually found too old with very high failure rated. From the limited reference that we can access, an estimate of the subway train lifetime is estimated to be around 40 to 50 years. For example, some lines of Singapore Mass Rapid Transit (SMRT) have been operating since 1987, 30 years from today. On the other hand, TRTC operated from 1996, which is only 21 years ago. There is a difference of 9 years. The assets' actual wear-out period may lie somewhere between 20 years (the oldest TRTC asset), and 40 years (New York City Subway). All these metropolitan metro systems are different in various aspects, thus, the performance of such MRT systems are not the same. Research attempts to establish a degradation curve model from the maintenance data has not been satisfactory.

The metro system is a complex system consisting of various components. For example, the rail track condition monitoring is an important technical concern of the MRT system [5]. However, it is infeasible to constantly inspect track conditions; an inspection once a month or less is the common maintenance. Severe track condition degradation is a potential threat to the railway system. Hence, more attention has been devoted to monitoring track condition via in-service vehicles [6]-[8]. The general goal of the research and technical modifications is to improve the performance and reliability of a mass rapid transit system.

Various approaches to analyze system performance have been reported [9]-[18], including the popular bathtub curve analysis [19]-[24]. The Bathtub curve model is widely used to assess system performance analysis [25]. Analysis based upon the bathtub curve has been extensively applied to various problems [11], [26]-[29]. Our research goal is to investigate the feasibility and validity to assess the performance of the Taipei MRT system based upon limited maintenance record.

We investigate and analyze the Taipei MRT data. We have data from Taipei MRT consisting of 11 systems: Electric Multiple Unit (EMU) propulsion, EMU Air Conditioner, EMU Communication, Switcher, Platform door, 22kV switchboard, Automated Fare Collection (AFC) door, Wenhu Line traffic control computer, Transmission system, elevator, and escalator. Specifically, we search for characteristics and compare with the bathtub degradation curve; the research objective is to acquire status information of the equipment and identify possible tendencies or features that may be indicative of the system performance.

This paper is organized as follows: Section I: Introduction with a description of the goal of this research project. Section II: Method. Section III: Data Analysis. Finally, Section IV: Conclusion and Future Work, followed by an acknowledgement.

II. METHOD

System condition analysis using the bathtub-shaped curve model [25] is commonly employed. It consists of a break-in trend as the system condition improves, followed by a plateau regime where the system condition is stable. After this stable regime, the system condition withers with increased malfunction rate, followed by a steep increase of malfunction rate where the malfunction rate increases with time rapidly whereas the system breaks down. Together, the bathtub-shaped curve represents the various stages of an ideal system.

However, not all system status can easily be compared to the bathtub-shaped degradation curve; it is an idealized theoretical model used in many problems. It is an idealized trend that depends on various factors. The feasibility of applying such bathtub-shaped curve may depend on the specific application and the various factors involved. Specifically, the system condition may not follow the same degradation curve, also, each equipment system may exhibit different characteristics depending on the specific application.

It is proposed that the maintenance data would yield a simple bathtub-shaped degradation curve for an equipment that is operated under normal condition. For systems that are affected by other factors, this theoretical degradation curve may be affected. Most cases do not follow the same degradation curve. For a complex system involving various brands, various models, and systems of various ages, the exhibited characteristics shall be different. In addition, as maintenance decisions involve human decision factors, such uncertainty further complicates the degradation curve, causing the exhibited characteristics further derailing from the possible universal bathtub-shaped curve.

Furthermore, each equipment in the Taipei metro system consists of various brands and various models that may possess different intrinsic characteristics. Since each equipment is maintained by human, the degradation curve is tampered with human factors and may exhibit characteristics differ from the original degradation curve without human influence. The research objective is to decipher whether such complex information can be extracted from the maintenance data of a limited time span.

III. DATA ANALYSIS

Maintenance data provided by TRTC is analyzed. We employ linear regression and various regression models to identify the trend. Through each method, our goal is to ascertain the general behavior of the dataset. The limited dataset showed diverse characteristics which is inconclusive. The recorded number of malfunction incidents of the MRT transmission system per month as a function of age is shown in Figure 1. The data is sporadic and gradually decrease with time.

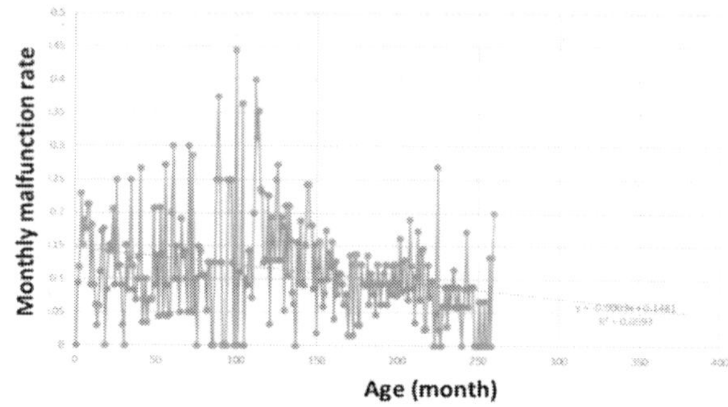

Figure 1. Average malfunction rate per month as a function of transmission system age (month).

As shown in Figure 1, the decreases with time is apparent. This could be due to the regular maintenance. in this mostly likely is due to the improvement of MRT maintenance. On the other hand, since the age of each equipment and the number of samples for each equipment are not consistent, the degradation curve exhibits mixed information of various complex factors.

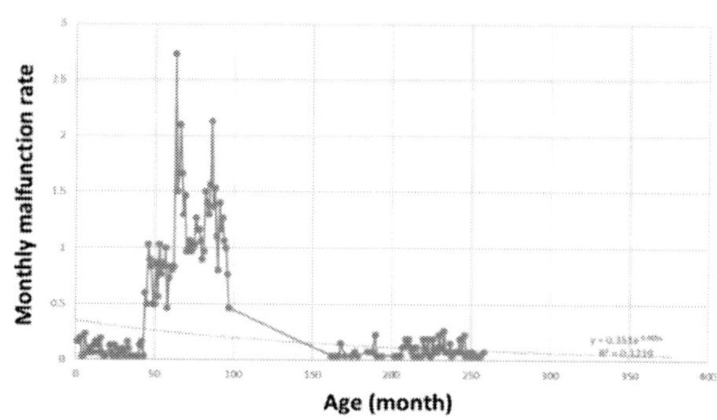

Figure 2. The average malfunction rate of the Wenhu Line central computers as s function of age (month).

The average malfunction rate of the Wenhu Line central computers as a function of age is shown in Figure 2. Due to incomplete record, there are some maintenance data is missing. Thus, the degradation trend may not be conclusive.

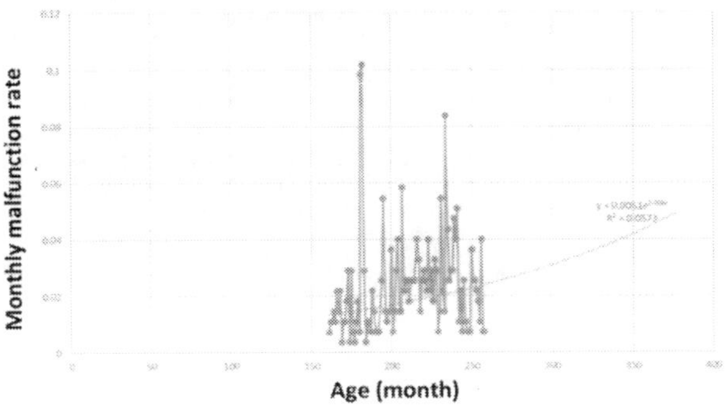

Figure 3. The average malfunction rate of the Muzha Line screen door as s function of age (month).

As shown in Figure 3, the average malfunction rate of the Muzha Line screen door as a function of age exhibits a gradual increase with age. The data span only covers short period of time, but it clearly increases with age. A more complete dataset may be required for conclusive results.

IV. Conclusion and Future Work

The goal of this paper is to assess the feasibility to extract status information of various Taipei MRT systems based upon the maintenance data. The maintenance data is limited and only consists of a single parameter: count of the number of malfunction incidents per month. By means of data analysis, our goal is to identify characteristics indicative of the current status of the metro system, remaining lifetime, and estimate its future trend. Yet, the system information may not be fully contained in the provided maintenance record. The validity of the estimation based upon incomplete data, may be limited.

The bathtub degradation curve could be affected by human factors; for example, if the asset retired in its early stage, the curve may not rise up during the wear-out period and may even descend. If properly maintained, the curve may not rise in the wear-out period, similar to the situation in airline industry. However, few MRT systems in reality exhibit degradation behavior similar to the bathtub curve model [30].

The degradation curve acquired from data analysis of the provided Taipei metro maintenance record has be assessed. however, the trend of each degradation curve exhibits various characteristics. By comparing with the bathtub curve model, we tried to assess the status of each system. However, the assessment is inconclusive. Possible factors include:

1) Each system has not reached the steady state.

2) Human factor such as maintenance tampers the natural trend.

3) More data, longer temporal span of maintenance record is required to reveal a degradation trend.

Based on the available maintenance records provided by TRTC, statistical analysis findings indicate that the Taipei metro is stable with no significant indication of degradation. Degradation curve acquired via statistical analysis is not conclusive. More data may be required to establish the general trend.

If the maintenance data contains severity information of each malfunction incident, data analysis may potentially yield more information to assess the status of the system. On the other hand, it is not ascertained that the desired status information is embedded in the malfunction incident record, which is further tampered by the regular maintenance. On a broader perspective, a fundamental question to be asked: Is the required information contained in the dataset? If it isn't, or perhaps only partial information is contained in the dataset, then even the most elaborate analysis approach cannot legitimately extract information that is not contained within the dataset.

For future work, we recommend the maintenance record consists of more than a single-parameter, such as the severity of the malfunction, the cost of the malfunction, maybe mileage of operation between each malfunction incidents. The maintenance record will be a resourceful dataset for assessing the status of a complex system. Such information may provide more direct information regarding the system status. We believe such approach may be more sensitive and indicative, and potentially be indicative of the system status and system lifetime.

Acknowledgment

We thank TRTC for providing information data for analysis and support to make this project possible. This research is supported by the Ministry of Science and Technology grant: MOST 107-2112-M-002-011 and MOST 108-2634-F-002-014.

References

[1] "Taipei Metro," *Wikipedia*. [Online]. Available: https://en.wikipedia.org/wiki/Taipei_Metro.

[2] H. Yin, K. Wang, Y. Qin, Q. Hua, and Q. Jiang, "Reliability analysis of subway vehicles based on the data of operational failures," *EURASIP Journal on Wireless Communications and Networking*, journal article vol. 2017, no. 1, p. 212, December 2017, doi: 10.1186/s13638-017-0996-y.

[3] Metropolitan Transportation Authority. "New York City Transit - History and Chronology." http://web.mta.info/nyct/facts/ffhist.htm (accessed.

[4] D. Rivoli, "Ancient subway trains on C and J/Z lines won't be replaced until 2022, documents say." http://www.nydailynews.com/new-york/ancient-subway-trains-won-replaced-2022-article-1.2323289

[5] X. K. Wei, F. Liu, and L. M. Jia, "Urban rail track condition monitoring based on in-service vehicle acceleration measurements," *Measurement*, vol. 80, pp. 217-228, Feb 2016, doi: 10.1016/j.measurement.2015.11.033.

[6] M. Molodova, M. Oregui, A. Nunez, Z. L. Li, and R. Dollevoet, "Health condition monitoring of insulated joints based on axle box

acceleration measurements," *Engineering Structures*, vol. 123, pp. 225-235, Sep 2016, doi: 10.1016/j.engstruct.2016.05.018.
[7] G. Lederman, S. H. Chen, J. Garrett, J. Kovacevic, H. Y. Noh, and J. Bielak, "Track-monitoring from the dynamic response of an operational train," *Mechanical Systems and Signal Processing*, vol. 87, pp. 1-16, Mar 2017, doi: 10.1016/j.ymssp.2016.06.041.
[8] R. Jiang *et al.*, "Network operation reliability in a Manhattan-like urban system with adaptive traffic lights," *Transportation Research Part C-Emerging Technologies*, vol. 69, pp. 527-547, Aug 2016, doi: 10.1016/j.trc.2016.01.006.
[9] Z. G. Li, J. G. Zhou, and B. Y. Liu, "System Reliability Analysis Method Based on Fuzzy Probability," *International Journal of Fuzzy Systems*, vol. 19, no. 6, pp. 1759-1767, Dec 2017, doi: 10.1007/s40815-017-0363-5.
[10] A. Z. Afify, G. M. Cordeiro, N. S. Butt, E. M. M. Ortega, and A. K. Suzuki, "A new lifetime model with variable shapes for the hazard rate," *Brazilian Journal of Probability and Statistics*, vol. 31, no. 3, pp. 516-541, Aug 2017, doi: 10.1214/16-bjps322.
[11] T. Kamel, A. Limam, and C. Silvani, "Modeling the degradation of old subway galleries using a continuum approach," *Tunnelling and Underground Space Technology*, vol. 48, pp. 77-93, Apr 2015, doi: 10.1016/j.tust.2014.12.015.
[12] D. Brancherie and A. Ibrahimbegovic, "Novel anisotropic continuum-discrete damage model capable of representing localized failure of massive structures: Part I: theoretical formulation and numerical implementation," *Engineering Computations*, vol. 26, no. 1-2, pp. 100-127, 2009, doi: 10.1108/02644400910924825.
[13] R. Tahmasbi and S. Rezaei, "A two-parameter lifetime distribution with decreasing failure rate," *Computational Statistics & Data Analysis*, vol. 52, no. 8, pp. 3889-3901, Apr 2008, doi: 10.1016/j.csda.2007.12.002.
[14] C. F. Daganzo and N. Geroliminis, "An analytical approximation for the macroscopic fundamental diagram of urban traffic," *Transportation Research Part B-Methodological*, vol. 42, no. 9, pp. 771-781, Nov 2008, doi: 10.1016/j.trb.2008.06.008.
[15] C. Kus, "A new lifetime distribution," *Computational Statistics & Data Analysis*, vol. 51, no. 9, pp. 4497-4509, May 15 2007, doi: 10.1016/j.csda.2006.07.017.
[16] C. D. Lai, M. Xie, and D. N. P. Murthy, "A modified Weibull distribution," *IEEE Transactions on Reliability*, vol. 52, no. 1, pp. 33-37, Mar 2003, doi: 10.1109/tr.2002.805788.
[17] O. O. Aalen and H. K. Gjessing, "Understanding the shape of the hazard rate: A process point of view," *Statistical Science*, vol. 16, no. 1, pp. 1-14, Feb 2001. [Online]. Available: <Go to ISI>://WOS:000169674200001.
[18] S. Kotz and D. N. Shanbhag, "Some new approaches to probability distributions," *Advances in Applied Probability*, vol. 12, no. 4, pp. 903-921, 1980 1980, doi: 10.2307/1426748.
[19] S. K. Maurya, A. Kaushik, S. K. Singh, and U. Singh, "A new class of distribution having decreasing, increasing, and bathtub-shaped failure rate," *Communications in Statistics-Theory and Methods*, vol. 46, no. 20, pp. 10359-10372, 2017, doi: 10.1080/03610926.2016.1235196.
[20] Q. H. Duan and J. R. Liu, "Modelling a Bathtub-Shaped Failure Rate by a Coxian Distribution," *IEEE Transactions on Reliability*, vol. 65, no. 2, pp. 878-885, Jun 2016, doi: 10.1109/tr.2015.2494374.
[21] W. J. Roesch, "Using a new bathtub curve to correlate quality and reliability," *Microelectronics Reliability*, vol. 52, no. 12, pp. 2864-2869, Dec 2012, doi: 10.1016/j.microrel.2012.08.022.
[22] J. Navarro and P. J. Hernandez, "How to obtain bathtub-shaped failure rate models from normal mixtures," *Probability in the Engineering and Informational Sciences*, vol. 18, no. 4, pp. 511-531, 2004 .
[23] S. Rajarshi and M. B. Rajarshi, "Bathtub distributions - a review," *Communications in Statistics-Theory and Methods*, vol. 17, no. 8, pp. 2597-2621, 1988 1988, doi: 10.1080/03610928808829761.
[24] M. V. Aarset, "How to identify an bathtub hazard rate," *IEEE Transactions on Reliability*, vol. 36, no. 1, pp. 106-108, Apr 1987, doi: 10.1109/tr.1987.5222310.
[25] K. L. Wong, "The bathtub does not hold water any more," *Quality and Reliability Engineering International*, vol. 4, no. 3, pp. 279-282, 1988, doi: 10.1002/qre.4680040311.
[26] H. T. Zeng, T. Lan, and Q. M. Chen, "Five and four-parameter lifetime distributions for bathtub-shaped failure rate using Perks mortality equation," *Reliability Engineering & System Safety*, vol. 152, pp. 307-315, Aug 2016, doi: 10.1016/j.ress.2016.03.014.
[27] F. K. Wang, "A new model with bathtub-shaped failure rate using an additive Burr XII distribution," *Reliability Engineering & System Safety*, vol. 70, no. 3, pp. 305-312, Dec 2000, doi: 10.1016/s0951-8320(00)00066-1.
[28] D. N. P. Murthy and R. Jiang, "Parametric study of sectional models involving two Weibull distributions," *Reliability Engineering & System Safety*, vol. 56, no. 2, pp. 151-159, May 1997, doi: 10.1016/s0951-8320(96)00114-7.
[29] G. S. Mudholkar, D. K. Srivastava, and M. Freimer, "The exponentiated Weibull family - A reanalysis of the bus-motor-failure data," *Technometrics*, vol. 37, no. 4, pp. 436-445, Nov 1995, doi: 10.2307/1269735.
[30] G. A. Klutke, P. C. Kiessler, and M. A. Wortman, "A critical look at the bathtub curve," *IEEE Transactions on Reliability*, vol. 52, no. 1, pp. 125-129, 2003, doi: 10.1109/TR.2002.804492.

Publishing and Retrieval System for Traffic Court Cases

Wei Kit Shiu
School of Computer Science and Engineering
Nanyang Technological University
Singapore
Email: shiu0003@e.ntu.edu.sg

Chai Kiat Yeo
School of Computer Science and Engineering
Nanyang Technological University
Singapore
Email: asckyeo@ntu.edu.sg

Abstract—**This paper details the design and development of a web-based publishing and retrieval system for traffic court cases. This proof-of-concept is meant to complement and in time to come, replace, existing manual processes of doing legal research for traffic court cases. Currently, legal staff have to manually browse through practitioners' library and motor accident guide books to look at precedents for the assessment of damages in personal injuries and fatal accidents. The system automatically extracts key information of the court cases to allow retrieving of relevant court cases from a search query term by professionals such as judges, lawyers, insurers, as well as the public for their research and references.**

Keywords-traffic court cases; intelligent document retrieval system; natural language processing; automated text extraction.

I. Introduction

With the general improvement in road safety over the years, the number of accidents resulting in injuries has dropped slightly [1]. Nevertheless, it still amounts to more than 7000 cases per year in Singapore, a dense city state with 5.8 million population and 9.5 million motor vehicles. This naturally leads to a huge number of traffic accident cases reaching the courts as well as claims for injuries suffered and deaths during the accidents.

Accident victims will naturally seek compensation for injuries incurred. However, depending on how co-operative the offender is, the process to seek compensation may be difficult. The situation may involve an investigation by the related insurers and may even escalate into legal cases to be settled in the courts. This can be a long and expensive process in which compensations that are eventually awarded may not even be sufficient to cover the legal expenses of the disputes.

Typically, if the claim is heard before the courts, it will involve a detailed re-accounting of the accident as well as medical reports of the injuries incurred by the plaintiffs. The judge will then consider all details together with relevant past cases to decide on a quantum of the damages to be awarded to the plaintiff [2] [3].

Every year, there are up to 12,000 accident claims that are heard in the courts and they are important precedents for the judges to use for future references. Since 2001, a book named "Practitioners' Library Assessment of Damages: Personal Injuries and Fatal Accidents", commonly known as the Blue Book has been published with the 3rd edition launched in Feb 2017 [4]. It is written by judges and serves as a reference for judges, lawyers and insurers when it comes to assessing the amount of damages that the court may award in cases involving personal injuries and death. It also gives road users an idea of the damage awards in an accident. The Blue Book is also used by practitioners and members of the insurance industry to negotiate and expedite the settlement of accident cases without escalating the case to the courts. The Blue Book is almost 800 pages and referencing it is a tedious task, let alone revising it to keep it as up-to-date as possible.

Another book, the Motor Accident Guide [5], written in simple English and illustrated by dozens of diagrams picked from past court cases serve to provide readers, especially layman, an idea of where they stand should they take an accident claim to court. The guide aims to keep a lid on claims arising from motor accidents. Similar to the Blue Book, the readers will have to go through the entire guide to look for the scenario that is most applicable to his/her case.

The motivation of this proof-of-concept (POC) is therefore to introduce digitalization of court documents and facilitate the search for precedent motor accident cases. The project will facilitate judges to publish past cases efficiently and in a timely manner and also enable others concerned to efficiently retrieve and review information of the past cases without the need to laboriously go through the physical Blue Book.

The rest of the paper is organized as follows: Section II details the design and development of the system. Section III shows the outputs from the system and discussion on its performance. Section IV concludes this paper.

II. System Design and Development

The project is divided into two main parts namely Case Publishing System and Case Retrieval System. The former requires the uploading of pdf versions of case documents as well as conversion of pdf to text for further processing. It also entails the extraction of key information such as plaintiff's name, age, gender, date of assessment, injuries, claims and amount awarded. The extracted information is also stored and serves as search engine index to provide results to the search queries. The Case Retrieval System involves retrieving of the relevant case documents based on the queries made to the system. Figure 1 shows the use case diagram for the system.

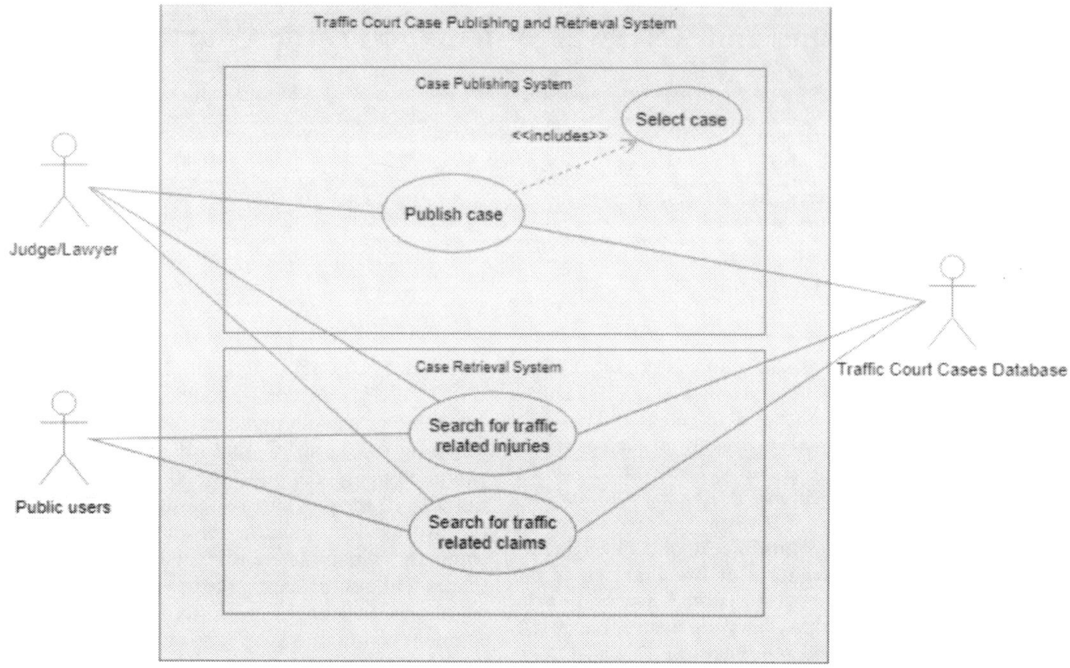

Figure 1. Use case diagram of the system.

The overall system comprises the Case Publishing System and the Case Retrieval System. The former allows the judges to upload past cases into the database and to edit or update published cases. The latter allows all concerned, namely, judges, lawyers and the public to access the databse and search for precedents matching the search terms entered such as the type of injuries, the award quantum.

A. Database

PyMySQL [6] is used to implement the system's database and the tools used to manage the database are Cross-Platform Apache, MariaDB, PHP and Perl (XAMPP) Control Panel [7] and phpMyAdmin [8]. The database is designed such that "cases" table holds a one-to-many relationship with the "injuries" table. Each case in the "cases" table is associated with one or more injury/claim in the "injuries" table. Each injury/claim in the "injuries" table uses its foreign key "case_ID" to identify its case mapping in the "cases" table. This design thus prevents data duplication.

B. Implementation

The system is fully written using Python.

PDF to text conversion: This function allows the uploaded PDF file to be converted to text format so that further processing can be done. A third-party library named "pdfminer.six" [9] is used here as it gives the best performance. It takes in an argument called [pdfname] where [pdfname] is the directory of the PDF file that is being uploaded and returns the text after the conversion is done. Many other libraries such as "PyPDF2" [10] have been used but the results are unsatisfactory as the converted text are either concatenated wrongly or there are missing text. However, "pffminer.six" is also not perfect and manual checking on the converted has to be performed. This is a big problem in the digitisation of past court cases and a one-off exercise will thus be needed to convert all the hard copies into digital form. Note that Natural Language Toolkit (NLTK) [11] is used to tokenize the converted text into sentences which are then parsed for the various extraction algorithms.

1) Extraction of plaintiff's name: Heuristic rule is applied in extracting the plaintiff's name after an analysis of the sample court cases on hand. The plaintiff's name will always appear at the top of every page in the document, in the form of "[Plaintiff Name] v [Defendant name]" and it is similar throughout all the cases. Therefore, the approach to this algorithm is to use regular expressions to extract the name. The *re.search* function takes [text] as a huge string and returns any substring that matches the pattern [r'(?P<PName>\b.*)\sv\s.*\b'], a regular expression created to match the format of the name given in the court document. Subsequently, symbolic group name *PName* is used to extract only the plaintiff's name. The code segment for the extraction is given in Figure 2.

We have explored the use of NLTK and pyenchant [9] for the plaintiff's name extraction. The algorithm is as follows: The converted text is tokenized into sentences and the sentences are parsed to extract those that contain the word "victim" or "plaintiff". The continuous name chunks are extracted using Name Entity Recognition with Regular Expressions and checked against those in the dictionary library. Name chunks with at least one word that is not a valid English word will be treated as a valid name but the result is not as good as the heuristic described above. Moreover, it is vulnerable to other word chunks that contain non-English words like national identity number and company name.

2) Extraction of plaintiff's age: The algorithm starts by tokenising the converted text into sentences. Next, it filters and extracts the sentences that contain keywords like "plaintiff" or "victim" and key phrases like "years old", "at the time", "accident happens", "when" etc. The reason of such key phrases is to improve the accuracy of extracting the plaintiff's age from neighbouring context. For example, "the plaintiff was 72 years old at the time of hearing". After obtaining the sentences that contain the keyword and key phrases, re.findall function is used to extract all the age numbers. The maximum of all the age numbers extracted will be set as the plaintiff's age at the time of assessment. An issue with this method is that the court documents may sometimes contain the age of more than one person. This will significantly increase the chances of extracting a wrong age number. Therefore, to reduce the odds of extracting a wrong age, a layer of filter is added to priortize the age number extracted from sentences that contain keywords like "plaintiff" or "victim" over others.

```
import re
#Algorithm starts here---
PlaintiffName = ""
#variable name [text] contains the text
converted from PDF
SearchPlaintiffName =
re.search(r'(?P<PName>\b.*)\sv\s.*\b',text
)
if(SearchPlaintiffName):
    PlaintiffName =
str(SearchPlaintiffName.group('PName'))
```

Figure 2. Code segment for extraction of plaintiff's name.

3) Extraction of plaintiff's gender: The main approach here is to identify the number of he/his and she/her pronouns that appears near to the keyword "plaintiff" or "victim" throughout the entire document. The higher count will be taken as the plaintiff's gender. First the converted text is tokenised into sentences. Next, for every sentence that contains the keyword "plaintiff" or "victim", the algorithm will count the number of times he/his and she/her appears. Finally, the gender with the higher count frequency will be taken as the plaintiff's gender.

4) Extraction of date of assessment: After analysing the cases on hand, it was found that the latest date shown in the traffic court cases is always the date of assessment. Therefore, the approach is to use re.findall function to extract every single date string that appears in the document and subsequently, extract the latest date out of all the date strings obtained. As the dates are extracted in the string format, an additional step is required to convert the date strings to numerical form so that the algorithm is able to compare every single date and recognise the latest date.

5) Extraction of injuries, claims and amount awarded: It is observed that every traffic court cases will have a section at the end of the document called "Conclusion". In the section, the injuries, claims and amount awarded will be listed out as a summary as shown in Figure 3. Therefore, the approach is to create two lists that store injuries/claims and amount awarded respectively, which is also shown in Figure 3. To implement the algorithm, a bag of words is created with all the relevant injuries/claims stored in it. With the help of the bag of words, the algorithm can identify and store the injuries/claims into the list "injuries_claims" while re.findall function is used to identify and store the amount awarded into the list "probable_award_amounts_main".

6) Case Retrieval: This function receives an input from the user and queries the database for matching results. User can searcj for traffic accident information by entering either the name of an injury or the name of a traffic accident claim. This function also allows substring search. For example, if the user enters "hand", cases that involved "left hand" injuries or "right hand" injuries will also be retrieved.

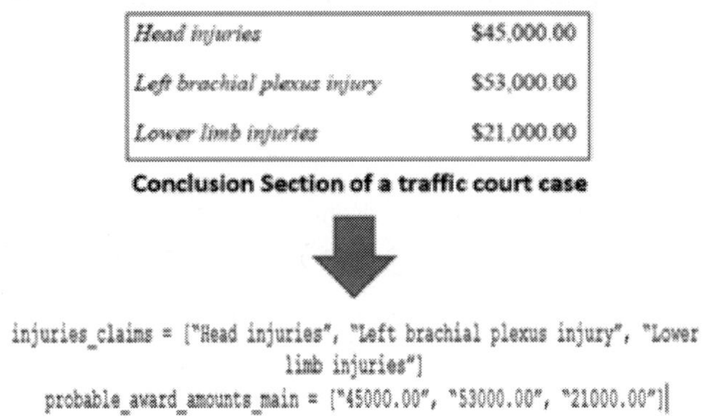

Figure 3. Illustration of the Conclusion section of the case summary.

III. Results and Discussion

The capabilities of the system are evaluated against the requirements specified. Functional testing is adopted to examine the functions of the system to ensure that it performs as required. Four available traffic court cases are used as test dataset [12] – [15] and they are all past judgements made by the Supreme Court of Singapore. Unfortunately, only four cases are made available online.

Table I shows the test results. Basically, extraction of plaintiff's name, age, gender and date of assessments works well for the 4 test dataset with the exception of the extraction of injuries, claims and amount awarded. This extraction is the most challenging as it requires much more sophisticated natural language processing techniques such as topic modelling to extract the different types of injuries and the medical terms. The simple technique adopted in this POC proves to be inadequate to address the entire spectrum of possible injuries.

TABLE I. SYSTEM TEST RESULTS

Functionality Test	Accuracy
Extraction of plaintiff's name	100%
Extraction of plaintiff's age	100%
Extraction of plaintiff' gender	100%
Extraction of date of assessment	100%
Extraction of injuries, claims and amount awarded	25%

Figure 4 shows the key information extracted from the test case in [15] while Figure 5 shows the retrieval results when a user types in the search term '*fracture*'.

This POC has set the trail in the digitalization of the legal domain. It is very useful in facilitating the search for precedent court cases of traffic injuries and the amount of damages awarded to reduce expensive law suits and court time. It also shows that automation of text extraction from voluminous case files is feasible. The premise for this POC is that the court cases have already been digitized and exist in pdf form. This is not the case as most, if not all, case documents exist in hard copies and have to be manually digitized and checked before being published in a system like the proposed system. Only then can accurate extraction of critical information be performed and retrieval of case documents be accurate.

A qualitative comparison is made against existing related work such as [16], [17] and [18]. Wyner et. al. [16] detail the use of text mining to automatically profile and extract arguments from legal cases and shows how context-free grammar can be used to extract arguments, and how ontologies and NLP can identify complex information such as case factors and participant roles. The approach applies linguistic analysis and stereotypical pattern of reasoning called argument schemes to identify argument sentences and semantically relevant sentences from a legal corpus. The arguments in the legal corpus need to be first analysed and represented in XML format for later mining. Compared to our POC, we do not need manual labelling of the legal documents. We extract precise entities such as injuries, plaintiff's details and damage awards while [16]'s extraction is very coarse-grained in the form of sentences of arguments. [16] also does not lend itself to retrieve cases based on search queries.

Wagh [17] merely proposes a study to group legal documents based on the contents using unsupervised text mining techniques. It only describes what the authors intend to do with no actual design and implementation. Andrew and Tannier [18] use a combination of both statistical and rule based techniques to enable journalists to automatically identify and annotate entities such as names of people, organizations, role and functions of people in legal documents. They also try to explore the relationship between these entities. The statistical method used is Conditional Random Fields while document and language specific regular expressions are used for the rule based technique. It is focused on extraction of specific entities from the documents but do not include the more complicated entities such as injuries, damages awarded and age. It also does not support search and retrieval of precedent cases based on input query terms unlike our POC.

In summary, in comparison with existing work, our POC supports more precise and fine-grained extraction of plaintiff's details, injuries and damage awards based on the search string input thereby greatly facilitates users of the system to easily extract and compare precedent cases closest to their query of interest. Another merit of our POC is we do not require labelled dataset.

There are however limitations in this POC which need to be addressed before a fully functional system can be deployed as it relies heavily on heuristic algorithms for the unstructured text mining. Much more sophisticated natural language processing techniques, namely, topic modelling using Latent Dirichlet Allocation (LDA) is needed not just to extract the injuries but also in the extraction of other plaintiff's details. The test cases used here are considered simple as they only involve a single plaintiff and a single defendant. Hence, extraction of plaintiff's details is very accurate as shown in Table I, which will not be the case for multiple plaintiffs. Another challenge is when the search query comprises a long sentence instead of a single word. In this case, the key words have to be extracted from the search string as well. Moreover, there is a lack of readily available court cases, preferably in the hundreds, to adequately stress test the POC.

IV. CONCLUSION

A POC for a web-based publishing and retrieval system for traffic court cases has been successfully developed. The system automatically extracts key information of the court cases to allow retrieving of relevant cases from a search query term by professionals such as judges, lawyers, insurers and the public. Such a system not only renders the legal research process for traffic court cases to be much more efficient but also relieves the judges of the laborious manual compilation and update of the Practitioners' Library Assessment of Damages (the Blue Book). Judges can publish past cases much more efficiently and keep the publication up to date compared to the manually compiled Blue Book which is published once after a few years.

A limitation of the POC is the adoption of heuristics in the text mining. Future work shall involve the introduction of topic modeling in NLP processing to handle the extraction of plaintiff's details and injuries for more complex cases than those shown in this paper as well as use of deep learning.

ACKNOWLEDGMENT

This work is supported in part by NTU Grant no. M4081329.020.

REFERENCES

[1] Public Affairs Department Singapore Police Force. *Annual Road Traffic Sitatuon 2018*, Singapore, 2019.

[2] State Courts Practice Directions, Section 40. Singapore: State Courts.

[3] Supreme Court of Judicature Act, Chapter 322, Section 80, Order 37. Singapore, 2014 edition.

[4] C. Chan et al., Practitioners' Library Assessment of Damages: Personal Injuries and Fatal Accidents, 3rd ed., LexisNexis, Feb 2017.

[5] States Court, Motor Accident Guide, Tusitala (RLS) Pte Ltd, Feb 2017.

[6] I. Naoki, PyMySQL. 2017. [Online]. Available from: https://pypi.python.org/pypi/PyMySQL. [retrieved: Dec 2019].

[7] Apache Friends, XAMPP,. [Online]. Available from: https://www.apachefriends.org/index.html. [retrieved: Dec 2019].

[8] Software Freedom Conservancy, phpMyAdmin. [Online]. Available from: https://www.phpmyadmin.net/. [retrieved: Dec 2019].

[9] Y. Shinyama, pdfminer.six, 2014. [Online]. Available from: https://pypi.python.org/pypi/pdfminer.six/20140915. M. Fenniak, PyPDF2. 2011. [Online]. Available from:, https://pypi.python.org/pypi/PyPDF2. [retrieved: Dec 2019].

[10] M. Fenniak, PyPDF2. 2011. Available from: https://pypi.python.org/pypi/PyPDF2. [retrieved: Dec 2019].

[11] S. Bird, E. Loper and E. Klein, Natural Language Toolkit. 2014. Available from: https://www.nltk.org/. [retrieved: Dec 2019].

[12] K. Ramesh, High Court Judgement: Lee Mui Yeng v Ng Tong Yoo. 2016. [Online]. Available from: https://www.supremecourt.gov.sg/docs/default-source/module-document/judgement/-2016-sghc-46-pdf.pdf. [retrieved: Dec 2019].

[13] K. C. Pang, High Court Judgement: Tan Hun Boon v Rui Feng Travel Pte Ltd and another. 2017. [Online]. Available from : https://www.supremecourt.gov.sg/docs/default-source/module-document/judgement/judgment-s662-2014-v2-pdf.pdf. [retrieved: Dec 2019].

[14] J. Y. Lee, Supreme Court Judgement: Ng Hua Bak v Eu Kok Thai. 2016. [Online]. Available from: https://www.supremecourt.gov.sg/docs/default-source/module-document/judgement/s1351-14-ad43-15-sghcr-12-by-jaylee-2nov2016-pdf.pdf. [retrieved: Dec 2019].

[15] C. Seow, High Court Judgement: Mullaichelvan s/o Perumal v Lee Heng Kah. 2013. [Online]. Available from: https://www.supremecourt.gov.sg/docs/default-source/module-document/judgement/2013-sghcr-3.pdf [retrieved: Dec 2019].

[16] A. Wyner, R. Mochales-Palau, M. F. Moens, D. Milward, Approaches to Text Mining Arguments from Legal Cases. In: E. Francesconi, S. Montemagni, W. Peters, D. Tiscornia (eds) Semantic Processing of Legal Texts. Lecture Notes in Computer Science, vol 6036. Springer, Berlin, Heidelberg, 2010.

[17] R. S. Wagh, Knowledge Discovery from Legal Documents Dataset using Text Mining Techniques, International Journal of Computer Applications 66(23):32-34, 2013.

[18] J. J. Andrew and X. Tannier, Automatic Extraction of Entities and Relation from Legal Documents, Proceedings of the Seventh Named Entities Workshop, Melbourne, pp. 1-8, Jul 2018.

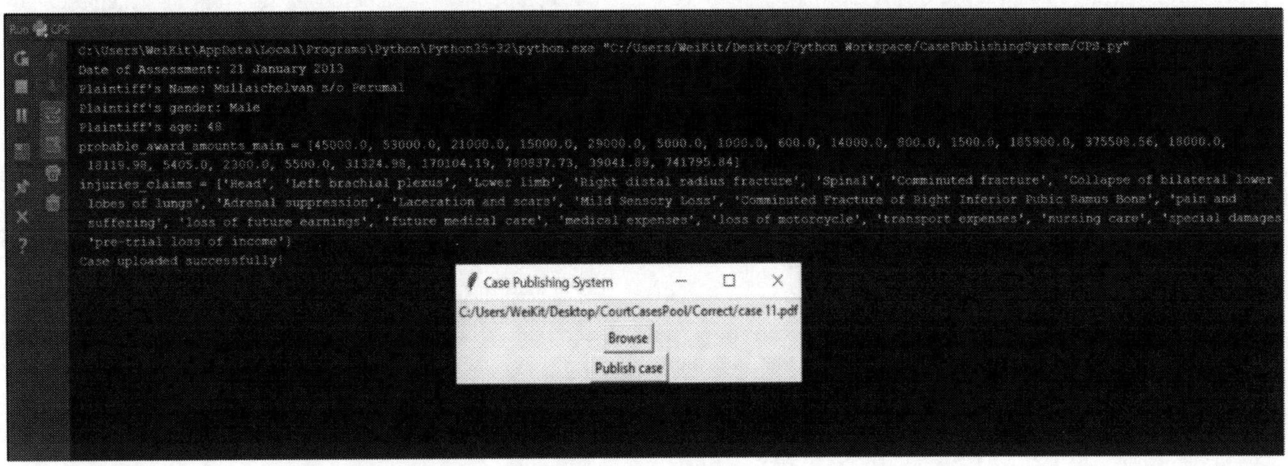

Figure 4. Extraction of key data from Test Case in [15].

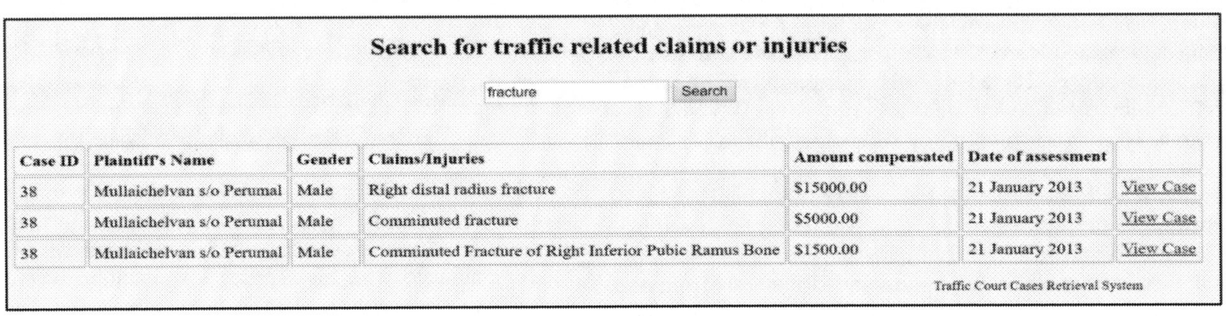

Figure 5. Case retrieval results for the search term 'fracture'.

BlueLab IoT Architecture

Vitor Vaz da Silva

Electronics Telecommunication and Computer Department
ISEL/IPL – Instituto Superior de Engenharia de Lisboa
Instituto Politécnico de Lisboa
Lisboa, Portugal
e-mail: vsilva@deetc.isel.ipl.pt

CTS-Centre of Technology and Systems,
UNL – Universidade Nova de Lisboa,
Caparica, Portugal.
e-mail: vvd.silva@campus.fct.unl.pt

Abstract—**Connected objects that build up the general idea of Internet of Things (IoT) need hardware and or a software structure to which they attach. There are many IoT solutions that are provided by companies, academia or independent developers. The BlueLab IoT platform is a possible solution for a set of different sensor devices that provide realtime data entries, which are stored in a database. Data entries for each station are organized as raw data sets. Those data sets can be processed later by applications and stored as processed data (P1), which can be further processed and stored producing higher level data. Data sets (raw and processed) marked as shared can then be used to form a data library (datalib). A BlueLab Iot project is composed by several datalibs; thus, the same data can be used by several users and projects without being replicated. Some physical devices that produce data (temperature, humidity, pressure, air quality) have been built and data stored within the BlueLab system, almost continuously for two years, providing a useful data resource to be used as a ground for further BlueLab characteristics. The novel contribution of this paper is the work in progress of the BlueLab system by presenting its architecture and available resources to developers. A hands on example is also presented.**

Keywords-IoT; CPS; Embedded Systems; BlueLab.

I. INTRODUCTION

Almost unstoppable are the things that can now be connected to the Internet as they are built with that intention, and older things that were present before the Internet of Things (IoT) concept can also be connected by a suitable interface; a Thing over Internet (ToI) that dilutes in the global IoT domain [1]. There are many different ideas of how to connect devices to each other, how to cooperate, synchronize, exchange, store and analyse data [2]. The BlueLab IoT system provides a platform for users to add their devices and store sensorial data. The data can also be visualized and processed to offer meaningful information. IoT systems need to consider security issues [3] and this awareness is also present on the BlueLab IoT system including user data and devices. The paper continues in section II with the system's architecture, both hardware and software, followed by section III where tested hardware has been used with different configuration sets in the stations, and then section IV with results and discussion from the whole system.

II. ARCHITECTURE

The BlueLab architecture has two domains, the logical and physical. The logical domain is composed by the conceptual components that build up the BlueLab and allow software interfaces to be built. The physical domain is mainly the hardware part of the BlueLab's overall system, which includes the possible communication and interconnection configurations.

A. Physical Architecture

The BlueLab IoT physical architecture is shown in Figure 1. The stations are fixed or mobile, have sensors and Wi-Fi connections. Data gathered is sent to the Database either directly through the Wi-Fi connection to a Gateway (or router) or by sending it through a Distributor (under development). A Distributor is a First In First Out (FIFO) data buffer system; it gathers data from specific stations and sends that data to the Database through a Gateway, whether through a Wi-Fi or cable connection to a Gateway. Stations are data sources and do not need data from other stations to provide their own data; they do not communicate with each other. In case of failure of communication with the server, it is the station (and or the Distributor) that has to cope with it; and data loss may eventually occur.

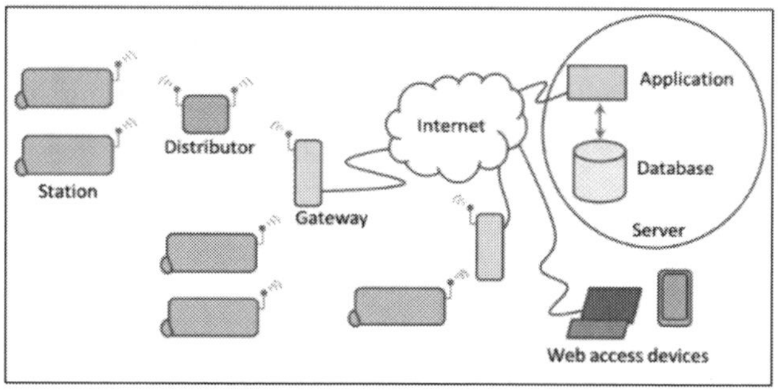

Figure 1. BlueLab's physical architecture.

The stations shown in Figure 1 can also be a smartphone with the BlueLab IoT system. Also shown in the figure are the user Web access devices, which use an Internet browser to communicate with the BlueLab Application where it is possible to manage the system by logging in successfully [4].

B. Logical Architecture

To get access to the BlueLab system, a user login interface is needed. The user login interface is modelled in a database and is shown in Figure 2.

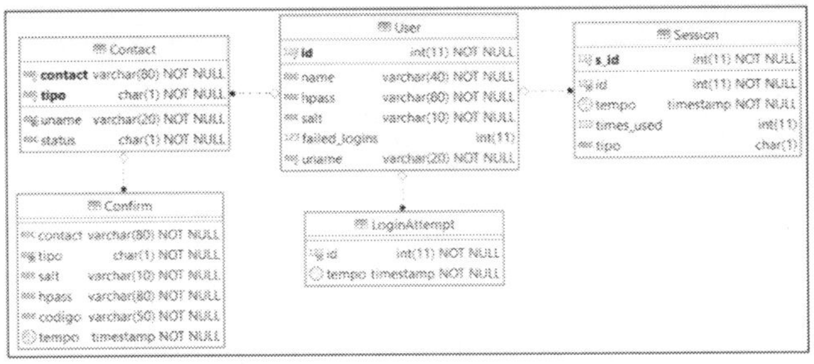

Figure 2. Database model for User access and authentication

A user account must have a contact which can be a phone number or an email and a name associated to it. Several strategies to recognize the authentic user are implemented, like password and associated hash procedures, email confirmation, phone confirmation by Short Message Service (sms), and failed login attempts within a time interval [5][6]. Those strategies are supported by the User, Contact, Confirm and LoginAttempt structures shown in Figure 2. For every valid login there is a random session number *sessionId* that has to be used in subsequent calls. The session is supported by the Session structure of Figure 2. A user may have more than one valid session. Each session may have a time limit, after which another login has to be issued to retrieve a different session number. A session may also be invalidated if a determined number of calls are exceeded.

Each user has a unique *uname* which is used as the database schema name which is associated to that user. After the creation of a new account the user has to build up the environment. The environment is composed by one or more stations; devices that are able to communicate with the BlueLab system and send values to be stored in the users' database schema. Each value is stored as a key value pair in the entry structure as shown in Figure 3.

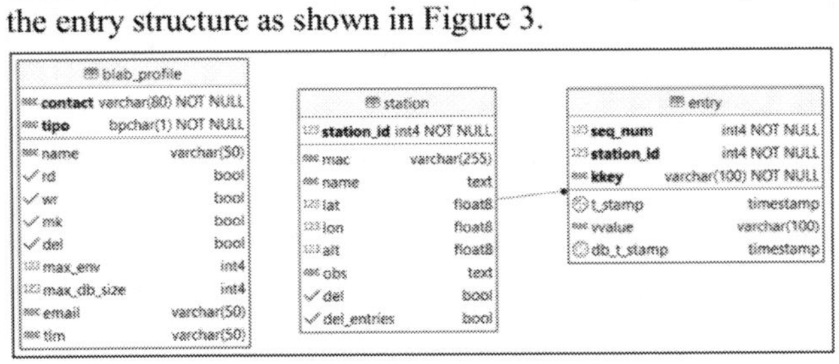

Figure 3. User profile and environment structures

A station has a structure where its identification is stored. The *station_id* is unique for each user and is system defined. The mac is user defined and it is not necessarily a mac address, it could be for example a phone's IMEI; and is unique for each user. Although latitude (*lat*), longitude (*lon*) and altitude (*alt*) are values that identify the position of a station, the station can still be mobile, and if needed the lat, lon and alt values can be sent and stored as an entry like any other sensor value. Any entry is identified by the station where it came from, the sequence number and a key, which can be the name of the physical reality that is being stored; e.g.: "temp". For that key the associated value is also stored; e.g.: "24.3", but the units are not, although the key can be used to hold the units; e.g.: "temp C". By using strings to store values the data type is not necessary because the context is in the key, and it allows storage to be uniform for all entries. Sequence numbers start at 1. Associated with an entry there are two timestamps, one belongs to the time at which the variable was sampled, and the other, database timestamp, the time at which the value was stored. A station that has different sensors and sends all values on the same frame will have all the entries with the same sequence number and same database timestamp. A station that uses the BlueLab system is not obliged to have a Real Time Clock (RTC) or any other time counting procedure, or it may or not have a buffer to hold samples prior to their sending to the database; which will in any of these situations have a significant difference between the station's timestamp and the database timestamp, besides the possibility of being in different timezones. Thus, it is easy to show or search for values belonging to keys in the time series using the sequence numbers and or the timestamps. The sequence number also ensures that the same value is not stored twice due to failures in the communication or the station, and also it is used for delivering values in order when the database is searched. A station can store entries without sequence, which means that there will not be a time series for those entries and they always have the last value. Those key value pairs are stored with sequence 0; values and their timestamps' are updated accordingly. This functionality can be used for the station to store values that it might use afterwards, like a memory. It can be used by the user to set parameters that are used by that station; and likewise values that a station communicates with the user: e.g., status or a sensor value. All these processes are asynchronous.

Within the database schema of a user there may exist one or more profiles supported by the *blab_profile* structure of Figure 3. These profiles help the stations to login into the BlueLab system. Logging in can be accomplished by the usual contact (email or phone number) and password, or only by a direct access code, which can be 80 characters long. By using the direct access code, a station does not need to store the user email or phone and password, which could jeopardize the users' account and entire database, should that station be captured for mischievous purposes. The user can change the direct access code at will. The same direct access code can be used by more than one station at a time; this kind of aggregation is a simple way to create a domain of stations. Each profile has flags that are set by the user when using the main profile and those flags indicate the privileges that that profile has for reading, writing or deleting data.

BlueLab IoT users can also share their data, or organize it in order to build up the architecture and provide different layers of meaning. For that a project has to be created as shown by the structures in Figure 4.

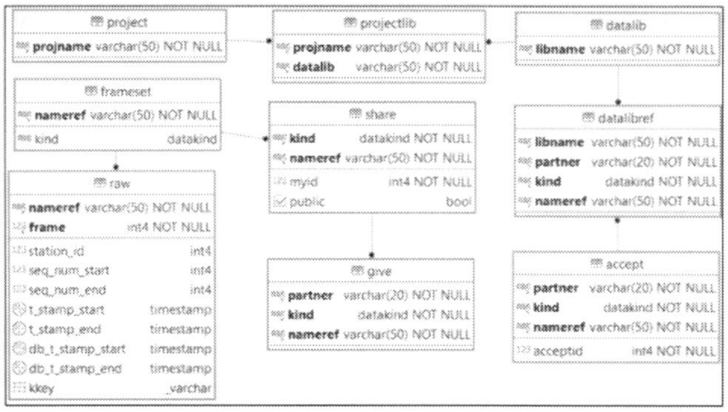

Figure 4. Project and data sharing structure

A user may have several projects, each one known by its unique name, and a project may use data libraries, as shown in the structures of Figure 4. Each data library has a unique name and references data which belongs to the user or to another user, known as partner. A partner is a BlueLab user that shares data; gives to or accepts from other users. A user does not share data that belongs to others; i.e. a user cannot give to a third user what was accepted from a second user. The partner identification is the same value as that of the database schema name, *uname*, referenced above in Figure 2. To share data acquired directly from the stations a user must build a raw set of frames. The raw is a set of selected frames from a station. A frame is the description of the data between two sequence numbers and or two timestamps (device and or database). All raw sets to be shared are on the share structure, and available to be given to partners and used by the user by adding them to the *datalibref* structure. The *datalibref* structure also holds the shared descriptions from the partners that were selected and stored on the accept structure. All this sharing strategy does not involve copying or storing data. When the data is needed, a request using the shared raw description is made to the original database schema.

Under development is the possibility of building processed data, which is data that results from processing raw data, from one or more stations, and eventually from partner's shared data. The reference to the processed data is also through the frameset and share structures (index *kind*). It is planned to add different layers of increasing meaning of processed data, P1, P2 and so on.

A station may issue an alarm which results on the sending of a sms by the BlueLab system. The sms alarm service is payed beforehand and credits or a number of available sms are stored in the operator structure shown in Figure 5. The structure allows support for several operators and offering them as payed services. Messages will be kept for the user to browse through and eventually delete the selected ones.

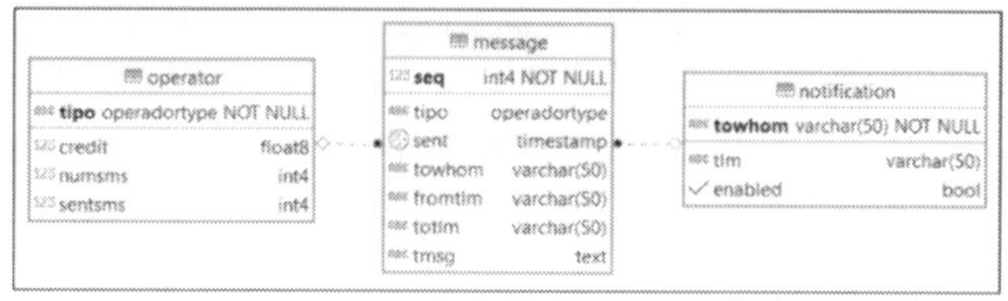

Figure 5. Alarm service structure

All destination sms numbers have to be previously entered and enabled in the notification structure of Figure 5 where they are identified by a token (*towhom*). Thus, a station can only send alarms by naming the destination token. A pre-existing token is "self", which means the users' phone (*tlm*) of the profile that was used for login.

III. MATERIAL AND METHODS

Several stations have been built using ESP8266 and ESP32 developer modules with the Arduino SDK. The stations are portable, and their power supply input is of 5V. The fixed stations are continuously connected to the mains electrical power distribution. Other stations use power packs or solar energy that charges a li-ion battery. Shown in Figure 6 is a fixed station out of its containing box.

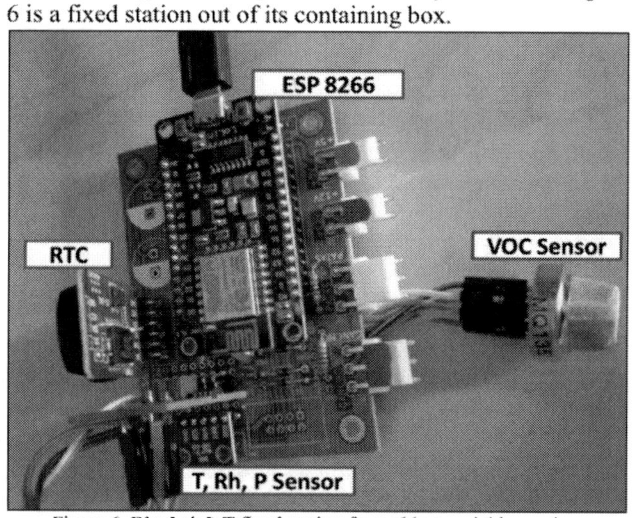

Figure 6. BlueLab IoT fixed station for ambient variable sensing

The device sensors are from a diverse set of sensor modules. The BME280 module provides temperature, relative humidity and air pressure values, and uses an I2C protocol for data retrieval [7]. The TLC555 module has a circuit that measures a capacitive moisture sensor for soil and translates its' value to an analogue output (0-3V), which has a response curve $moisture = A * response^{B}$ with constant values A and B found by calibration procedures [8]. An Hall effect current sensor with a 20 A range, ACS712, with analogue output (0-5 V) directly proportional to the sensed current [9]. Air quality sensor MQ135, that can detect ammonia, sulphide, benzene series steam, smoke and other toxic gases [10][11]. The circuit for the air quality sensor can also be used for similar type of Volatile Organic Compound (VOC) sensors [12].

The fixed station of Figure 6 is composed by an ESP8266 microcontroller, a RTC with battery, a MQ135 sensor and a BME280 module. This fixed station is acquiring in-house data since July 2018. Note that the sensor's calibration *A* and *B* values can be stored with sequence number 0, defining them as constants with an appropriate identification string.

There is a hands on example at github [13]. The code can be downloaded into an ESP8266 or ESP-32 microcontroller and it uses as sensors a digital input, and an analogical input, which is floating if not connected, so that touching it will produce different readings. On the above mentioned user link there is an Android app that can use the phone's light sensor and the latitude, longitude and altitude values of the GPS to send to the BlueLab IoT system; everything can be safely deleted.

IV. Results and Discussion

Two graphs are displayed in Figure 7 showing the values stored by the fixed station in a house from 25.08.2019 00:00 till 07.09.2019 23:59, totalling 12526 samples each.

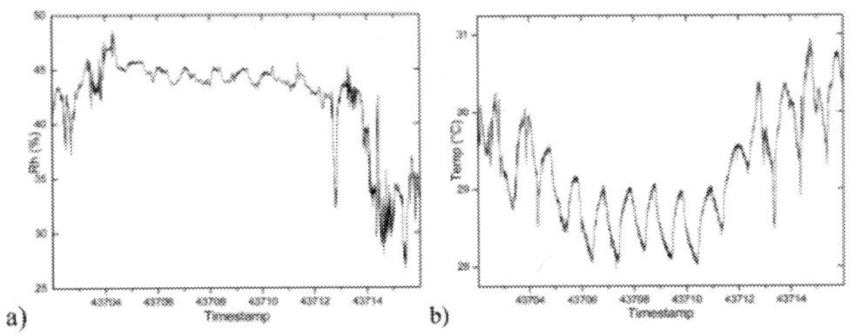

Figure 7. Graphs for a) relative humidity and b) temperature (ºC) values

Samples were obtained every 3 s smoothed by a 4-point moving average filter, for all sensors. The resulting waveforms were then sampled every 90 s and its values sent through the communication link to the BlueLab IoT database. This continuous process can then be searched, and displayed as shown in Figure 7. The data displayed is classified as raw. This raw data could then be processed (not yet done) on a first stage and be classified as P1. For example, from the figures, the circadian rhythm can be extracted, and characteristics like the min, max and mean values stored as P1. By interpretation of the circadian data, it would be easy to conclude with high probability that during 7 days the house had no human intervention; maybe occupants were on holidays.

V. Conclusion

BlueLab Iot system is a possible solution for developers to add a station that gathers data in any format, stores and retrieves it from a database. It has been working continuously since July 2018. All improvements made to the system since then have not compromised the acquired data. Frequently, tests are made by adding different devices with several combinations of sensors, and power requirements, including battery packs and solar panels. Users can access the BlueLab IoT system using an Internet browser and configure their profile and options, and can also visualize and delete their data received from their stations. Data can be shared among users of the system; this allows a user to include on a project its own and shared data. Presently each user has a different schema on the same database, but in future, each user can define its own database on different servers. A station is a device with the BlueLab IoT system, for example a smartphone application, or an embedded system or a computer program that gathers data from several sources and sends them to the BlueLab Iot system. As future work, it is planned the processing of data to produce P1 framesets, real time use case scenarios, and improvement of the user interface.

References

[1] T. Kramp, R. van Kranenburg, and S. Lange, "Introduction to the internet of things," in *Enabling Things to Talk: Designing IoT Solutions with the IoT Architectural Reference Model*, 2013, pp. 1–10.

[2] J. Mineraud, O. Mazhelis, X. Su, and S. Tarkoma, "A gap analysis of Internet-of-Things platforms," *Comput. Commun.*, vol. 89–90, pp. 5–16, 2016.

[3] S. Vashi, J. Ram, J. Modi, S. Verma, and C. Prakash, "Internet of Things (IoT): A vision, architectural elements, and security issues," in *Proceedings of the International Conference on IoT in Social, Mobile, Analytics and Cloud, I-SMAC 2017*, 2017, pp. 492–496.

[4] V. Vaz da Silva, "BlueLab IoT," 2020. [Online]. Available: https://bluelab.pt/iot. [Accessed: 21-Jan-2020].

[5] P.-H. Kamp, "LinkedIn Password Leak: Salt Their Hide," *Queue*, vol. 10, no. 6, p. 20, Jun. 2012.

[6] A. Conklin, G. Dietrich, and D. Walz, "Password-based authentication: a system perspective," in *37th Annual Hawaii International Conference on System Sciences, 2004. Proceedings of the*, 2004, pp. 1–10.

[7] "BME280 - Combined humidity and pressure sensor (and temperature) datasheet," *Bosch*, 2015. [Online]. Available: https://www.digchip.com/datasheets/parts/datasheet/1727/BME280-pdf.php. [Accessed: 29-Sep-2019].

[8] R. Radi, M. Murtiningrum, N. Ngadisih, F. S. Muzdrikah, M. S. Nuha, and F. A. Rizqi, "Calibration of Capacitive Soil Moisture Sensor (SKU:SEN0193)," in *2018 4th International Conference on Science and Technology (ICST)*, 2018, pp. 1–6.

[9] V. Miron-Alexe, "Comparative study regarding measurements of different AC current sensors," in *2016 International Symposium on Fundamentals of Electrical Engineering (ISFEE)*, 2016, pp. 1–6.

[10] "MQ135 Semiconductor Sensor for Air Quality," *Winson*, 2015. [Online]. Available: https://www.winsen-sensor.com/d/files/PDF/Semiconductor Gas Sensor/MQ135 (Ver1.4) - Manual.pdf. [Accessed: 30-Sep-2019].

[11] K. Vandana, C. Baweja, Simmarpreet, and S. Chopra, "Influence of Temperature and Humidity on the Output Resistance Ratio of the MQ-135 Sensor," *Int. J. Adv. Res. Comput. Sci. Softw. Eng.*, vol. 6, no. 4, pp. 423–429, 2016.

[12] C. Durán, J. Benjumea, and J. Carrillo, "Response Optimization of a Chemical Gas Sensor Array using Temperature Modulation," *Electronics*, vol. 7, no. 4/54, 2018.

[13] V. Vaz da Silva, "BlueLab IoT at GitHub," 2020. [Online]. Available: https://github.com/tektonia/bluelab_iot. [Accessed: 21-Jan-2020].

Automated Greenhouse Using Arduino Mega

Badour AlAbri, Hawa AlSaraai, Roghaieh Parvizsedghy

Department of Engineering, German University of Technology in Oman, Oman.
RoghaiehParvizsedghy@gutech.edu.om

Ali Al-Humairi[12],
[1]Department of Computer Science, German University of Technology in Oman, Oman.
[2]Department of Communication Technologies, University of Duisburg-Essen, Duisburg, Germany.
ali.alhumairi@gutech.edu.om
ali.al-humairi@stud.uni-duisburg-essen.de

Hayat El Asri[3], Laila Benhlima[4]
Department of Computer Science
Mohammadia School of Engineering
Mohammed V University
Rabat, Morocco
[3]hayatelasri@research.emi.ac.ma,
[4]benhlima@emi.ac.ma

Abstract— **Greenhouses are especially important in hot climates. In fact, there are some plants that cannot survive in hot climates; for instance, strawberries, peaches, and pomegranates. In general, Greenhouses are a closed and transparent structure that can be used in home gardens and farms, creating a suitable environment for plants to grow in a relatively cold environment. Furthermore, greenhouses offer some other factors of extreme importance for plants to grow rapidly; to name but a few, cold temperature, suitable humidity, soil moisture, and a cover from harmful winds. A greenhouse is designed in such a way to increase the production of crops and harvest seasons. Moreover, greenhouses are mobile, which makes them easy to transfer from one place to another if need arises. Besides, a greenhouse is not limited to a specific size, but can be adjusted based on the available surface area and number of crops. Unlike traditional greenhouses, the automated greenhouse proposed in this paper will have an automatic irrigation system and a weather controller.**

Keywords-Greenhouse, Design, Construction, Control System, Automated System, Agriculture, Irrigation.

I. INTRODUCTION

The consumption of fruits and vegetables has become of vital importance in most societies. A large number of different kinds of fresh fruits and vegetables are available anytime of the year. However, in a dry climate such as Oman's, growing fruits and vegetables is a big challenge because of different factors such as the low humidity and the lack of rain. A suitable greenhouse that takes into account the challenges aforementioned is needed to grow fruits or vegetables. A greenhouse is defined as a simply designed house whose ceiling can be made of different materials like, plastic or glass. The selected material depends on the climate condition requirement.

Structure and design of greenhouses affects the crop production. Many developments have appeared related to greenhouse design recently. Those early structured was made to control parameters like temperature and humidity. Nonetheless, these latter did not meet the needed requirements of quality control criteria. Nowadays, the surrounding environment faces many issues and challenges regarding the climate condition. Global warming and weather changes are considered to be the main causes of these latter. Farmers, and the agriculture industry in general, are facing many obstructions regarding the aforementioned issues. Therefore, the automated greenhouse is the best solution to overcome these issues in the agriculture sector. There are several advantages that come with building a structure like that. To mention but a few, its suitability to grow any type of plants, its ability to provide the ideal weather condition and conserve the water, and its ability to decrease the need for technicians since the greenhouse is fully automated. The remaining of this paper is structured as follow. Section II discusses the literature review. Section III, presents the implementation objectives. Section IV, describes the design and the implementation. Section V, present the results. Finally, the conclusion and the future work of the paper are presented.

II. LITRATURE REVIEW

This section will introduce the relevant literature and research projects that have been done before. The concept of the greenhouse is to provide a suitable environment for many different plants. The greenhouse is a method to provide plants such fruits and vegetables all year round with the different weather conditions by control and monitor different parameters such as, humidity and temperature [6].

Waaijenberg [5] conducted a research about the greenhouse design, construction, and the covered materials. Generally, there are many material properties to evaluate the covered material of a greenhouse. For example, the fire behavior, the mechanical strength, the investment costs, the permeability for humidity, and the available dimensions. Another parameter which will be affected by a covering material is the light transition. Light transition relies on the covered material of the greenhouse.

The concept of growing different types of plants in a monitored and controlled environment came from "Rome under the reign of Emperor Tiberius"[13]. It was found that similar papers only focus on the temperature, the humidity, and the irrigation system. For a plant to grow with a good quality, it needs enough space to develop its roots, an appropriate amount of water, adequate lighting, oxygen, a suitable temperature, and mineral. Kumar et al [8] suggested the usage of microcontrollers for controlling greenhouses. The aim of this project was to enhance plants' growth by providing a suitable environment and a controlled irrigation system to offer a sufficient amount of water. The sensors utilized in this project are: a soil moisture sensor, a temperature sensor, and a humidity sensor. Each and every recorded value is presented on a Liquid Cristal Display (LCD) that enables the farmers to easily maintain the environmental parameters environment of the greenhouse.

On the other hand, Shaker et al. [1] built a greenhouse project to control the climate and the irrigation system inside the greenhouse by using Wireless Sensor Network (WSN). The structure of this project aimed at providing environment where the climate can be fully controlled in order to protect the plants from any external weather condition.

III. Implementation objectives

The main purpose of this automated greenhouse is to design and implement a greenhouse for plants that can be automatically controlled and monitored by using a microcontroller.

The detailed objectives of this project are as follow:

- Optimizing the usage of Energy by controlling the energy consumption.
- Minimizing the usage of water by controlling the irrigation system, and providing the needed amount of water.
- Designing and constructing the structure of the greenhouse by selecting efficient and appropriate materials.
- Designing and implementing an Automated Irrigation System.
- Maintaining the climate factors inside the greenhouse's environment.

The greenhouse will be fully automated system so there is no need for human interventions. In addition, it will be open source which, make it unique and different from the others projects.

IV. Design and implementation

To achieve the project objectives, using Arduino as a microcontroller seems to be the best choice since it supports open hardware and software systems. In addition, it has a very low cost and it is available on the local market. The choice of materials was as follows. A Field Control System: this step depends on the working of different sensors used in this project which are the soil moisture, the temperature and the humidity, the lighting, the water flow, the gas, a SIM card and electric current. The testing and programming for every sensor was done separately. The first sensor used is the temperature and humidity sensor and then we added the other different sensors which are the soil moisture, PH level, light, SIM card, MQ-7, flow meter, and current. However, different actuators such, pump, light, and fan are installed to. The second step is the project preparation. For the purpose of building the structure of this project, plastic and aluminum were used.

A. Design Process

Selecting of structural material of the greenhouse depends on the cost and availability, technical characteristics, and local climate. Furthermore, the selection of these materials is based on the requirements of design strength, physical properties, life expectancy, and cost of construction materials

a)Frame:

The frames for the greenhouse are essential because without good solid frames, any greenhouse would not stand properly. There are a variety of materials that may be used for the frames of the greenhouse. Each material has advantages and disadvantages. Selecting the suitable choice of frames will have a good impact on the greenhouse structure.

Aluminum is the selected material for the greenhouse frame. It is considered as a low maintenance material, and can be used for a long time. This material cannot break or rust easily. It supports the members which are made from the heaviest pieces. Moreover, it supplies good rigid for the plastics, and it can be painted in any color. It has several advantages such as its lightness and robustness. Also, it is suitable in any environmental condition and will not face any corrosion, unlike iron.

b)Covered material:

Covering material of the greenhouse is also an essential part that affects the productivity of the crops and the structure performance of the greenhouse. It also affects the amount of light needed for growing plants. Several characteristics should be considered in choosing the most suitable covering material such as, weight, amount of transmitted light, cost, amount of transmitted energy, and the ease of maintenance.

Polycarbonate plastic is the selected material for covering the greenhouse. It has better insulation and a natural light filter which conserves the plants from harmful radiations. This plastic consists of UV radiations, which is used in outdoor areas. UV radiations help the plastic to prevent the deterioration and yellowing from sun radiation. It is available anywhere there is strong wind and other mechanical stress. It is a fully transparent material. The transparent corrugated plastic provides strength and a protection from high temperature. Also, it consists of clear bubble insulation which provides a protection from cold weather.

The greenhouse profile is generally of lean type design, with 60 cm width, 80cm length and 80 height. The last step was to assemble all parts together to finalize the project construction besides the last step in the coding process was to gather all codes in one single program and run it in a large-scale project to make sure that everything is working perfectly.

B. System block diagram

Figure 1 shows the system block diagram. The greenhouse environment in this project is controlled and monitored by the microcontroller Arduino Mega. This latter controls and monitors the plants within this greenhouse, which is lettuce in this case, by utilizing the sensors, mainly the humidity, temperature, and current sensors. The fan and water pumps are the actuators used in this project. In addition, the Arduino software or "Arduino Integrated Development Environment" was used to develop the different codes that are used in this project the language of this software based on C++ language. The first sensor utilized is the humidity and temperature sensor. This sensor is responsible for sending the value of the temperature and the humidity inside the greenhouse. If a temperature higher than 26 degrees Celsius is recorded, fan will be activating it to regulate it. On the other hand, if a temperature lower than 26 C is recorded, the fan will be deactivated and the lamp will be turned on to work as “sun” in order to regulate the temperature. The same goes for the humidity, the humidity will be sensed during the system operation. If the humidity level exceeds 34%, the fan will be turned on, and if it goes below 31%, the lamp will be activated. The second sensor is the soil moisture sensor this sensor detects the soil moisture percentage. If the detected moisture percentage is less than 35%, it is concluded that the soil is very dry and the water pump machine will be turned on to irrigate the plants inside the greenhouse. However, if the sensor detects a soil moisture percentage higher than 35 %, it is concluded that the soil is wet, and there is no need for irrigation. Regarding the light sensor (LDR), it will work if it senses that the value of the LDR is lower than threshold. Then, the light will turn on, and vice versa. following to that, the PH sensor will work if the PH inside the main tank become less than 8, then the second water pump will operated to stabilize the PH value. In addition, the carbon monoxide sensor will detect the amount of CO inside the greenhouse. If the CO concentration is more than 120 ppm, the SIM sensor will be activated and a message will be sent to the greenhouse' owners. Finally, the water flow detector is installed to sense the water flow rate record the water consumption in liters.

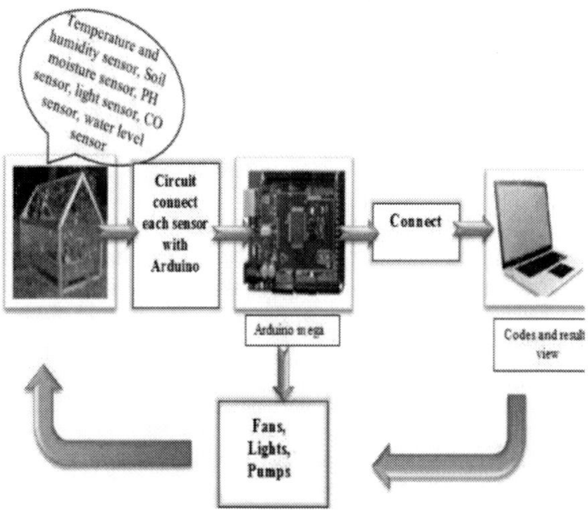

Figure 1. System block diagram

C. Automated greenhouse flowchart

The flowchart in Figure 2 presents the different sensors and how each of them works. The flowchart represents the used sensors and how they operate. The environment of the lettuce crop is monitored by the Arduino Mega microcontroller that controls the needed sensors for the plant and offers the suitable environment. These sensors are PH, soil moisture, light, temperature, and humidity. Moreover, there are some actuators which are installed in the greenhouse in order to maintain the suitable environment. These actuators are fan, lamps and pumps. Firstly, the humidity and temperature sensors are used to measure the temperature and humidity value. If the temperature is more than 26 degree, then the fan will work to reduce it and if it is less than 26 then the lamps will work to heat the greenhouse. The second sensor provides the suitable value of the PH value. If the PH value is more than 8 in the main tank, then the pump will work to provide more water from the other tank until it reaches 8. Thirdly, the light sensor detects the brightness inside the greenhouse. If the LDR value is less than threshold then the lamps will work. Furthermore, Furthermore, soil moisture sensor detects the amount of water in the soil. If the soil moisture is less than 35%, then the pump will work to provide the needed water for lettuce. Then, if the carbon monoxide sensor records that the value of CO more than 120ppm, a message will be sent to the owner of the greenhouse. Finally, both values of the current sensors will be represented on the LCD during the fan and the pump operation.

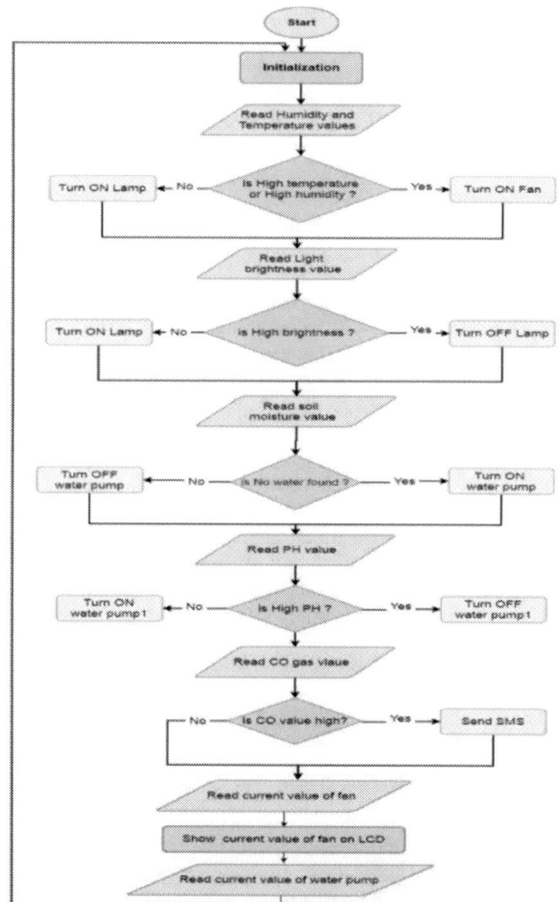

Figure 2. Flow chart of the project

V. RESULTS AND DISCUSSION

Selecting the materials:

1. Aluminium: it is very light in weight which is needed to build the greenhouse structure to handle it

everywhere, and to protect it from the climate conditions such as strong wind.

2. Polycarbonate plastic: it is easy to fit and handle. Replacing polycarbonate plastic sheets from the greenhouse is much easier, but to be more careful when installing any material in polycarbonate plastic because it gets damaged quickly.
3. Light bulb: incandescent lights are reliable and have a full brightness as soon as the key switches on. The quantity of lose heat is very high which increases the temperature inside the greenhouse and affects the growth of the plants.
4. Fan: it is one of the high performance cooling products.

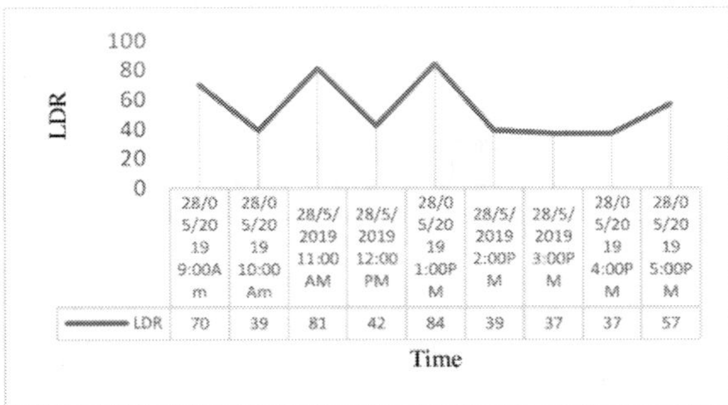

Figure 3. LDR Sensor

The line graph in Figure 3 illustrates the values of the LDR sensor that detect the brightness inside the greenhouse from 9:00 AM to 5:00 PM. It can be clearly seen that the LDR values are fluctuating during that period. Moving on to the details, the highest values were recorded at 9, 11 and 1:00PM, while the lowest values were recorded at 3:00 and 4:00PM.These changes happened because the LDR sensor detects the brightness from the lights which are installed inside the location of greenhouse.

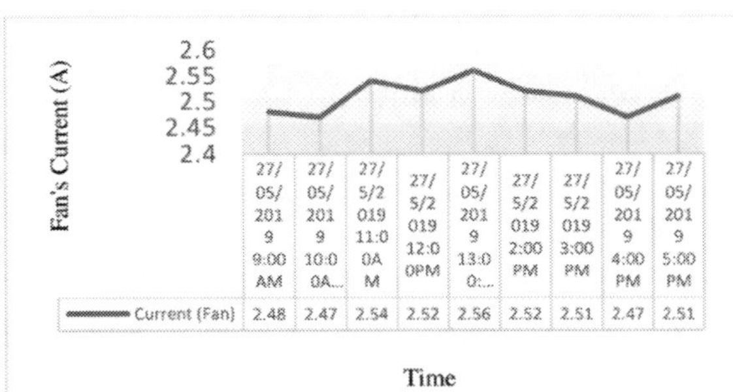

Figure 4. Fan's current

The line graph from Figure 4 presents the values of current sensor that monitors the fan consumption with the time from 9:00 AM to 5:00 PM. The overall trend shows a fluctuation in the fan's current values. Back to the details, the highest value was recorded at 1:00 PM, whereas the lowest value was recorded at 4:00 PM. These fluctuations happened because the fan was switched on and off during the period due to a temperature change.

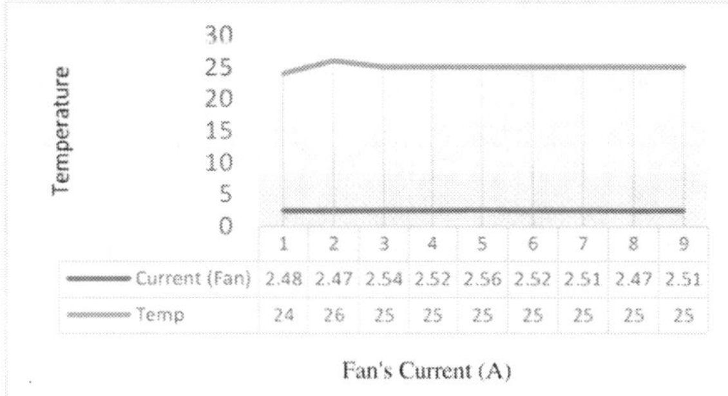

Figure 5. Fan's Current & Temperature

Figure 5 presents the comparison between the fan's current and temperature from 9:00 AM to 5:00 PM. The y-axis presents the temperature values while the x-axis shows the fan's current in Ampere. It can be clearly observed that both lines are constant during the period.

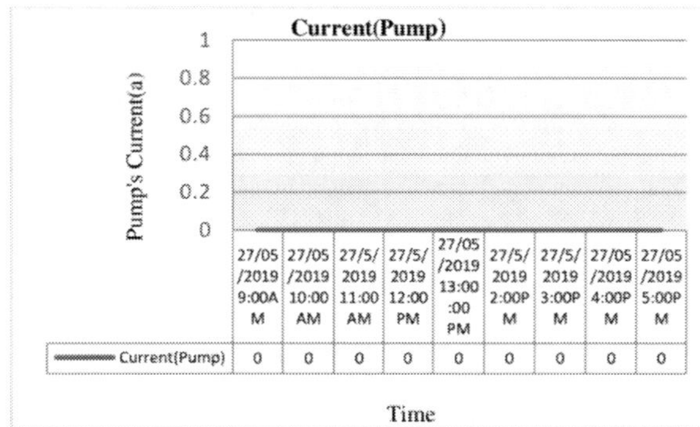

Figure 6. Pump's (OFF) Current

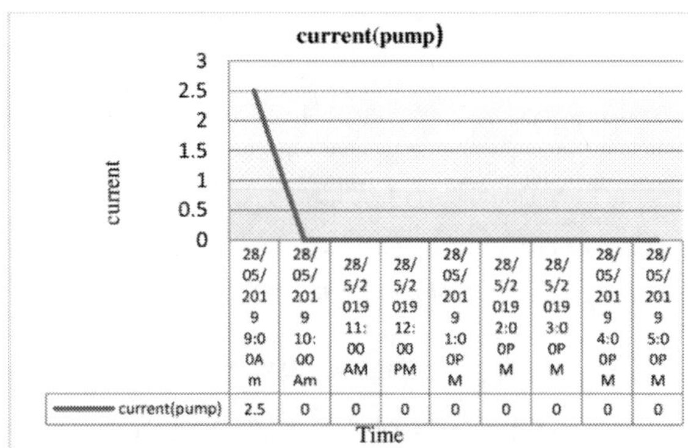

Figure 7. Pump's (ON) Current during Irrigation

The two-line graph in Figures 6 and 7 shows the current sensor for the pump with the time from 9:00AM to 5:00 PM. In the first graph, it can be observed that the pump's current values are almost zero because the pump was switched off. Whereas in the second graph, the value for the pump's current was 2.5 Ampere because the pump was switched on. The pump was switched on because the soil was dried. In the remaining time the values are almost zero because the soil had enough water.

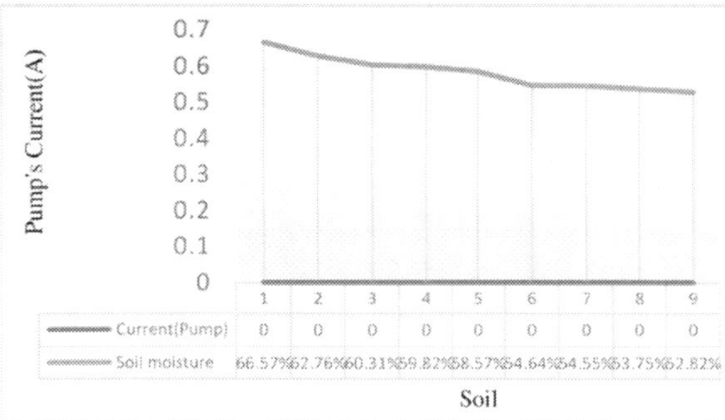

Figure 8. Pump's (OFF) Current & Soil Moisture

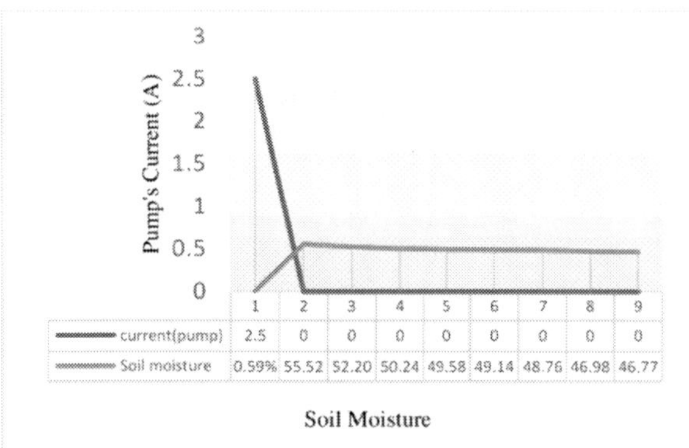

Figure 9. Pump's (ON) Current & Soil Moisture

The two graphs in Figures 8 and 9 show the comparison between the pump's current and soil moisture. The x-axis represents the pump's current while the y-axis represents the percentage of soil moisture. In the first graph, the values of soil moisture were decreased gradually but the pump's current values were almost zero during the period. Whereas in the second graph, the value for the pump's current was 2.5 ampere at the first period. The soil moisture value was recorded in that time was 0.59%. In this situation, the pump was switched on to irrigate the plants. In the remaining time, the pump's current values are almost zero.

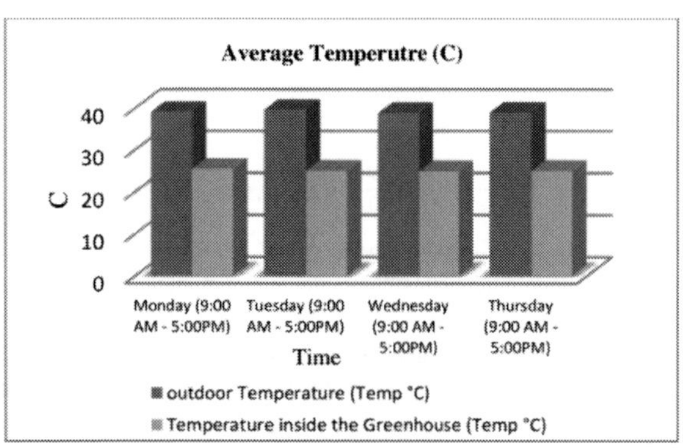

Figure 10. Temperature Average

For the humidity and temperature sensor, it has been noticed that if the value of the temperature that appears in the LCD Screen becomes more than the fixed temperature number in the system, the sensor shows response to that and the Fan will be switched on to decrease the value of the temperature. The chart in Figure 10 shows the average temperature in Celsius for outside and inside the greenhouse. The results were recorded for 4 days (Monday, Tuesday, Wednesday, Thursday), each day from 9:00AM to 5:00PM. Looking to the graph, the temperature inside the greenhouse was recorded with a constant value 25 for whole the days. On the other hand, the outside temperature recorded an average value between 38 and 39 for the same period.

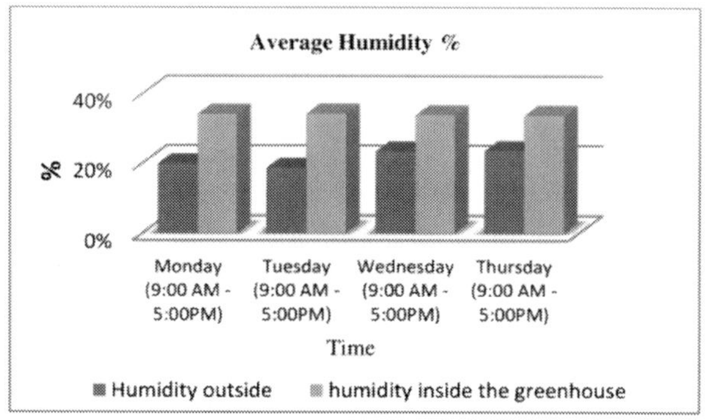

Figure 11. Average Humidity

Regarding the humidity controls, if the percentage of humidity is either less or more than the fixed point in the system which is 35%, the sensor will detect that and the fan will be operated in order to decrease the value of the humidity inside the greenhouse. The next chart in Figure 11 shows the average percentage of the humidity for a period of four days beginning with 27/5/2019 until 30/5/2019 for each day from 9:00 AM to 5:00 PM. The humidity in the greenhouse environment was compared with the outside humidity. In general, it is clear from the graph that the humidity inside the greenhouse was constant during that time for all the mentioned days, which means that the control system works efficiently. On the other hand, the outside humidity was varying with a range of 19% to 23% during the same time of the change in the other condition outside.

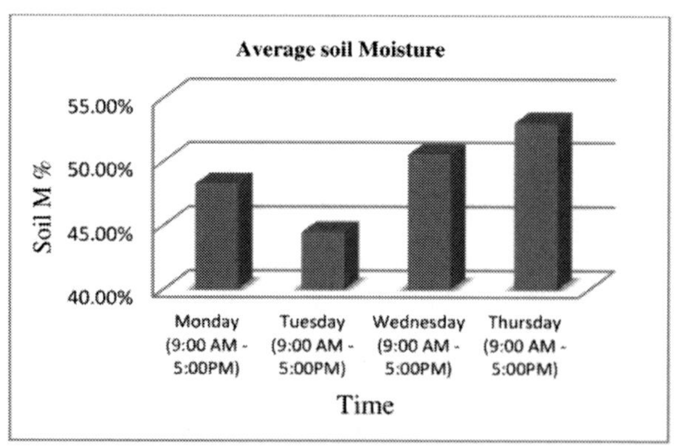

Figure 12. Soil Moisture Average

In this test, it has been noticed that when the percentage of the soil moisture becomes lower than the limited value (35%), it was detected by the sensor and a signal was sent to operate the pump to irrigate the plants in the controlled greenhouse. Nevertheless, if the soil moisture sensor sense that the value of the moisture exceeds 35%, a signal is sent to the system to stop the irrigation process as the plants have enough water. Moreover, Figure 12 shows the average percentage of the soil moisture for a period of 4 days between 9:00 AM and 5:00 PM daily. Looking into the graph, it can be recognized that the soil moisture average has declined on Tuesday due to the results that was recorded during the day has the lowest value between the four days. However, the percentage of the soil moisture increased gradually on Wednesday and Thursday.

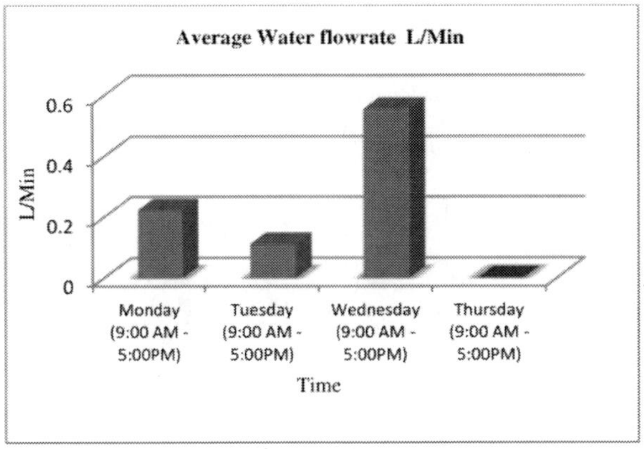

Figure 13. Water Flow Average

In Figure 13, the water flow sensor works to detect the water flow that enters the greenhouse. When the soil becomes dry, the sensor of soil moisture sends a signal to operate the pump. During that time, the water flow sensor will record the water flow. The chart above in Figure 13 illustrates the average water flow amount during the aforementioned period. It is clear from the graph that the water flow rate recorded the lowest amount on Wednesday with a value of 0.557 L/Min. Nonetheless, it has the lowest value on Thursday because the plants were not irrigated during the system operation. On the fourth day, the data of the water flow was 0 L/Min for the whole period because the soil has enough water and there is no need to irrigate the plants.

Figure 14 compares the soil moisture to the water flow rate for the first day. What is noticeable is that there is a direct relationship between the water flow and the soil moisture. When the water pump works to irrigate the plants, the amount of water increased sharply to reach its peak. During that same time, the soil wetness percentage increased and the same was noticed during the whole days.

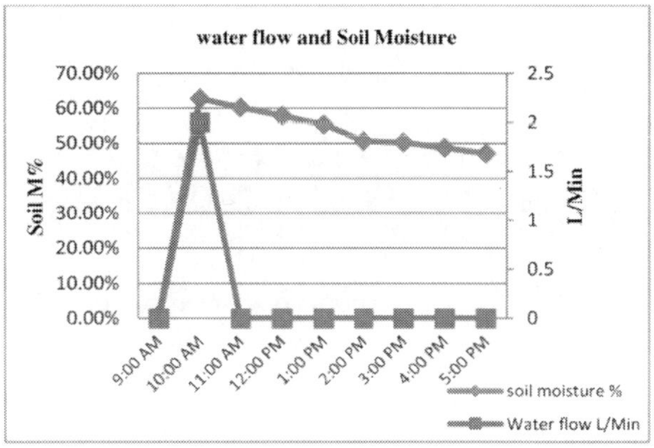

Figure 14. Water Flow & Soil Moisture

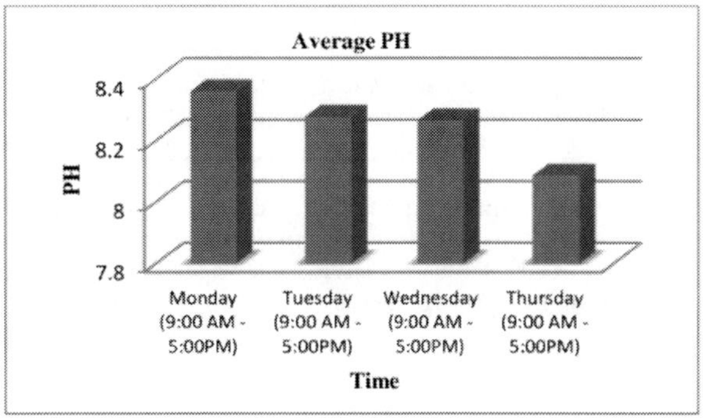

Figure 15. PH Average

The PH sensor works to sense the PH level into the main tank which is used for the irrigation system. When the value of the PH becomes more than threshold, the sensor detects that and the second pump is operated to push water into the main container to decrease the PH level. Figure 15 demonstrates the daily PH level. Overall, the PH level is at its highest on Monday because the water was not used before. In contrast, the lowest value was in Thursday with a value of 8.08. In general, the water that used in the tank considered basic.

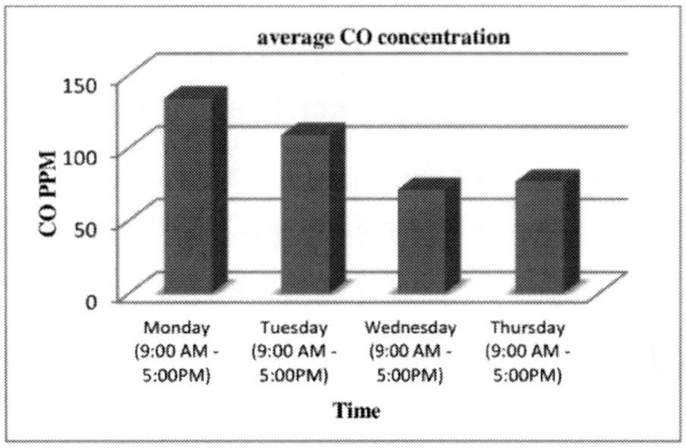

Figure 16. CO Average

The MQ-7 sensor is used. This sensor detects that the value of the gas (CO). If the said value is more than the threshold, a message will be sent to the owner in order to quickly check the greenhouse. The above chart in Figure 16 demonstrates the average value of the gas (CO) in PPM for a period of 4 days, each day between 9:00 AM to 5:00 PM. What is noticeable on Monday the CO concentration recorded as the highest value its reach 133 ppm. On the other hand, the lowest value was recorded on Wednesday with a value of 70 ppm.

VI. CONCLUSION AND FUTURE WORK

The main purpose of this research project is to construct, design, and implement a fully automated greenhouse with an efficient design to provide a suitable environment for growing plants using an Arduino microcontroller. The greenhouse is constructed using Aluminum as a supported frame and polycarbonate plastic as a cover material. The choice these materials is based on the previous studies about constructing a greenhouse. The selected design is lean-to type greenhouse that is mobile and easily transferrable. We achieved successful results with this project. In fact, the sensors used showed very promising response with a success percentage reached to 90% in detecting and sending signals to Arduino, to control the climate parameters and the irrigation system. By having this efficient system inside greenhouse, the lettuce productivity increased, water and energy consumption were optimized, and manpower decreased.

Regarding the future works, intelligence with data processing and prediction will be carried out to improve the result. In addition, a possible extension of this project would involve creating a knowledge management system, where several cases are going to be fed into the system for future predictions and recommendation purposes.

REFERENCES

[1] A. Imran, and S. Mahmoud, Greenhouse micro climate monitoring, Electronic and Communication Engineering vol: 7, no: 12, 2013.

[2] B. Kendirli, Structural analysis of greenhouses, a case study in Turkey, Building and Environment, Retrieved from https://www.Oecd.Org/Env/Outreach/Kg_Study_Irrigation.Pdf 2006.

[3] B. Basic Greenhouse Design and Planning for a Location, Retrieved from Enesco: https://greenhouses-etc.net/gh_guide/greenhouses.html 2006.

[4] D. Attalla, and J Tannfelt WU, Automated Greenhouse, no.44, SWEDEN, 2015.

[5] D. Waaijenberg, Design, construction and maintenance of greenhouse structures, Acta Horticulturae, no.710, pp. 31-42, 2006.

[6] H. MOHAMED, Automation of greenhouses by using microcontroller, Microprocessor and Electronic Control, pp.1-72, (2015).

[7] H. T. Jadhav, Economic and Environmental Analysis, Iowa State University Digital Repository, 2017, DOI:10.13031/aim.201701178.

[8] K., Pradeep, Greenhouse Monitoring and Automation, International Journal of Engineering Trends and Technology (IJETT), Vol.45, no. 5, 2017.

[9] M. Teitel, Greenhouse Design: Concepts and Trends, Acta horticulturae, no.952, pp.605-620, Jun. 2012, doi: 10.17660/ActaHortic.2012.952.77

[10] M. Woods, and A. Swartz Warren, Glass Houses, Hardcover, London, pp. 216, 1988.

[11] N. E. Hassan, an Automatic monitoring and control system, conference and workshop proceeding, Bangladesh, Brac University, 2015.

[12] P. S. Dhaknel, PLC based greenhouse automation, Vol. 5, ISSN. 2321-9653, April. 2017.

[13] G.Bruno, rimol blog, retrieved from rimol greenhouses, https://www.rimolgreenhouses.com/blog/the-first-greenhouses-from-rome-to-america, 2013- 2014.

Smart Chair for Mitigation of Skin Pressure Ulcers

Miguel Gomes[a], Pedro Rebelo[b], Vitor Vaz da Silva[c]
[a,c]Electronics Telecommunication and Computer Dpt. ISEL/IPL – Instituto Superior de Engenharia de Lisboa
Instituto Politécnico de Lisboa, Lisboa, Portugal
[b]ESTeSL – Escola Superior de Tecnologia da Saúde de Lisboa,
Instituto Politécnico de Lisboa, Lisboa, Portugal
[c]CTS – Centre of Technology and Systems,
UNL – Universidade Nova de Lisboa, Caparica, Portuga
e-mail[a]: miguelfpgomes.92@gmail.com
e-mail[b]:pedro.rebelo@estesl.ipl.pt
e-mail[c]:vsilva@deetc.isel.ipl.pt

Abstract—Pressure Ulcers are still a great health problem, even in developed countries, that usually appear in impaired individuals as result of long periods of immobilization. It is estimated that the European prevalence rates range from 8.3 % to 22.9 % in hospitalized patients and is estimated that this kind of wounds represent 2 % of the European budget for primary health care. To mitigate this problem, a working device was built in order to assess the microclimate created between a sited individual and where he is sited on. To that end, the device was composed by pressure, temperature and humidity sensors, controlled by a microprocessor that made all the data management, sending it wirelessly to a platform on the Internet that stores all the information acquired, having also a user interface that shows up the data.

Keywords-Pressure; Ulcer; Sensors; Ischial; Smart Seat.

I. INTRODUCTION

Pressure Ulcers (PU) are injuries located at the top layer of the skin, and/or at its underlying tissues, as consequence of an ischemic process and tissue necrosis. They are normally chronic wounds frequently related to long periods on hospitals where most of their time patients happen to be on a laying position, compressing the soft tissues between a bony prominence and the external surface of the body.

The pressure ulcers can be classified according to the National Pressure Ulcer Advisory Panel (NUPAP) [1] and the European Pressure Ulcer Advisory Panel (EPUAP) [2] grades, where 4 stages can be defined and each stage can provide a different standard for treatment and prevention for pressure ulcers:

Stage 1 – Non-blanchable erythema at skin: In this stage, the skin is intact only with the presence of a located erythema (usually associated to a bony prominence) [1].

Stage 2 - Partial loss of skin thickness: Dermis partial loss of thickness [1].

Stage 3 - Full loss of skin thickness: At this third stage, the tissues lose their total thickness. The ears, occipital region, nose cane and malleoli does not present subcutaneous tissue, so the PU are more superficial at these zones [1].

Stage 4 – Full loss of tissue thickness: At this stage, the full loss of tissue thickness can lead to an exposed bone, tendon or muscle, yet, the depth, depends on the wound's anatomical location[1].

A. Risk factors on Pressure Ulcer creation

The pathologic conditions that lead to PU are multifactorial and integrate several pathogenic ways; moreover, the individual's weakness (generally on elder individuals) can be one catalyser of this whole process.

The risk factors can be divided into intrinsic and extrinsic factors: Extrinsic factors create skin damage through external conditions, while intrinsic factors are related physiological and body function factors [3], [4].

1) Extrinsic factors:

Between all the extrinsic factors, excessive pressure forces, friction, shear forces, and excessive humidity are considered the most important and more likely to lead to skin wounds and PU development [5].

a) Pressure: A long duration pressure at soft tissues between two surfaces (usually between a bony surface and rigid surface), generates a pressure higher than that of the surface capillary vessels, creating occlusion on these vessels and consequently tissue hypoxia, and ischemia, which can lead to an ulceration process [6]. The human organism response to this situation of excessive compression is the frequent change of position, relieving this way the compressed zone, re-establishing the blood flow [6].

b) Shear forces: Shear forces happen when two surfaces slide over each other. Relating to PU, shearing forces are created by the gravity felt upon the body, pulling it down, and at the same time there is a force, parallel to the body, creating a resistance to the gravity force, and these two forces combined create a friction and shear forces at the individual's skin [4]. This kind of forces are usually related to incorrect body transfers and mobilization on impaired individuals [5].

c) Humidity: is the chemical change on skin's pH, alternating the epidermis's resistance, making it more likely to develop wounds created by other factors [6][10].

2) Intrinsic factors:

These kinds of factors are directly related to body structure and its function; more precisely the immobilization, sensibility malfunctions, gender, age, nutritional state, incontinence and a bad tissue perfusion rate can trigger the PU development [7].

Some systems for mapping the pressures felt under a seated individual's body can be found on the market, and those systems usually provide a visual perception for the pressure felt under the bony prominences relatively to other body segments with greater amount of soft tissues. Those systems have great utility when choosing an efficient wheelchair cushion, or even to find the best position to the seated individual (in terms of anterior/posterior and side leaning) so an effective pressure relief can be achieved. Although those mentioned systems have great utility, their lack of interaction with the wheelchair user and attendant makes those systems less useful, as they are not designed for a whole day of utilization. Our concept is a system that not only monitors the pressure under the individual's body all day long, recording the values, but also monitors the microclimate generated under the seated individual, warning the attendant if any risk values are being reached, and with all this information, measures can be taken in order to prevent wounds to appear.

This work is divided in five sections, such as section I, where an introduction to the studied problematic have been made; section II explains the architecture of the study, and the approach to the study, and the materials used in the study are present in section III. Section IV and Section V present the discussion of the problematic and the solutions found on this study, and the conclusion respectively.

II. Architecture

Our approach to solve this positional issue consists of a smart electronic seat; a chair that monitors the environment that is created between the seated individual and the base of the chair, in order to quantify the values of pressure, temperature and humidity that may represent a risk to skin integrity, and also a response for the necessity to mobilize an impaired individual that lacks that capacity.

This smart seat collects data that is processed and stored in a server, and warns the attendants identifying which of their patients has a risky environment underneath, and needs to be mobilized in order to shift weight to another body part (most of the times the pressure is transferred to the back if the chair/wheelchair has a tilt in space option). The system architecture can be seen bellow on Figure 1.

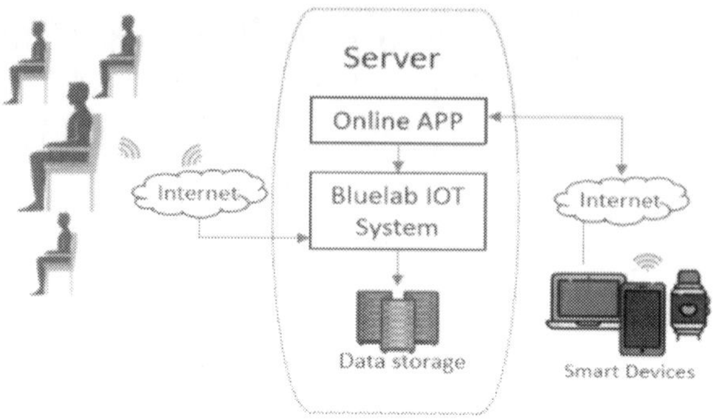

Figure 1. System configuration with the chair system being in contact with the server by wireless and can be accessed by smart devices through internet connection.

The architecture of this work, seen on Figure 1, uses the chair explained above as the centre piece of the whole data acquisition and processing system. After the data acquired by the sensors embedded in the seat, a microprocessor manages the data processing by reducing its noise with a low pass filter, and sends that data by Wi-Fi through an internet connection to the BlueLab IoT system where it is stored [8]. The stored data can then be retrieved and displayed graphically for user comprehension. The system is scalable as the replication of the smart chairs on the same location can be achieved by the same internet connection and different chair ids. Each chair is identified within the BlueLab IoT system as a different station. If needed, geographically different locations can be monitored by the same access to the BlueLab IoT system. Furthermore, each chair can send an alarm (SMS) to the attendant that will aid the sitting person in finding a new position. The system would be suitable for users from every ethnicity, gender weight and age, as the sensors provide absolute values for temperature humidity and pressure, and those values will be compared with the surrounding environment.

III. Material and Methods

The hardware used on each seat is composed by a microcontroller, Analogue to Digital Converters (ADC), batteries, and several sensors for temperature, pressure, and relative humidity. The sensors are set on a mat and it is called the shieldboard.

Microcontroller: is a NodeMCU lolin V3, designed by Espressif Systems, with a processor Tensilica L106 32-bit, speed at 80~160 MHz, flash memory of 16 Mb. It has also ESP8266 communication built in for internet connectivity with 802.11 b/g/n protocol. The whole microprocessor itself has a current consumption between 10 uA and 170 mA with a 3.3 V voltage supply. This microcontroller was programmed with Arduino IDE V1.8.9, and the program stored within the microcontroller's flash memory. Executed whenever the microcontroller starts up, sampling the sensors every 3 to 30 seconds; the sampling rate will be defined in future by the results. The sampled data is sent over the Wi-Fi connection.

The program can also emit an alarm that will result on the sending of a SMS by the BlueLab IoT system.

Sensors and Shieldboard: for monitoring the micro-environment created between the individual's body and the surface where he is sited; two kinds of sensors are used: Resistive Pressure Sensor, and Digital Temperature and Humidity Sensor. For pressure quantification, three FSR 406 (Force Sensing Resistor), from Interlink sensors with size 43.69 x 43.69 mm, and a sensitivity range from 0.1N to 100 N [9]. The sensors surface area is wide enough to cover all the skin area that lies under the ischial bony prominence. The location of the three sensors is designed to be adaptable to the "wearer ", as the sensors can be easily repositioned to be right under the bone tip. In the main configuration, two sensors are placed under each ischial bone, and the remaining sensor is placed further front to the first ones, this way, this third sensor records the pressure under the thigh, as a reference for the values of the first two sensors. The temperature and humidity sensors were placed in way that one of the sensors stays under the person to monitor the environment created at the zone that is expected higher values of temperature and humidity, and the second sensor were placed outside the shiedboard, in order to monitor the values of temperature and humidity of the surrounding environment for the person. This way we can have both quantified results for the microclimate under the person and also relative results, depending on the surrounding environment. This configuration is schematized on Figure 2.

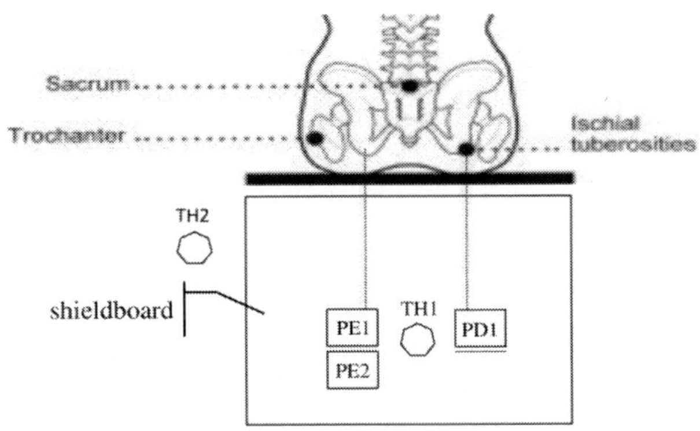

Figure 2. Seat sensors: PE1, PE2, and PD13 are pressure sensors, while TH1 and TH2 are temperature and relative humidity sensors.

Regarding temperature and humidity sensors, two sensors were used: model DHT11 from Vellemam manufacture [10] with temperature range from 0 to 50 degrees (+/- 0.2 degrees error), and a relative humidity range from 20% to 90% (+/- 5 RH error). These two digital sensors provide the temperature and relative humidity of the environment created bellow the individual's body, and their disposition on the shieldboard above the chair's seat can be seen on Figure 2. The main objective with the integration of these two sensors is to quantify the values of temperature and relative humidity, in order to understand the influence that the body heat and moisture has on the ulcer development that makes the tissues more vulnerable and susceptible to become damaged.

The DHT11 has one digital pin for both input and output 1-wire communication. It is connected directly to one of the GPIO (General Purpose Input Output) pins.

The number of sensors can be increased, and with that in aim the I^2C communication protocol is used for the ADC. Module ADS 1115 with 16-bit resolution is used in a module from Adafruit [11] directly connected to the appropriate GPIO pins. The module has 4 ADCs one for each pressure sensor.

To power the smart chair device, two 2600 mAh @ 3.37 V batteries each with a 5V converter, connected in parallel, are able to supply up to 5000 mAh @ 5V. As the system itself consumes around 170 mA, the batteries should maintain the system active for around 29 hours, which is enough for a whole day use, as they should be charged every day.

As a proof of concept, an experiment was performed with the following phases:

A – 3 min of no pressure applied to the shieldboard,
B – 5 min of person sitting still,
C – 40 min of sitting person relaxed,
D – Sitting person repositioning; pressure pattern change,
E – 40 min of sitting person relaxed,
F – 3 min of no pressure applied to the shieldboard.

IV. Results and Discussion

An experiment was performed to evaluate the use of the shieldboard and to identify the different circumstances of the sitting subject by analysing the data logged through the BlueLab IoT system. The collected data is presented as a graph on Figure 3.

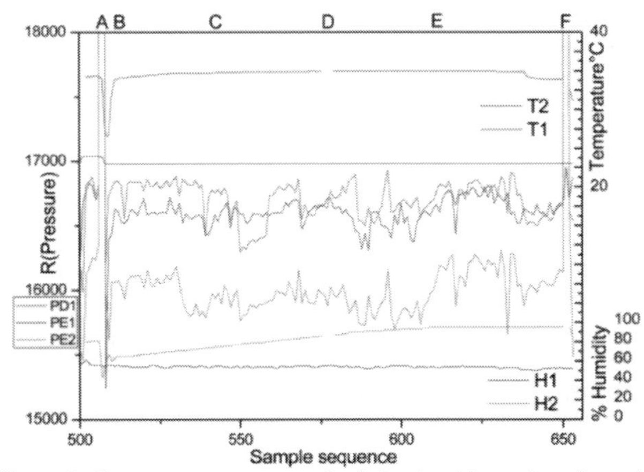

Figure 3. Pressure, temperature and relative humidity values from the experiment.

The graphical representation of the data presented in Figure 3 has on its X axis the sample sequence of the data frames; consecutive samples are 30 s apart. The Y axis has three different scales: on the left the resistance value, R, which is proportional to the pressure exerted on the sensors (PD1, PE1 and PE2), on the top right temperature between 20 and 40 ºC for sensors (T1 and T2), and on the bottom right the relative humidity 0 to 100% for the humidity sensors (H1 and H2). At the top of the graph letters A to F represent the different phases of the experiment.

Sensors T1 and H1 are ambient sensors and their values are almost constant as they represent the condition of the room. Sensors T2, H2, PE1, PE2, PD1 are positioned on the shieldboard under the sited person.

Results show a rapid increase in temperature of the seat and a gradual increase of the humidity under the seated person, reaching values that may result in a microclimate dangerous to the top layers of the skin, if this condition remains through time. Pressure signals show that the sensors are sufficiently sensitive to capture unnoticed movements of a person sitting still. Some of those variations in pressure, for example around sample 550, may indicate a change of position of the individual; an unintentional repositioning as the conscious repositioning occurred in D. In D missing values of T2 and H2 are NaN (not a number) probably due to fault contact of the sensors during the repositioning. The fact that temperature and humidity present high values, indicate a dangerous microclimate to the skin that can lead to ulceration, and the recorded values at the time of mobilization 34.8 degrees and 77% humidity, and those values endanger skin integrity. Temperature and humidity kept increasing with time reaching the max values of 35 degrees Celsius and 95% humidity, values that can be highly dangerous to skin and can lead to ulceration, if there is no mobilisation. The pressure felt under the ischial tuberosity is expected to be greater that the felt on the thigh [12], and the results have also corroborated that fact.

Although the system proved to be functional, there is still room for improvement, as the sensors used may be more accurate in order to improve the data acquisition on the bony tip of the ischial tuberosity, and also the environment. The possibility to link the system to a module on a power wheelchair could be an important improvement for user to change its own position in situations where no attendants would be around.

V. Conclusion

The device proved to be functional as it is able to record the microclimate generated under a seated individual, indicating values of pressure, temperature and humidity as direct data. It is also possible to indirectly know if for example the person has fallen as it can be identified by absence of pressure on the sensors, and such event can be immediately sent to the attendant (by SMS for example). Storing data online enables the use of several stations where each can be associated to a smart chair, and the acquired data can be linked to the person who is using the chair. This is helpful in a scenario where multiple patients are being treated at the same time as in hospitals and nursing homes, once the attendant will be warned to change the patient's position, and therefore, distribute the pressure location felt on the body, creating a relief and preventing the appearing of pressure ulcers.

Also, other events can be monitored, like the sudden absence of pressure, that can indicate that the patient have left the chair without permission or has fallen off the chair.

For future studies, the creation of a predictive algorithm could be an important improvement for the prevention of PU, and the whole system could be that way much more intuitive and effective. Force Sensors should also be increased in quantity in order to cover more body surface and relate the pressure felt at some location to the forces applied to the forces registered to the other sensors, having that way a relative pressure from one location regarding the surrounding areas.

References

[1] L. E. Edsberg, J. M. Black, M. Goldberg, L. McNichol, L. Moore, and M. Sieggreen, "Revised National Pressure Ulcer Advisory Panel Pressure Injury Staging System," *J. Wound, Ostomy Cont. Nurs.*, vol. 43, no. 6, pp. 585–597, 2016.

[2] G. W. Cherry, "The European Pressure Ulcer Advisory Panel: A Means of Identifying and Dealing with a Major Health Problem with a European Initiative," in *Science and Practice of Pressure Ulcer Management*, London: Springer-Verlag, pp. 183–187.

[3] M. Stephens and C. A. Bartley, "Understanding the association between pressure ulcers and sitting in adults what does it mean for me and my carers ? Seating guidelines for people , carers and health & social care professionals," *J. Tissue Viability*, vol. 27, no. 1, pp. 59–73, 2018.

[4] D. A. Hobson, "Comparative effects of posture on pressure and shear at the body-seat interface," *J. Rehabil. Res. Dev.*, vol. 2, no. 4, 1992.

[5] D. Menezes, "Do risco ao desenvolvimento de Úlceras por Pressão : a realidade de um serviço de medicina," Universidade de Coimbra, 2015.

[6] R. Almeida and S. Maia, "Úlceras de pressão: Prevalência e Caracterização em Hospitais na Região Norte de Portugal," Universidade Católica Portuguesa do Porto, 2012.

[7] P. Chiari, C. Forni, M. Guberti, D. Gazineo, S. Ronzoni, and F. D'Alessandro, "Predictive factors for pressure ulcers in an older adult population hospitalized for hip fractures: A prognostic cohort study," *PLoS One*, vol. 12, no. 1, pp. 1–12, 2017.

[8] V. Vaz da Silva, "BlueLab IoT, a Universal Software Platform for IoT Data Acquisition Devices," *i-ETCISEL Acad. J. Electron. Comput.*, no. IoT as a Field Revolution-Special Issue 2018, p. ID-4, 2018.

[9] Interlink, "Force Sensing Resistor 406." [Online]. Available: https://www.interlinkelectronics.com/fsr-406. [Accessed: 14-Feb-2020].

[10] Velleman, "Digital Temperature and Humidity sensor." [Online]. Available: https://www.velleman.eu/products/view/?id=435536. [Accessed: 14-Feb-2020].

[11] Adafruit, "ADS 1115." [Online]. Available: https://www.adafruit.com/product/1085. [Accessed: 14-Feb-2020].

[12] E. Kwong and G. Pang, "Development of an Intelligent Seat for the Alleviation of Pressure Ulcers," *BMEiCON 2018 - 11th Biomed. Eng. Int. Conf.*, pp. 1–5, 2019.

Teaching Machines to Understand Urban Networks

Maria Coelho and Mark A. Austin
Department of Civil and Environmental Engineering,
University of Maryland, College Park, MD 20742, USA
E-mail: memc30@hotmail.com; austin@isr.umd.edu

***Abstract*—Next-generation urban systems will be enabled by technological (cyber) advances deeply embedded within the physical domain. The volume and variety of collected data in years to come is only going to grow and diversify, making the task of urban system design and management much more difficult than in the past. We believe these challenges can be addressed by teaching machines to understand urban networks. This paper explores opportunities for using recently developed graph embedding procedures to encode the structure and associated network attributes as low-dimensional vectors. These embeddings can be later used to advance various learning tasks. We exercise the proposed approach on a problem involving identification of leaks in an urban water distribution system. The Dynamic Attributed Network Embedding (DANE) framework is used to generate low-dimensional vectors for a water distribution network, whose pressure attributes are simulated with EPANET. The embeddings are then fed to a Random Forest algorithm trained to identify water leaks.**

Keywords-Systems Engineering; Machine Learning; Graph Embeddings.

I. INTRODUCTION

This paper is concerned with integrating recently developed graph embedding procedures with machine learning tasks that can enhance decision making in urban settings.

A. Problem Statement

Modern societal-scale infrastructures are going through an interesting time where the digital wave (e.g., the Internet, smart mobile devices, cloud computing) has opened up new avenues for enhancing the development of urban systems (e.g., transportation, electric power, wastewater facilities and water supply networks, among others) whose operations and interactions have superior levels of performance, extended functionality and good economics. While end-users applaud the benefits that these digital technologies afford, model-based systems engineers are faced with a multitude of new design challenges that can be traced to the presence of heterogeneous content (multiple disciplines), network structures that are spatial, multi-layer, interwoven and dynamic, and behaviors that are distributed and concurrent. In the past, engineers have kept these difficulties under control by designing subsystems that operate as independently as possible from each other. Today, however, it is acknowledged that subsystem independence and inferior levels of situational awareness imply sub-optimal functionality and performance. Communication and information exchange establishes common knowledge among decision makers which, in turn, enhances their ability to make decisions appropriate to their understanding, or situational awareness, of the system state, its goals and objectives. Overcoming these barriers makes future challenges in urban system design and management a lot more difficult than they used to be.

B. Scope and Objectives

Our work is motivated by the premise that next-generation cities are transitioning to an information-age fabric, where highly efficient sensing and communication technologies are deeply embedded within the physical urban domain. Present-day trends indicate that the flow and variety of urban data is only going to grow and diversify, making the task of system design, analysis and integration of multi-disciplinary concerns much more difficult than in the past.

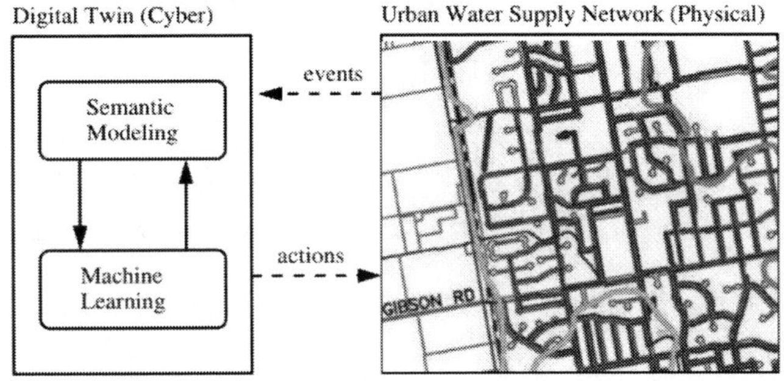

Figure 1. High-level representation for an urban water supply network digital twin (cyber) working alongside a physical urban water supply network.

As illustrated in Figures 1 and 2, we believe that these challenges can be addressed by combining Machine Learning (ML) formalisms and semantic model representations of urban systems that work side-by-side in collecting data, identifying events, and managing city operations in real-time. To this end, Figure 3 shows a preliminary classification of the strengths/weaknesses of AI/ML. The proposed approach builds upon our recent work in semantic modeling for (multi-domain) system of systems [1] [2] and exploration of a combined semantic and ML approach to the monitoring of energy consumption in buildings [3].

This paper explores opportunities for using recently developed graph embedding procedures to encode the structure and associated network attributes as low-dimensional vectors. These embeddings can be later used to advance various learning tasks. We exercise the proposed approach on a problem involving identification of leaks in an urban water distribution

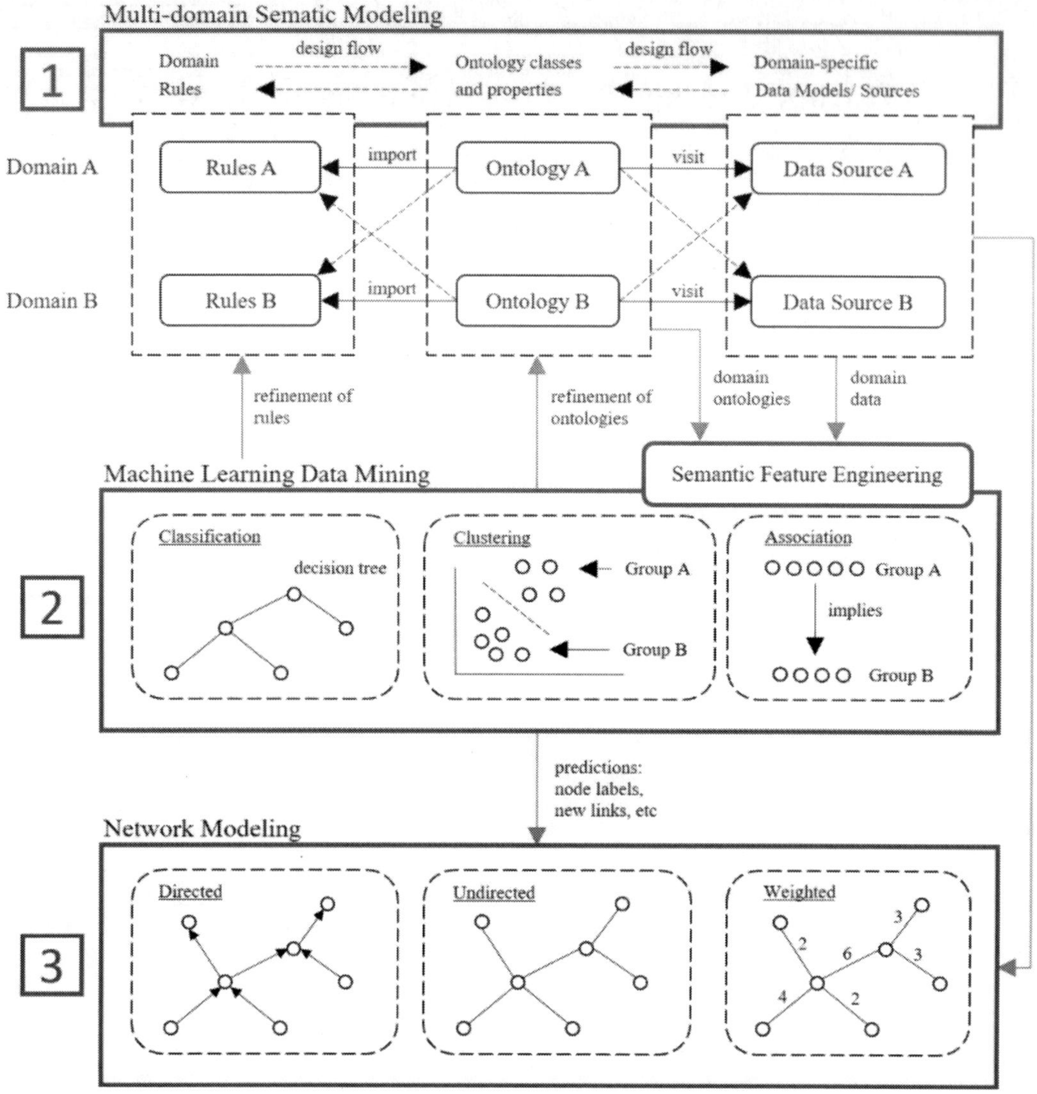

Figure 2. Digital twin architecture.

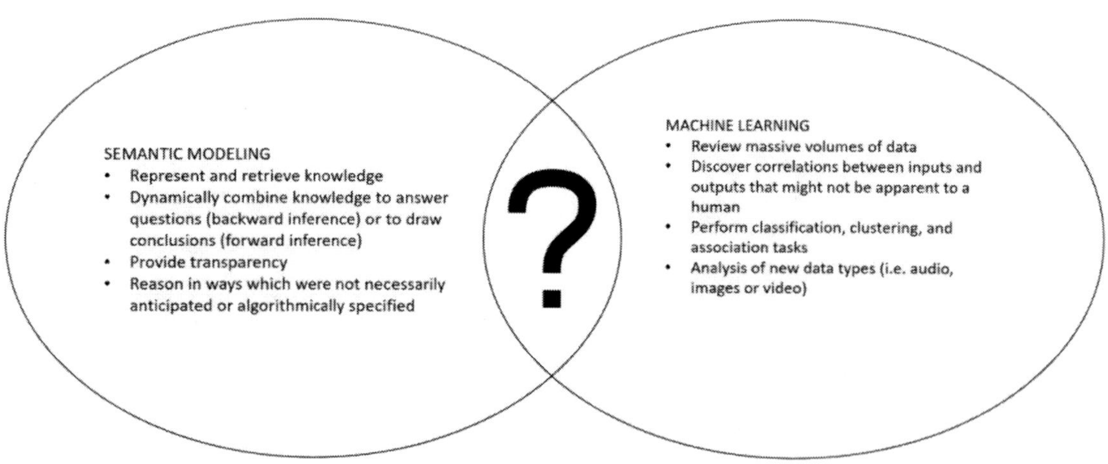

Figure 3. Venn diagram of semantic modeling capabilities versus machine learning capabilities.

system. The remainder of this paper proceeds as follows: Related work in ML algorithms for graphs is covered in Section II. Our work in progress is described in Section III. Conclusions and directions for future work are located in Section IV.

II. Related Work

This section covers the relationship of graph embedding procedures to our related work in integration of semantic modeling and ML approaches for the design of "city digital twins".

A. Architectural Template for Combined AI/ML

The proposed architectural template for a combined multi-domain semantic modeling and ML approach is shown in Figure 2. It is an extension of our work in 2018 [4]. Box 1 covers a framework for multi-domain semantic modeling, where concurrent development of ontologies, rules and data models placed on an equal footing. Box 2 shows ML for three classes of problems – classification, clustering and association – found in the data mining domain. Traditionally, ML approaches rely on user-defined heuristics to extract features encoding information about a graph (e.g., degree statistics or kernel functions). However, recent years have seen a surge in approaches that automatically learn to encode graph structure and attributes into low-dimensional embeddings, using techniques based on deep learning and nonlinear dimensionality reduction. Box 3 is the starting point for our investigation and the focus of this work-in-progress paper.

B. Graph Embeddings for Urban Networks

A prerequisite to network data mining is to find an effective representation of networks. Established network representations, such as adjacency matrices, suffer from data sparsity and high-dimensionality, and a lack of support for capturing semantics. During the most recent decade, however, there has been a strong surge of interest in learning to encode continuous and low-dimensional representations of networks as graph embeddings. Graph embedding provides an effective and efficient way to solve the graph analytics problem, by learning a continuous vector space for the graph, assigning each node (and/or edge) in the graph to a specific position in the vector space. This process provides users a deeper understanding of what is behind the data, and thus can benefit a lot of useful applications such as node classification, node clustering, node recommendation, link prediction, and so forth [5].

Embedding urban graphs into a low-dimentional space is not a trivial task. A key challenge in the design of graph embeddings for urban networks stems from the observation that the information to be preserved is strongly affected by the underlying characteristics of the graph. Urban networks may be homogeneous, heterogeneous, and carry auxiliary information modeled as attributes. Graph edges may be undirected, directed and/or weighted. In a comprehensive survey of graph embedding problems, techniques and applications, Hongyun and co-workers [5] propose two taxonomies of graph embedding which correspond to what challenges exist in different graph embedding problem settings and how the existing work address these challenges in their solutions.

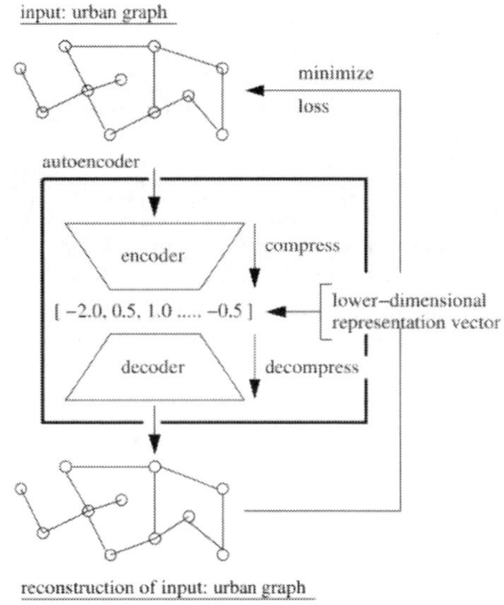

Figure 4. Traditional encoder-decoder approach.

One of the challenges described is capturing the diversity of connectivity patterns in the graph. When embedding a graph with topology information only, the connections between nodes are the target to be preserved. However, for a graph with edge weight or direction, the connectivity pattern provides graph property from other perspectives, and thus should also be considered during the embedding. Different types of objects (e.g., nodes, edges) are embedded into the same space in heterogeneous graph embedding. Therefore, another challenge is conserving global consistency and addressing imbalance between objects of different types. Some urban graphs (e.g., urban water supply networks) contain auxiliary information of a node/edge/whole-graph in addition to the structural relations of nodes (i.e., labels, attributes, node features, information propagation, knowledge base). The auxiliary information helps to define node similarity in addition to graph structural information. The challenges of embedding graph with auxiliary information is how to combine these two information sources to define the node similarity to be preserved.

In addition to the graph embedding input considerations, output format also pose challenges. Different types of embedding facilitate different applications. Output can be categorized into node embedding, edge embedding, hybrid embedding and whole-graph embedding. The challenge is determining suitable embedding output to meet the needs of a specific application or task. The task may be node classification, node clustering, node recommendation/retrieval/ranking, link prediction, triple classification, graph visualization, etc.

C. Autoencoders

Autoencoders are neural networks that are trained to reconstruct their original input. Figure 4 shows a high-level architecture for an autoencoder designed to work with graphs. First, an encoder takes a graph as its input and systematically compresses it into a low-dimensional (embedding) vector. The decoder then takes the vector representation and attempts to generate a reconstruction of the original (graph) input. Encoder-decoder pairs are designed to minimize the loss of information between the input graph and the output (i.e., reconstructed) graph, and then use the embeddings for downstream ML tasks. These frameworks may be deterministic or probabilistic [6].

III. Work in Progress

In this section we exercise a graph embedding procedure that can encode both structure and network attributes on a problem involving the identification of leaks in an urban water distribution system.

Topic 1. Use Case

This use case aims to explore ML techniques for the detection and localization of leakages in very simple water distribution systems (WDSs). See Figure 5. Figure 6 is a flowchart of the process for detecting the location of the leak and taking actions to restore the system. We start by extracting a graph representation of the WDS and determining the initial hydraulic parameters of the system. The following topics describe: (1) the generation of hydraulic data, in particular node pressure, by the hydraulic simulation software EPANET [7]; (2) the preservation of the network topology and node pressure information in the encoding of node embeddings by the DANE framework [8]; (3) the training and testing of a Random Forest algorithm [9] with the node embeddings to infer leak location; and (4) the resulting performance obtained using this proposed framework.

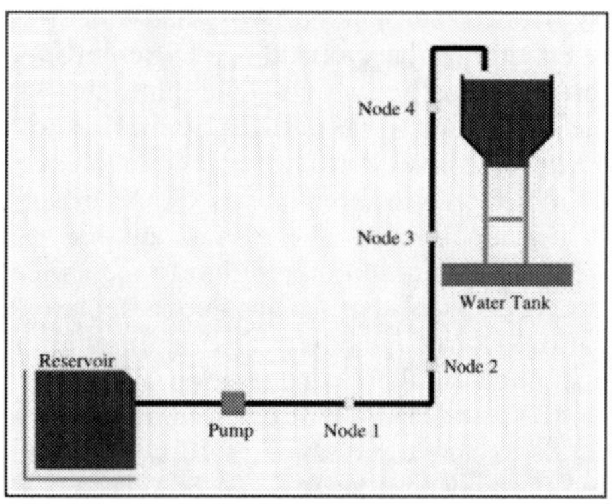

Figure 5. Elevation view of urban water distribution network and junction (node) numbers used by EPANET simulation.

Topic 2. Data Generation

ML algorithms for automatic water leakage detection requires training data. The data should involve hydraulics parameters at different locations in the WDS, pertaining to previous leaks that occurred in the past. However, for security reasons WDS data, which includes geographical layout of pipes, tanks, and demands are kept confidential by the water utility companies and are not readily available in public domain. Alternatively, the training sets can be generated by simulation of the pipe network under consideration. The simulation tool EPANET [7] can be used to achieve this goal

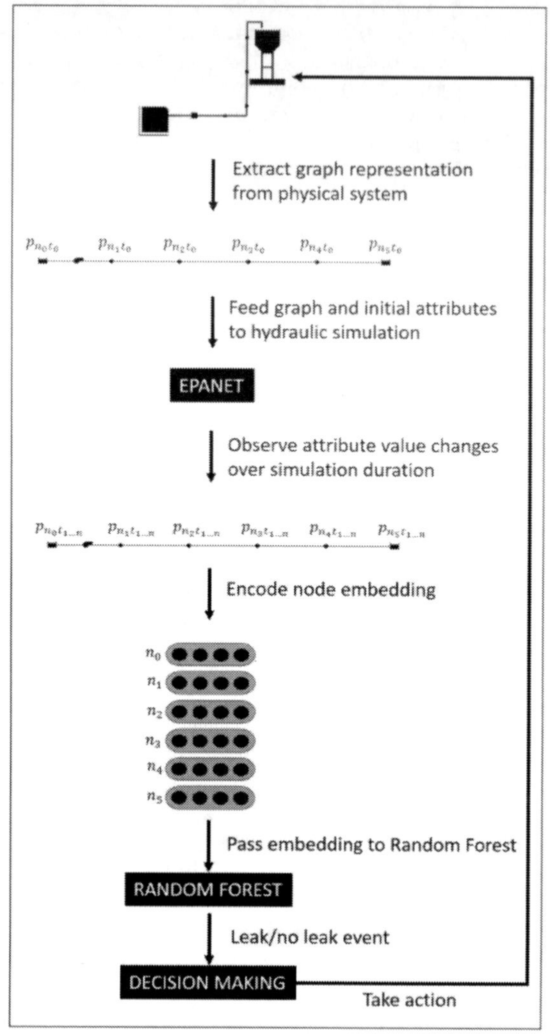

Figure 6. Process flowchart for training and executing machine.

[10]. EPANET is a computerized simulation model produced by the Environmental Protection Agency of the USA that predicts the dynamic hydraulic and water quality behavior within a drinking water distribution system operating over an extended period of time. Pipe networks consist of pipes, nodes (junctions), pumps, valves, and storage tanks or reservoirs. EPANET tracks the flow of water in each pipe, the pressure at each node, the height of the water in each tank, the type of chemical concentration throughout the network during a simulation period, the age of the water, and source tracing. A user can edit various characteristics of a network element and perform simulation to observe its effect on the overall system.

One of the main features of EPANET is that its hydraulic calculation engine is demand-driven. The water output data at each node is defined as the base demand. Although the software does not have direct tool to induce leakage in the system, it is still possible to model leaks as an additional demand, independent of the pressure in a consumption node. The demand can be increased at different times during the simulation. The virtual WDS layout used to perform the simulations is shown in Figure 5. with location of the 4 junctions, 4 links, pump station, water source, and tank. In this work, we assume sensor nodes are deployed in each junction of the network; however, in our resource limited world, placing as many sensors as there are junction nodes to monitor all of the nodes in real time is extremely infeasible. An opportunity for future work would be to investigate how many sensor nodes are needed and where to place them in the network. Placement of sensor node would have direct impact on the efficacy of locating the leakage in the WDS.

In order to generate the large number of cases required for the ML training sets, the implementation of EPANET can be automated by developing a program which calls EPANET many times with varying leak locations. In this work, we will use the EPANET-Python Toolkit to perform this task. The toolkit is an open-source software, originally developed by the Flood Resilience Group (a multidisciplinary research group affiliated to UNESCO-IHE and Delft University of Technology), that operates within the Python environment, for providing a programming interface for the latest version of EPANET. It allows the user to access EPANET within python scripts. The toolkit is useful for developing specialized applications, such as water distribution network models that require running many network analyses. For simplicity, we will limit the parameter of interest to node pressure, although we recognize other parameters such as flow may be helpful in the indication of a leak as well. We obtain the pressure data by making some underlying assumptions: (1) The data obtained through simulation does not involve any noise in it (i.e., the sensors are ideal), (2) At-most one leakage can occur in the WDS in a simulation run, and (3) Water leakage is assumed to occur at the junction nodes only.

Topic 3. Node Embedding

With the data obtained from the hydraulic simulation through EPANET-Python Toolkit, graph embedding can be performed. In this use case we are interested in obtaining a low-dimensional node vector representation for each node in the network. The learned embeddings could advance various learning tasks, particularly leak detection by node classification. WDSs' networks are associated with a rich set of node attributes, and their attribute values are naturally changing, with the emerging of new content patterns and the fading of old content patterns. In addition, it has been widely studied and received that there exists a strong correlation among the attributes of linked nodes [11]. These node correlations and changing characteristics motivate us to seek an effective embedding representation to capture network structure and attribute evolving patterns, which is of fundamental importance for learning in a dynamic environment. In 2018, Li et al. proposed a novel DANE framework that first provides an offline method for a consensus embedding and then, in order to capture the evolving nature of attributed networks, leverages matrix perturbation theory to maintain the freshness of the end embedding results in an online manner [8]. Applying DANE to the pressure data outputted from EPANET simulation, yields a six dimensional node embedding vectors for each node. How to determine the optimal number of embedding dimensions is still an open research problem, thus we chose a set up for which the best results were reported.

Topic 4. Node Classification

With the node embeddings obtained from DANE, leakage detection can be performed. Leakage detection in this work pertains to finding the corresponding junction where the leakage has occurred, therefore the target function assigns a value of 1 to the node where leakage has occurred, and a value of 0 to the remaining nodes. The input and output data are prepared, and passed to a Random Forest classification algorithm. Random forest is considered a highly accurate and robust method because of the number of decision trees participating in the process. It does not suffer from the overfitting problem often encountered in other ML methods, since it takes the average of all the predictions, and cancel out the biases. Random forests can also handle missing values, by using median values to replace continuous variables, or computing the proximity-weighted average of missing values. It also provides the relative feature importance, which helps in selecting the most contributing features for the classifier [9].

The training set needs to capture as much of the expected variation in the target and environment as possible, therefore we generate training set from a simulation where all of the nodes are leaking for half of the simulation duration, and for the other half of the simulation duration none of the nodes are leaking. Since the simulation was set to last 24 hours, with pressure readings at every hour, the training set contains 24 cases for each node. Figure 7 shows the plots for each node in this scenario, where the first of the embedding dimensions is plotted against time. Note that at the time step where the leak occurs, the embedding value for that dimension changes; therefore, the problem can be framed as anomaly detection. In order to test the trained machine, we generate a test set from a simulation where none of the nodes are leaking for half of the simulation duration, and for the other half of the simulation duration only one of the nodes is leaking. Similar to the training set, the test set also contains 24 cases for each node. Figure 8 shows the first of the embedding dimensions plotted against time. Note that the embedding values change slightly compared to the previous scenario where all the nodes where leaking; therefore, the goal of the ML process is not only to detect the anomalies, but also identify which anomalies are actual leaks and which ones are just a propagation of the leak effects. Also note that we keep the leak duration constant through all simulations, since the initial objective of this work is not to identify when the leak occurs but where it occurs. However, we do aknowledge that the time domain is relevant and future work will need to address variations in not only space but time as well.

Topic 5. Preliminary Results

By training the Random Forest algorithm with both leak and non leak data for each node, we were able to test whether the algorithm is able to detect a leak in the system. The test was performed by feeding the algorithm data for a scenario where initially none of the nodes was leaking, and later introducing the leak only at node number 3, as shown in Figure 8. Classification problems are perhaps the most common type of ML problem and as such there are a myriad of metrics that can be used to evaluate predictions for these problems. Classification accuracy is the most common evaluation metric for classification problems, and it is the ratio of number of correct predictions to the total number of input samples. We

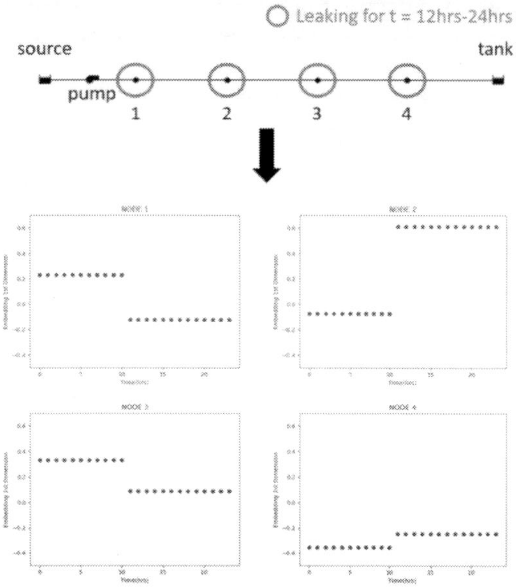

Figure 7. Node embeddings (1st dimension) obtained for train data set plotted against time.

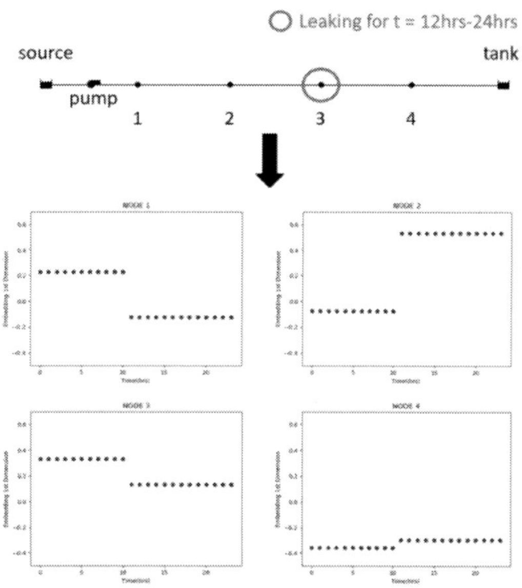

Figure 8. Node embeddings (1st dimension) obtained for test data set plotted against time.

found that the Random Forest algorithm used to train and test has a classification accuracy of 100 percent. We recognize such a high performance may be due to the simplicity of our network and the presence of only one leak when testing. Future work will investigate the influence of size and complexity of the network to the performance of the leak detection.

IV. Conclusions and Future Work

The long term objective of this research is to understand how ML and semantic-modeling can work hand-in-hand to enhance the collection of data, identification of events, and management of city operations. By exploring potential applications of ML to the identification of leaks in urban networks, this work work-in-progress paper takes a tiny step towards realization of the goal. Note that no validation set was used in this work because the simplicity of the network did not provide enough dimensionality to partition the cases into separate training, validation and testing sets without losing significant modeling or testing capability. In addition, we have used only one basic scenario for training and one for testing. Looking forward, our investigation will explore other possible simulations where different leak combinations and larger network sizes will be used. Future work will also explore the accuracy of the learned model when facing dynamic topologies, where edges are removed or created. We also aim to understand what types of graphs (e.g., undirected, directed, weighted) are easy for the ML to learn. Lastly, to the best of our knowledge, the DANE framework does not incorporate a decoder; therefore, extensions of the DANE framework to incorporate this capibility will be needed.

References

[1] M. Coelho, M. A. Austin, and M. R. Blackburn, "Distributed System Behavior Modeling of Urban Systems with Ontologies, Rules and Many-to-Many Association Relationships," The Twelth International Conference on Systems (ICONS 2017), April 23-27 2017, pp. 10–15.

[2] ——, The Data-Ontology-Rule Footing: A Building Block for Knowledge-Based Development and Event-Driven Execution of Multi-Domain Systems. Proceedings of the 16th Annual Conference on Systems Engineering Research, Systems Engineering in Context, Chapter 21, Springer, 2019, pp. 255–266.

[3] P. Delgoshaei, M. Heidarinejad, and M. A. Austin, "Combined Ontology-Driven and Machine Learning Approach to Monitoring of Building Energy Consumption," in 2018 Building Performance Modeling Conference and SimBuild, Chicago, IL, September 26-28 2018, pp. 667–674.

[4] M. A. Austin, P. Delgoshaei, M. Coelho, and M. Heidarinejad, "Architecting Smart City Digital Twins: A Combined Semantic Model and Machine Learning Approach," Journal of Management in Engineering (Special Issue on Smart City Digital Twins), ASCE, 2019, (In Press).

[5] H. Cai, V. W. Zheng, and K. C. Chang, "A Comprehensive Survey of Graph Embedding: Problems, Techniques and Applications," IEEE Transactions on Knowledge and Data Processing, vol. 30, no. 9, 2018, pp. 1616–1637.

[6] W. L. Hamilton, R. Ying, and J. Leskovec, "Representation Learning on Graphs: Methods and Applications," CoRR, vol. abs/1709.05584, 2017. [Online]. Available: http://arxiv.org/abs/1709.05584

[7] L. Rossman, EPAnet 2 Users Manual, January 2000, vol. 38.

[8] J. Li et al., "Attributed Network Embedding for Learning in a Dynamic Environment," in Proceedings of the 2017 ACM on Conference on Information and Knowledge Management, ser. CIKM '17. New York, NY, USA: ACM, 2017, pp. 387–396. [Online]. Available: http://doi.acm.org/10.1145/3132847.3132919

[9] L. Breiman, "Random Forests," in Machine Learning, vol. 45, no. 1. Norwell, MA, USA: Kluwer Academic Publishers, October 2001, pp. 5–32.

[10] J. Mashford, D. Silva, S. Burn, and D. Marney, "Leak Detection in Simulated Water Pipe Networks using SVM," Applied Artificial Intelligence, vol. 26, May 2012, pp. 429–444.

[11] J. J. Pfeiffer, S. Moreno, T. La Fond, J. Neville, and B. Gallagher, "Attributed Graph Models: Modeling Network Structure with Correlated Attributes," in Proceedings of the 23rd International Conference on World Wide Web, ser. WWW '14. New York, NY, USA: ACM, 2014, pp. 831–842. [Online]. Available: http://doi.acm.org/10.1145/2566486.2567993

Point Cloud Mapping Using Only Onboard Lidar in GNSS Denied and Dynamic Environments

Misato Yamaji, Seiya Tanaka
Graduate School of Science and Engineering
Doshisha University
Kyotanabe, Kyoto 610-0394 Japan

Masafumi Hashimoto, Kazuhiko Takahashi
Faculty of Science and Engineering
Doshisha University
Kyotanabe, Kyoto 610-0394 Japan
e-mail: {mhashimo, katakaha}@mail.doshisha.ac.jp

Abstract— **This paper presents a 3D point cloud mapping in Global Navigation Satellite Systems (GNSS) denied and dynamic outdoor environments using only a scanning multilayer lidar mounted on a vehicle. Distortion in scan data from the lidar is corrected by estimating the vehicle's pose (3D positions and attitude angles) in a period shorter than the lidar scan period based on Normal Distributions Transform (NDT) scan matching and Extended Kalman Filter (EKF). The corrected scan data are mapped onto an elevation map; static and moving scan data, which are originated from static and moving objects, respectively, in the environments, are classified using the occupancy grid method. Only the static scan data are applied to generate a point cloud map using NDT-based Simultaneous Localization And Mapping (SLAM) and graph-based SLAM. Experimental results in a public road environment show the performance of the proposed method.**

Keywords-lidar; point cloud map; distortion correction; NDT SLAM; graph SLAM; GNSS denied environment; dynamic environment.

I. INTRODUCTION

Recently, studies have been conducted on autonomous driving and active safety of vehicles, such as automobiles and personal mobility vehicles, and on autonomous robots for last-mile and first-mile automation. Important technologies in these studies include environmental map generation [1] and map-matching based self-pose estimation by vehicles using the generated maps [2]. A lot of their related studies using cameras, lidars, and radars have been actively conducting [3][4].

In this paper, we focus on map generation with a lidar mounted on a vehicle. When compared with camera (vision) based map generation, lidar based map generation is robust to lighting conditions and require less computational time. Furthermore, lidar based map generation provides mapping accuracy better than radar based map generation due to higher spatial resolution of lidar. From these reasons, we focus on lidar based map generation.

In Intelligent Transportation Systems (ITS) domains, mobile mapping systems are utilized to map generation in wide road environments, such as highways and motorways [5]. We have been studying a method for point cloud mapping (map generation) using only a lidar mounted on a vehicle in narrow road environments, such as at community and scenic roads in urban and mountainous areas [6]. The generated map could be applied to autonomous driving and navigation of various smart vehicles, such as intelligent wheelchairs, personal mobility vehicles, and delivery robots [7]. The generated maps may also be utilized in various social services, such as disaster prevention and mitigation.

In urban and mountainous environments, the information of Global Navigation Satellite Systems (GNSS) is often disturbed and denied. For map generation in GNSS denied environments, Simultaneous Localization And Mapping (SLAM) using Normal Distributions Transform (NDT) [8] or Iterative Closest Points (ICP) [9] methods have been applied. In their scan matching based SLAM, the accuracy in mapping wide area degrades due to the accumulation error. To reduce the accumulation error, the graph-based SLAM [10] is usually applied. Recently, we presented a map generation method using NDT-based SLAM and graph-based SLAM [6]. A vehicle equipped with a lidar was moved so that loops could be made in road network topology, and several submaps (maps of different small areas) were generated using recursive NDT-based SLAM and graph-based SLAM. Several submaps were also merged using graph-based SLAM. Such approach in submap generation and merging makes it easy to update and maintain maps.

In environments, moving objects, such as automobile, two-wheeled vehicles, and pedestrians, exist. In such dynamic environments, the lidar scan data are therefore classified into two types: scan data originated from moving objects (referred to as moving scan data), and those originated from static objects (static scan data), such as buildings, trees, and traffic poles. For accurate map generation, the moving scan data should be removed, and only the static scan data should be utilized. Several methods for mapping in dynamic environments have been presented [11][12][13]; however, map generation in dynamic environments still represent a significant challenge compared with map generation in static environments. Our map generation method [6] was also applicable in static environments. Apart from map generation, we have been studying moving object detection and tracking in crowded dynamic environments [14][15]. The detection and tracking methods can contribute in accurately generating maps by extracting the static scan data from the lidar data.

Map generation using the onboard lidar is performed by mapping lidar scan data captured in a sensor coordinate frame onto a world coordinate frame using the vehicle's self-pose (position and attitude angles) information. The lidar obtains range measurements by scanning lidar beams. Thus, when the vehicle moves, the entire scan data within one scan (lidar beam rotation of 360° in a horizontal plane) cannot be obtained at the same pose of the vehicle. Therefore, if the entire scan data obtained within one scan is mapped onto the world coordinate frame using the vehicle's pose information, distortion arises in environmental maps. To correct this distortion, the vehicle's pose should be determined more frequently than the lidar scan period, i.e., for every lidar measurement in the scan. Many methods for distortion correction have been proposed [16][17][18]. We also presented a distortion correction method using only the lidar information; the NDT scan matching and Extended Kalman Filter (EKF) were applied to estimate the vehicle's pose, and the distortion in the lidar scan data was corrected using the pose estimates [19].

In this paper, to generate a 3D point cloud map in GNSS denied and dynamic environments using only the onboard scanning lidar, we integrate three methods that we previously proposed: distortion correction in the lidar scan data, extraction of the static scan data from the entire lidar scan data, and point cloud mapping based on NDT and graph-based SLAM. The mapping performance is shown through experimental results in public road environments.

The rest of this paper is organized as follows. In Section II, we give the experimental system and overview a map generation method based on NDT-based and graph-based SLAM. In Section III, we explain a correction method of distortion in the lidar scan data, and in Section IV, we describe an extraction method of the static scan data. In Section V, we conduct experiments to verify the proposed method, followed by conclusions in Section VI.

II. EXPERIMENTAL SYSTEM AND SLAM OVERVIEW

In this section, we show our experimental system and briefly describe the scan data mapping using NDT scan matching (NDT-based SLAM) and graph-based SALM.

A. Experimental System

As shown in Fig. 1, our experimental small vehicle is equipped with a scanning 32-layer lidar (Velodyne HDL-32E). The maximum range of the lidar is 70 m, the horizontal viewing angle is 360° with a resolution of 0.16°, and the vertical viewing angle is 41.34° with a resolution of

Figure 1. Overview of the experimental vehicle.

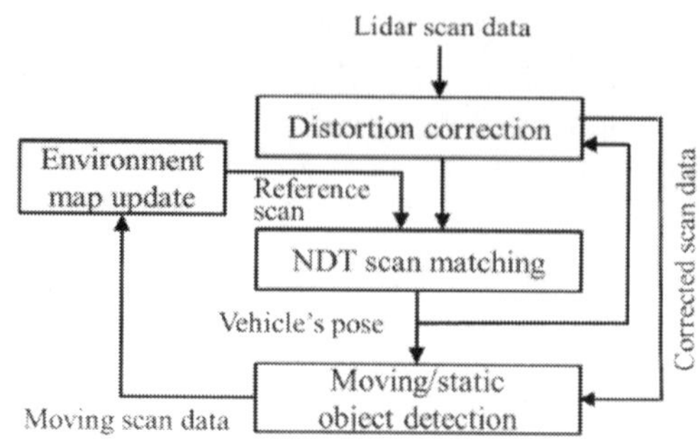

Figure 2. Overview of NDT-based SLAM.

1.33°. The lidar provides 384 measurements (the object's 3D position and reflection intensity) every 0.55 ms (at 2° horizontal angle increments). The period for the lidar beam to complete one rotation (360°) in the horizontal direction is 100 ms, and 70,000 measurements are then obtained in one rotation.

In this paper, one rotation of the lidar beam in the horizontal direction (360°) is referred to as one scan, and the data obtained from this scan is referred to as scan data. Moreover, the lidar scan period (100 ms) is denoted as τ and scan data observation period (0.55 ms) as $\Delta\tau$.

B. NDT-based SLAM

The process for NDT-based SLAM is shown in Fig. 2. To be clear, the NDT scan matching [8] is described in this subsection. Distortion correction method is detailed in the following section.

First of all, the scan data related to road surfaces are removed, and the scan data related to objects are mapped onto a 3D grid map (a voxel map) represented in the vehicle's coordinate frame, Σ_b. A voxel grid filter is applied to downsize the scan data. The voxel used for the voxel grid filter is a tetrahedron with a side length of 0.2 m.

In the world coordinate frame, Σ_W, a voxel map with a voxel size of 1 m is used for NDT scan matching. For the i-th (i = 1, 2, …n) measurement in the scan data, we define the position vector in Σ_b as $\boldsymbol{p}_{bi}$ and that in Σ_W as $\boldsymbol{p}_i$. Thus, the following relation is given by the homogeneous form:

$$\begin{pmatrix} \boldsymbol{p}_i \\ 1 \end{pmatrix} = \boldsymbol{T}(\boldsymbol{X}) \begin{pmatrix} \boldsymbol{p}_{bi} \\ 1 \end{pmatrix} \quad (1)$$

where $\boldsymbol{X} = (x, y, z, \phi, \theta, \psi)^T$ is the vehicle's pose. $(x, y, z)^T$ and $(\phi, \theta, \psi)^T$ are the 3D position and attitude angle (roll, pitch, and yaw angles) of the vehicle, respectively, in Σ_W. $\boldsymbol{T}(\boldsymbol{X})$ is the following homogeneous transformation matrix:

$$T(\boldsymbol{X}) = \begin{pmatrix} \cos\theta\cos\psi & \sin\phi\sin\theta\cos\psi - \cos\phi\sin\psi & \cos\phi\sin\theta\cos\psi + \sin\phi\sin\psi & x \\ \cos\theta\sin\psi & \sin\phi\sin\theta\sin\psi + \cos\phi\cos\psi & \cos\phi\sin\theta\sin\psi - \sin\phi\cos\psi & y \\ -\sin\theta & \sin\phi\cos\theta & \cos\phi\cos\theta & z \\ 0 & 0 & 0 & 1 \end{pmatrix}$$

The scan data obtained at the current time $t\tau$ ($t = 0, 1, 2, \ldots$), $\boldsymbol{p}_{b(t)} = \{\boldsymbol{p}_{b1(t)}, \boldsymbol{p}_{b2(t)}, \cdots\}$, are referred to as the new input scan, and the scan data obtained in the previous time before $(t-1)\tau$, $\boldsymbol{P} = \{\boldsymbol{P}_{(0)}, \boldsymbol{P}_{(1)}, \cdots, \boldsymbol{P}_{(t-1)}\}$, are referred to as the reference scan (environmental map).

NDT scan matching conducts a normal distribution transformation for the reference scan data in each grid on a voxel map. It calculates the average value and covariance of the lidar measurement positions. By matching the new input scan at $t\tau$ with the reference scan data obtained prior to $(t-1)\tau$, the vehicle's pose, $\boldsymbol{X}_{(t)}$, at $t\tau$ is determined. The vehicle's pose is used for conducting a coordinate transform with (1), and the new input scan can then be mapped to Σ_W, and the reference scan is updated.

C. Graph-based SLAM

To reduce the accumulation error of the map generated by NDT-based SLAM, we apply the graph-based SLAM [20]. The vehicle's poses obtained by NDT-based SLAM are mapped onto a factor graph. To detect the loop (revisit area), we first obtain the candidates of the revisit areas using the information on self poses of the vehicle. Thereafter, the loop probability indicator (LPI) [21] and matching distance indicator (MDI) are calculated using the lidar scan data captured during the initial visit and revisit of the vehicle. A higher degree of similarity between the lidar scan data of the initial visit and revisit of the vehicle will lead to a larger LPI and a smaller MDI. Thus, we detect the loop using the LPI and MDI values.

When the loop is detected, the vehicle's pose is calculated at the revisit area relative to that at the first-visit area based on NDT scan matching. The relative poses of the vehicle are inputted to the factor graph as loop constraints. We then minimize the objective function of (2) so that the accuracy in the map generated by the NDT-based SLAM can be improved [21]:

$$F(\chi) = \sum_{i,j} (\Delta\boldsymbol{X}_{ij} - \Delta\hat{\boldsymbol{X}}_{ij})^T \boldsymbol{\Omega}_{ij} (\Delta\boldsymbol{X}_{ij} - \Delta\hat{\boldsymbol{X}}_{ij}) \tag{2}$$

where $\chi = (\boldsymbol{X}_1^T, \boldsymbol{X}_2^T, \cdots, \boldsymbol{X}_i^T)^T$. $\boldsymbol{X}_i$ is the vehicle's pose at the $i\tau$. $\Delta\boldsymbol{X}_{ij}$ is the pose of the vehicle at the $j\tau$ relative to that at the $i\tau$, which is calculated from NDT scan matching. $\Delta\hat{\boldsymbol{X}}_{ij}$ is the estimate of the relative pose. $\boldsymbol{\Omega}_{ij}$ is the information matrix.

III. DISTORTION CORRECTION OF LIDAR SCAN DATA

In this section, we describe a motion model of the vehicle for EKF and EKF-based correction method of distortion in lidar scan data.

A. Motion Model

As shown in Fig. 3, the vehicle's linear velocity in Σ_b is defined as V_b (the velocity in the x_b-axis direction), and the angular velocities about the x_b-, y_b-, and z_b- axes are defined as $\dot{\phi}_b$, $\dot{\theta}_b$, and $\dot{\psi}_b$, respectively. If the vehicle is assumed to move at nearly constant linear and angular velocities, the following motion model can be derived:

$$\begin{pmatrix} x_{(t+1)} \\ y_{(t+1)} \\ z_{(t+1)} \\ \phi_{(t+1)} \\ \theta_{(t+1)} \\ \psi_{(t+1)} \\ V_{b(t+1)} \\ \dot{\phi}_{b(t+1)} \\ \dot{\theta}_{b(t+1)} \\ \dot{\psi}_{b(t+1)} \end{pmatrix} = \begin{pmatrix} x_{(t)} + a_{1(t)}\cos\theta_{(t)}\cos\psi_{(t)} \\ y_{(t)} + a_{1(t)}\cos\theta_{(t)}\sin\psi_{(t)} \\ z_{(t)} - a_{1(t)}\sin\theta_{(t)} \\ \phi(t) + a_2(t) + \{a_3(t)\sin\phi(t) + a_4(t)\cos\phi(t)\} \\ \cdot\tan\theta(t) \\ \theta(t) + \{a_3(t)\cos\phi(t) - a_4(t)\sin\phi(t)\} \\ \psi(t) + \{a_3(t)\sin\phi(t) + a_4(t)\cos\phi(t)\} \\ \cdot\dfrac{1}{\cos\theta(t)} \\ V_{b(t)} + \tau w_{\dot{V}_b} \\ \dot{\phi}_{b(t)} + \tau w_{\ddot{\phi}_b} \\ \dot{\theta}_{b(t)} + \tau w_{\ddot{\theta}_b} \\ \dot{\psi}_{b(t)} + \tau w_{\ddot{\psi}_b} \end{pmatrix} \tag{3}$$

where t and t+1 are time steps. $a_1 = V_b\tau + \tau^2 w_{\dot{V}_b}/2$, $a_2 = \dot{\phi}_b\tau + \tau^2 w_{\ddot{\phi}_b}/2$, $a_3 = \dot{\theta}_b\tau + \tau^2 w_{\ddot{\theta}_b}/2$ and $a_4 = \dot{\psi}_b\tau + \tau^2 w_{\ddot{\psi}_b}/2$. $w_{\dot{V}_b}$, $w_{\ddot{\phi}_b}$, $w_{\ddot{\theta}_b}$, and $w_{\ddot{\psi}_b}$ are the acceleration disturbances.

Equation (3) is expressed in the vector form as follows:

$$\boldsymbol{\xi}_{(t+1)} = \boldsymbol{f}[\boldsymbol{\xi}_{(t)}, \boldsymbol{w}, \tau] \tag{4}$$

where $\boldsymbol{\xi} = (x, y, z, \phi, \theta, \psi, V_b, \dot{\phi}_b, \dot{\theta}_b, \dot{\psi}_b)^T$ and $\boldsymbol{w} = (w_{\dot{V}_b}, w_{\ddot{\phi}_b}, w_{\ddot{\theta}_b}, w_{\ddot{\psi}_b})^T$.

We define the vehicle's pose obtained at $t\tau$ using NDT scan matching as $\boldsymbol{z}_{NDT(t)} \equiv \boldsymbol{X}_{(t)}$. The measurement equation is then

$$\boldsymbol{z}_{NDT(t)} = \boldsymbol{H}\boldsymbol{\xi}_{(t)} + \Delta\boldsymbol{z}_{NDT(t)} \tag{5}$$

where $\Delta\boldsymbol{z}_{NDT}$ is the measurement noise, and $\boldsymbol{H}$ is the measurement matrix.

B. EKF-based Distorion Correction

The flow of distortion correction of the lidar scan data is shown in Fig. 4. The lidar scan period (τ) is 100 ms, and the scan data observation period ($\Delta\tau$) is 0.55 ms. When the scan data are mapped onto Σ_W using the vehicle's pose

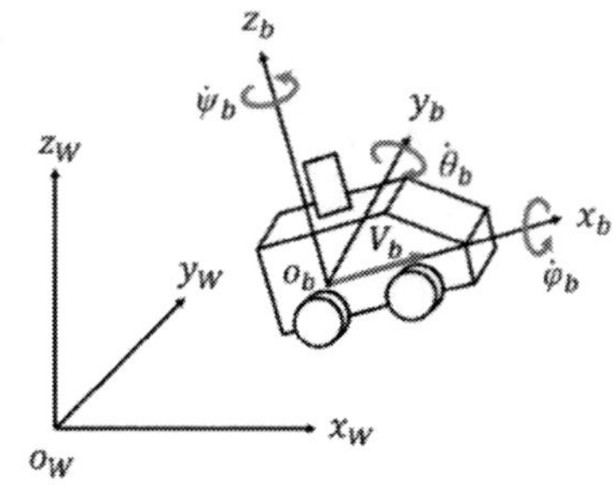

Figure 3. Notation related to vehicle motion.

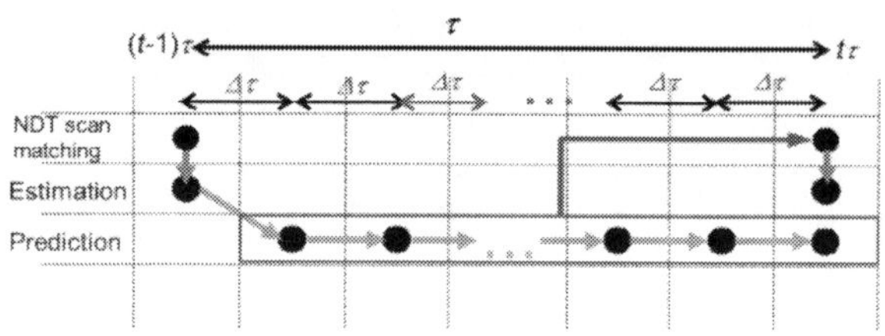

Figure 4. The flow of distortion correction.

calculated every lidar scan period, the distortion arises in environmental maps. We therefore correct the distortion in the lidar scan data by estimating the vehicle's pose using EKF every scan data observation period.

The state estimate and its error covariance obtained at $(t-1)\tau$ using EKF are denoted as $\hat{\xi}_{(t-1/t-1)}$ and $\boldsymbol{\Gamma}_{(t-1/t-1)}$, respectively. From these estimates, EKF gives the state prediction, $\hat{\xi}_{(t-1,1/t-1)}$, and its error covariance, $\boldsymbol{\Gamma}_{(t-1,1/t-1)}$, at $(t-1)\tau+\Delta\tau$ as follows:

$$\left.\begin{aligned} \hat{\xi}_{(t-1,1/t-1)} &= f[\hat{\xi}_{(t-1/t-1)}, 0, \Delta\tau] \\ \boldsymbol{\Gamma}_{(t-1,1/t-1)} &= \boldsymbol{F}_{(t-1/t-1)}\boldsymbol{\Gamma}_{(t-1/t-1)}\boldsymbol{F}_{(t-1/t-1)}^T \\ &\quad + \boldsymbol{G}_{(t-1/t-1)}\boldsymbol{Q}\boldsymbol{G}_{(t-1/t-1)}^T \end{aligned}\right\} \quad (6)$$

where $\boldsymbol{F} = \partial f/\partial\hat{\xi}$, $\boldsymbol{G} = \partial f/\partial \boldsymbol{w}$, and $\boldsymbol{Q}$ is the covariance matrix of the plant noise, $\boldsymbol{w}$.

By a similar calculation, the state prediction, $\hat{\xi}_{(t-1,j/t-1)}$, and its error covariance, $\boldsymbol{\Gamma}_{(t-1,j/t-1)}$, at $(t-1)\tau+j\Delta\tau$ (where $j = 1, 2, \ldots, 180$) can be obtained by

$$\left.\begin{aligned} \hat{\xi}_{(t-1,j/t-1)} &= f[\hat{\xi}_{(t-1,j-1/t-1)}, 0, \Delta\tau] \\ \boldsymbol{\Gamma}_{(t-1,j/t-1)} &= \boldsymbol{F}_{(t-1,j-1/t-1)}\boldsymbol{\Gamma}_{(t-1,j-1/t-1)}\boldsymbol{F}_{(t-1,j-1/t-1)}^T \\ &\quad + \boldsymbol{G}_{(t-1,j-1/t-1)}\boldsymbol{Q}\boldsymbol{G}_{(t-1,j-1/t-1)}^T \end{aligned}\right\} \quad (7)$$

In the state prediction $\hat{\xi}_{(t-1,j/t-1)}$, we denote the elements related to the vehicle's pose, $(x, y, z, \phi, \theta, \psi)$, as $\hat{\boldsymbol{X}}_{(t-1,j/t-1)}$. Using (1) and the pose prediction, the scan data, $\boldsymbol{p}_{bi}(t-1,j)$, in Σ_b obtained at $(t-1)\tau+j\Delta\tau$ can be transformed to $\boldsymbol{p}_i(t-1,j/t-1)$ in Σ_W as follows:

$$\begin{pmatrix} \boldsymbol{p}_i(t-1,j/t-1) \\ 1 \end{pmatrix} = \boldsymbol{T}(\hat{\boldsymbol{X}}_{(t-1,j/t-1)}) \begin{pmatrix} \boldsymbol{p}_{bi}(t-1,j) \\ 1 \end{pmatrix} \quad (8)$$

Because the lidar scan period (τ) is 100 ms, and the scan data observation period ($\Delta\tau$) is 0.55 ms, the time $t\tau$ is almost equal to $(t-1)\tau+180\Delta\tau$. Using the pose prediction, $\hat{\boldsymbol{X}}_{(t-1,180/t-1)}$ at $t\tau$, the scan data, $\boldsymbol{p}_i(t-1,j/t-1)$, at $(t-1)\tau+j\Delta\tau$ in Σ_W is transformed into the scan data, $\boldsymbol{p}^*_{bi}(t)$, at $t\tau$ in Σ_b as follows:

$$\begin{pmatrix} \boldsymbol{p}^*_{bi}(t) \\ 1 \end{pmatrix} = \boldsymbol{T}(\hat{\boldsymbol{X}}_{(t-1,180/t-1)})^{-1} \begin{pmatrix} \boldsymbol{p}_i(t-1,j/t-1) \\ 1 \end{pmatrix} \quad (9)$$

Using the corrected scan data, $\boldsymbol{p}^*_b(t) = \{\boldsymbol{p}^*_{b1}(t), \boldsymbol{p}^*_{b2}(t), \cdots\}$, within one scan (lidar beam rotation of 360° in a horizontal plane), as the new input scan, NDT scan matching can accurately calculate the vehicle's pose, $z_{NDT}(t)$, at $t\tau$. Based on (4) and (5), EKF then gives the state estimate, $\hat{\xi}_{(t/t)}$, and its error covariance, $\boldsymbol{\Gamma}_{(t/t)}$, at $t\tau$ by

$$\left.\begin{aligned} \hat{\xi}_{(t/t)} &= \hat{\xi}_{(t-1,180/t-1)} + \boldsymbol{K}_{(t)}\{z_{NDT}(t) - \boldsymbol{H}\hat{\xi}_{(t-1,180/t-1)}\} \\ \boldsymbol{\Gamma}_{(t/t)} &= \boldsymbol{\Gamma}_{(t-1,180/t-1)} - \boldsymbol{K}_{(t)}\boldsymbol{H}\boldsymbol{\Gamma}_{(t-1,180/t-1)} \end{aligned}\right\} \quad (10)$$

where $\hat{\xi}_{(t-1,180/t-1)}$ and $\boldsymbol{\Gamma}_{(t-1,180/t-1)}$ are the state prediction and its error covariance at $t\tau$ (= $(t-1)\tau+180\Delta\tau$), respectively. $\boldsymbol{K}_{(t)} = \boldsymbol{\Gamma}_{(t-1,180/t-1)}\boldsymbol{H}^T\boldsymbol{S}^{-1}_{(t)}$ and $\boldsymbol{S}_{(t)} = \boldsymbol{H}\boldsymbol{\Gamma}_{(t-1,180/t-1)}\boldsymbol{H}^T + \boldsymbol{R}$. $\boldsymbol{R}$ is the covariance matrix of Δz_{NDT}.

The corrected scan data $\boldsymbol{P}^*_b(t)$ are mapped onto Σ_W using the pose estimate calculated by (10), and the distortion in environmental maps can then be removed.

IV. EXTRACTION OF STATIC SCAN DATA

In dynamic environments wherein moving objects, such as cars, two-wheeled vehicles, and pedestrians, exist, the lidar scan data related to moving objects (referred to as moving scan data) should be removed from the entire scan data, and only the scan data related to static objects (static scan data), such as buildings and trees, should be utilized in map generation.

To extract the static scan data, first, we classify the lidar scan data into two types: scan data that are originated from road surfaces (referred to as road surface scan data) and scan data that are originated from objects (referred to as object scan data) based on a rule-based method. The object scan data are mapped onto an elevation map represented in Σ_W. In this study, the cell of the elevation map is a square with a side length of 0.3 m.

A cell in which scan data exist is referred to as an occupied cell. For the moving scan data, the time to occupy the same cell is short, whereas for the static scan data, the time is long. Therefore, using the occupancy grid method based on the cell occupancy time [14][15], we identify two types of cells: moving and static cells, which are occupied by the moving and static scan data, respectively. Since the scan data related to an object usually occupy more than one cell, adjacent occupied cells are clustered. Then, the scan data in clustered static cells are applied to map generation.

When moving objects pause, the occupancy grid-based method mentioned above often misidentifies their scan data as the static scan data. To address this problem, the road surface scan data are mapped onto the elevation map, and the cells in which the road surface scan data are occupied for a while are determined as the road surface cells. If the object scan data exist on the road surface cells, we always determine the object scan data as the moving scan data and remove the moving scan data from the entire scan data.

V. Experimental Results

Although as mentioned in Section I, our study focuses on map generation in narrow road environments, such as at community roads and scenic roads in urban and mountainous areas, we conducted experiments of map generation in highly traffic road environments (Fig. 5(a)) to discuss the performance of our method in dynamic environments.

The traveled distance of the vehicle was about 2903 m, and the maximum speed of the vehicle was 40 km/h. In the urban road environment, there were 114 cars, 26 two-

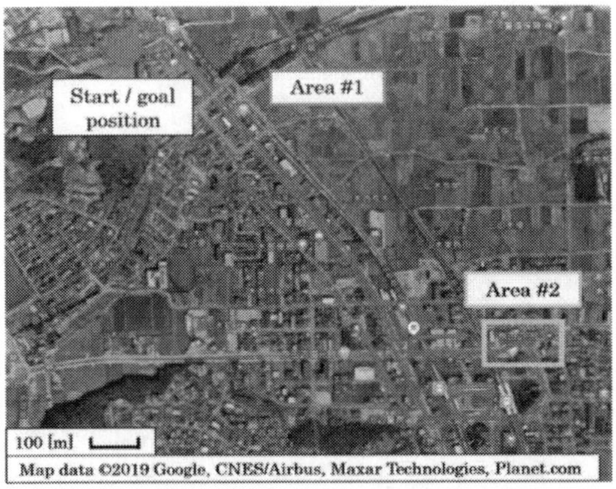

(a) Moved path (red line) of the vehicle (top view).

(b) Photo of area #1 (bird-eye view). Red line indicates moved path of the vehicle

(c) Photo of area #2 (bird-eye view). Red line indicates moved path of the vehicle

Figure 5. Experimental environment.

Figure 6. Point cloud map (top view)

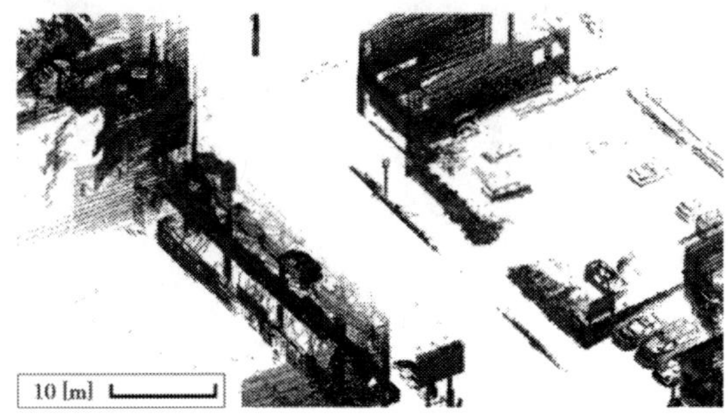

(a) Case 1

(b) Case 2

(c) Case 3

Figure 7. Mapping result of area #1 (bird-eye view). Black and red dots indicate the static and moving scan data, respectively.

(a) Case 1

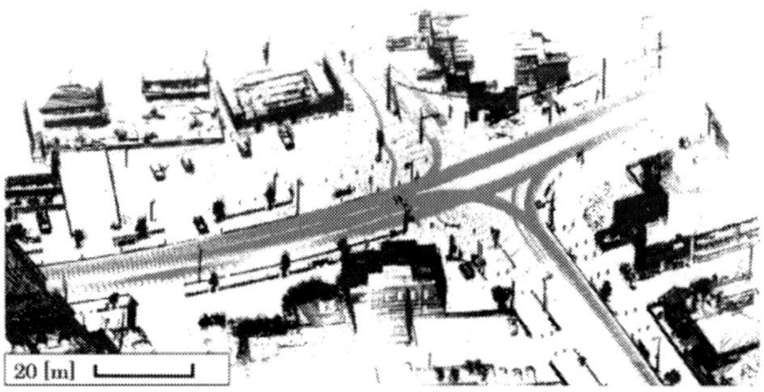

(b) Case 2

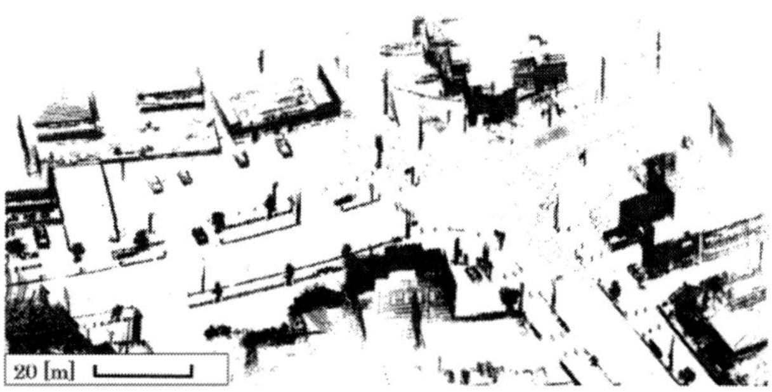

(c) Case 3

Figure 8. Mapping result of area #2 (bird-eye view). Black and red dots indicate the static and moving scan data, respectively.

(a) Photo of traffic sign

(b) Case 1

Figure 9. Mapping result of a tree in area #2.

(c) Case 2

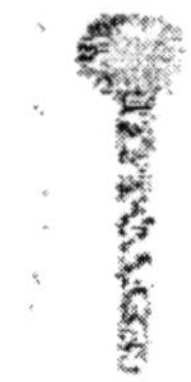

(d) Case 3

Figure 9. Continued.

TABLE I. DEVIATION BETWEEN START AND GOAL POSITIONS OF THE VEHICLE

True	NDT-based SLAM			NDT and graph-based SLAM
	Case 1	*Case 2*	*Case 3*	
2.88 [m]	22.41 [m]	18.48 [m]	132.16 [m]	4.98 [m]

wheeled vehicles, and 37 pedestrians.

Figure 6 shows the mapping result using the NDT-based SLAM in conjunction with the methods of distortion correction of the lidar scan data and extraction of the static scan data. To evaluate the mapping performance using the NDT-based SLAM in detail, Figs. 7 and 8 show the enlarged map of area #1 (Fig. 5 (b)) and #2 (Fig. 5 (c)), respectively. Figure 9 also shows the mapping result of a traffic sign in area #2. For comparison purpose, the maps were generated in the following three cases:

Case 1: Mapping by the proposed method; NDT-based SLAM with the methods of correcting distortion in the lidar scan data and extracting the static scan data,

Case 2: NDT-based SLAM with the distortion correction method and without the method of static scan data extraction, and

Case 3: NDT-based SLAM without the distortion correction method and with the method of static scan data extraction.

In Figs. 7 and 8, case 1 (proposed method) and 3 more significantly remove the track of moving objects than case 2. In Fig. 9, the mapping results by case 1 and 2 are more crispness than the result by case 3. It is concluded from these figures that the proposed method provides better mapping result than case 2 and 3.

Table I shows the positioning performance of the vehicle by SLAM; deviation between the start and goal positions of the vehicle. The true deviation is calculated from the position information using the onboard Real Time Kinematic-Global Positioning Systems (RTK-GPS) unit. It is clear from the table that distortion correction of the lidar scan data provides better mapping accuracy in NDT-based SLAM. In addition, it is clear that graph-based SLAM further improves the mapping accuracy.

VI. Conclusion

This paper presented lidar based map generation in GNSS denied and dynamic outdoor environments using only the onboard scanning lidar. The 3D point cloud mapping was performed by integrating three algorithms that we previously proposed: distortion correction in the lidar scan data, extraction of the static scan data (removal of the moving scan data) from the entire lidar scan data, and NDT-based and graph-based SLAM. The performance of the map generation was shown through experimental results in urban road environments.

We are currently improving performance of removal of moving scan data. We are also evaluating the proposed method in various environments, including large-scale residential environments.

Acknowledgment

This study was partially supported by the KAKENHI Grant #18K04062, the Japan Society for the Promotion of Science (JSPS).

References

[1] C. Cadena, et al., "Past, Present, and Future of Simultaneous Localization and Mapping: Toward the Robust-Perception Age," IEEE Trans. on Robotics, vol. 32, no. 6, pp. 1309–1332, 2016.

[2] L. Wang, Y. Zhang, and J. Wang, "Map-Based Localization Method for Autonomous Vehicles Using 3D-LIDAR," IFAC-Papers OnLine, vol. 50, issue 1, pp. 276-281, 2017.

[3] B. Huang, J. Zhao, and J. Liu, "A Survey of Simultaneous Localization and Mapping," eprint arXiv:1909.05214, 2019.

[4] S. Kuutti, et al., "A Survey of the State-of-the-Art Localization Techniques and Their Potentials for Autonomous Vehicle Applications, " IEEE Internet of Things Journal, vol.5, pp.829–846, 2018.

[5] H. G. Seif and X. Hu, "Autonomous Driving in the iCity—HD Maps as a Key Challenge of the Automotive Industry," Engineering, vol. 2, pp.159–162, 2016.

[6] K. Morita, M. Hashimoto, and K. Takahashi, "Point-Cloud Mapping and Merging using Mobile Laser Scanner," Proc. of the third IEEE Int. Conf. on Robotic Computing (IRC 2019), pp.417–418, 2019.

[7] D. Schwesinger, A. Shariati, C. Montella, and J. Spletzer, "A Smart Wheelchair Ecosystem for Autonomous Navigation in Urban Environments," Autonomous Robot, vol. 41, pp. 519–538, 2017.

[8] P. Biber and W. Strasser, "The Normal Distributions Transform: A New Approach to Laser Scan Matching," Proc. of IEEE/RSJ Int. Conf. on Intelligent Robots and Systems (IROS 2003), pp. 2743–2748, 2003.

[9] P. J. Besl and N. D. McKay, "A Method of Registration of 3-D Shapes," IEEE Trans. on Pattern Analysis and Machine Intelligence, vol. 14, no. 2, pp. 239–256, 1992.

[10] G. Grisetti, R. Kummerle, C. Stachniss, and W. Burgard, "A Tutorial on Graph-based SLAM," IEEE Intelligent Transportation Systems Magazine, pp. 31–43, 2010.

[11] G. Bresson, Z. Alsayed, L. Yu, and S. Glaser, "Simultaneous Localization and Mapping: A Survey of Current Trends in Autonomous Driving," IEEE Trans. on Intelligent Vehicles, vol. 2, pp.194–220, 2017.

[12] J. P. Saarinen, H. Andreasson, T. Stoyanov, and A. J. Lilienthal, "3D Normal Distributions Transform Occupancy Maps: An Efficient Representation for Mapping in Dynamic Environments," Int. J. of Robotics Research, vol.32, no.14, pp.1627–1644, 2013.

[13] X. Ding, Y. Wang, H. Yin, L. Tang, and R. Xiong, "Multi-session Map Construction in Outdoor Dynamic Environment," Proc. of the 2018 IEEE Int. Conf. on Real-time Computing and Robotics (IRC2018), pp. 384–389, 2018.

[14] S. Sato, M. Hashimoto, M. Takita, K. Takagi, and T. Ogawa, "Multilayer Lidar-Based Pedestrian Tracking in Urban Environments," Proc. of IEEE Intelligent Vehicles Symp. (IV2010), pp. 849–854, 2010.

[15] S. Kanaki, et al., "Cooperative Moving-Object Tracking with Multiple Mobile Sensor Nodes -Size and Posture Estimation of Moving Objects using In-vehicle Multilayer Laser Scanner-," Proc. of 2016 IEEE Int. Conf. on Industrial Technology (ICIT 2016), pp. 59–64, 2016.

[16] S. Hong, H. Ko, and J. Kim, "VICP: Velocity Updating Iterative Closest Point Algorithm," Proc. of 2010 IEEE Int. Conf. on Robotics and Automation (ICRA 2010), pp. 1893–1898, 2010.

[17] F. Moosmann and C. Stiller, "Velodyne SLAM," Proc. of IEEE Intelligent Vehicles Symp. (IV2011), pp. 393–398, 2011.

[18] J. Zhang and A. Singh, "LOAM: Lidar Odometry and Mapping in Real-time," Proc. of Robotics: Science and Systems, 2014.

[19] K. Inui, M. Morikawa, M. Hashimoto, and K. Takahashi, "Distortion Correction of Laser Scan Data from In-vehicle Laser Scanner based on Kalman Filter and NDT Scan Matching," Proc. of the 14th Int. Conf. on Informatics in Control, Automation and Robotics (ICINCO), pp. 329–334, 2017.

[20] R. Kümmerle, G. Grisetti, H. Strasdat, K. Konolige, and W. Burgard, "G2o: A General Framework for Graph Optimization," Proc. of 2011 IEEE Int. Conf. on Robotics and Automation, pp. 3607–3613, 2011.

[21] F. Martín, R. Triebel, L. Moreno, and R. Siegwart, "Two Different Tools for Three-dimensional Mapping: DE-based Scan Matching and Feature-based Loop Detection," Robotica, vol. 32, pp. 19–41, 2017.

Multiview-Fusion-Based Crowd Density Estimation Method for Dense Crowd

Liu Bai, Cheng Wu, Yiming Wang and Feng Xie
School of Rail Transportation
Soochow University, Suzhou, P. R. China 215139
Email:20174246009@stu.suda.edu.cn, cwu,ymwang,fengxie@suda.edu.cn

Abstract—**Crowd gathering places are prone to crowd stampede and other public emergencies, resulting in large numbers of casualties and property losses, then, leading to negative social impact. At present, the research on dynamic assessment of crowd gathering safety situation mainly relies on isolated real-time video monitoring, and lacks reliable methods to deal with plenty of video data from different sources, perspectives and granularities. Based on the traffic Internet of things infrastructure, this paper explores the fusion technology of multi-sensor source homogeneous video data. On the basis of the static model of crowd aggregation based on the high-altitude perspective, this paper studies the different source and multi granularity real-time dynamic monitoring video cooperative perception methods in the middle and low altitude and different perspectives. The dynamic scene crowd statistical perception including motion prediction mechanism is used to extract the global coarse-grained motion situation of the crowd from the perspective of high altitude. The multi column convolution depth neural network is used to extract the local fine-grained density features of the crowd with line of sight occlusion in low altitude perspective, thus establishing the holographic model of the temporal and spatial evolution of crowd situation, and proposing a new method of crowd aggregation safety situation assessment. This method is applied to the crowd gathering safety situation assessment of Suzhou city life fountain square, and achieves good results, which provides theoretical support for the safety control of crowd gathering place based on the Internet of things.**

Keywords–Crowd gathering safety situation; Video monitoring; Accident analysis and early warning; Traffic safety.

I. Introduction

When the flow of people in space is highly concentrated for a long time, the crowd density will rise sharply and the distribution is extremely unreasonable, which increases the potential safety hazards and seriously threatens the personal safety. After the spread of the flow, it will even affect the circulation and control of the surrounding traffic. Typical such events, such as the example occurring in the Shanghai Chen Yi Bund Square on December, 2014. The opposite ow of people formed a hedging caused a crowded stampede accident, resulting in 36 deaths and 49 injuries. In addition, according to incomplete statistics, from 2001 to 2014, there were more than 150 people trampling events around the world, all of which occurred in crowded places. Such incidents are sudden, complex and low-level control, which is extremely lightly to cause large-scale casualties. This also makes the prevention and research against crowded stampede accidents become the urgent needs to developing countries with rapid crowd and relatively backward management.

At present, the monitoring of the crowding degree and trend of population is beneted from the mature use of intelligent surveillance video systems, and its comprehensive perspective coverage provides more data support for crowd density estimation. Some scholars have processed the video frame image, and finally got the number of people and the density of the crowd, with good accuracy [1]. To a certain extent, such detection methods have solved the accuracy problems existing in the current crowd density detection, However, the safety of the current location cannot be determined. On the other hand, in the related research on group disaster dynamics, we are more concerned with pedestrian flow simulation and individual motion models. Helbing et al. analyzed the two phenomena of laminar flow from the laminar flow to the stop flow and turbulent flow after analyzing the video of the Mina/Mecca crowd disaster during the 1426 hours pilgrimage on January 12, 2006 [2]. Insights into the causes of these key population conditions are important for organizing safer group events. Johansson et al. discussed how to study high-density conditions based on appropriate video data on the basis of Helbing, and explained the critical conditions of crowd turbulence, and proposed corresponding measures to improve population safety [3]. Moussaid et al. proposed a cognitive heuristic based cognitive science method that predicts individual trajectories and collective movement patterns [4]. The essence of the pedestrian movement model is to study the spatial and temporal evolution trend of the crowd. The input of the model comes from some simple rules and hypotheses. In practice, these inputs often rely on the help of human experience. In fact, with the continuous development of sensor technology, real-time crowd gathering information can effectively replace artificial experience and become the input of a group disaster model. In view of the above problems, this paper combines the analysis of the overall crowd situation and individual model of the crowd gathering place in the context of the intelligent traffic key technology of multi-layer domain collaborative intelligent sensing and data fusion. The focus is transferred from accurately estimating the number of people on the current picture or signal to the reasonable distribution of crowd density. Considering the distance of the crowd within the space from the attraction point and the psychological state of the crowd and other factors, the individual model and the static model of the crowds gathering are established, and the spatial-temporal evolution of the crowd situation is extracted from the real-time monitoring video, thus proposing the crowds gathering early warning method for multi-domain information. The method is used to analyse the crowd density distribution of Suzhou City Life Squares on a certain day with certain guiding significance.

The structure of this paper is as follows: Section II introduces the work related to crowd density detection and individual motion models; Section III establishes the static model of crowd gathering based on the theory of personal space, and analyses the crowd situation from the low-altitude local perspective and the high-altitude global perspective respectively, then, establishing the dynamic model of the spatial-temporal evolution of the crowd situation. Section IV applies the static and dynamic model to Suzhou City Life Squares, which guides crowd monitoring and evacuation, and achieves good results. Section V discusses the results.

II. Related Work

This section introduces the crowd density detection methods in the field of machine vision in recent years, and also summarizes the pedestrian model in crowd disaster dynamics. This has inspired the work of this paper.

A. Crowd Density Detection

The core of crowd density model is to calculate and estimate the crowd density. So many methods have been used to estimate the crowd density, and abundant results have been achieved. From the perspective of computer vision research, the crowd density estimation and counting methods in visual surveillance can be divided two classes. That is crowd density detection based on model labeling and crowd density detection based on feature extraction [5].

The methods using model labeling directly can label and count the human model in the image. Luo et al. mapped the crowd image directly to its crowd density map, then, obtained the total number of people by integral [6]. Zhao et al. divided the human body into multiple objects and used the ellipsoidal model for global tracking to calculate the crowd density [7]. Ge et al. proposed a bayesian method for estimating the number and location of individuals in video frames, which combines a spatial stochastic process that controls the number and location of individuals with a conditional marking process for selecting body shape, shape and direction, and nally gives the number of individuals [8]. Rao et al. proposed a method of estimating crowd density by motion hints and hierarchical clustering, which uses optical ow for motion estimation, contour analysis for crowd contour detection, and gets crowd density by clustering [9]. Although this method retains the features of detection targets to the greatest extent, it is easy to cause inaccurate detection results and difcult to meet the requirements due to the blurred individual contour and inaccurate positioning for dense crowds.

The methods using feature extraction can estimate the crowd density by extracting human features or using other parameters instead of human behavior, then, using normalized method. Koki et al. used the rotational angular velocity of human body as test data, and used continuous wavelet transform and machine learning methods to measure crowd density [10]. Ven et al. learned to distinguish crowd characteristics from granules and tted the contours between crowd and background (i.e., non-crowd) regions for density estimation [11]. Oliver et al. compared the application of two texture classification methods of bow and Gabor filters on aeronautical image plaque datasets to distinguish different crowd densities [12]. Zhang et al. proposed a simple and effective Multi-column Convolution Neural Network (MCNN) structure to map the image to its population density map [13]. By using filters with different size of receiving fields, the features of each column of Convolution Neural Network (CNN) can adapt to the changes of head size caused by perspective effect or image resolution and the effect is remarkable. Although the method of calculating individual density by extracting individual characteristics improves the accuracy of population density detection, the uneven distribution of population density leads to the identication of regional safety hazards not only by estimating the accuracy of population density.

B. Pedestrian Behavior Estimation

As mentioned above, on the basis of high-precision crowd density, we also need to pay attention to the position and state information of each individual. On the micro level, we divide the pedestrian motion model into cellular automata model, social force model, agent-based model and so on.

Based on the individual movement analysis of the cellular automata model, Claudio et al. proposed an improved version of the cellular automaton floor field model, using a sub-grid system to increase the maximum density allowed during the simulation and to reproduce the observed phenomena in dense crowd [14]. Ji et al. proposed a new triangular mesh cellular automaton model for the characteristics of high-density crowd evacuation, and accurately simulated the evacuation process of high-density crowd [15]. The advantage of the kinds of model is relatively simple and suitable for pedestrian behavior simulation in large-scale scenes. But its disadvantage is still obvious. That is, the algorithm itself is a heuristic algorithm, whose results with statistical signicance is unpredictable. And it can not be explained rationally due to divergent rule setting.

Based on the individual movement analysis of the social force model, Helbing et al. suggested that pedestrian movement be described as "social forces", which are not directly imposed by the pedestrian's personal environment, but the measurement of the intrinsic motivation of the individual to perform the task [16]. Yang et al. proposed a pedestrian dynamics correction method based on social force model. By comparing the density-velocity and density-flow maps with the basic maps, it was verified that the guided crowd model can better reflect the pedestrian behavior characteristics in emergency situations [17]. However, the social force model lacks a clear and effective mechanism to ensure that pedestrians do not excessively contact (also known as overlap), so anti-overlap mechanism needs to be introduced.

Based on the individual motion analysis of the agent model, Tak et al. proposed an Agent-based Redestrian Cell Transmission Model (A-PCTM), which shows the flexibility of switching destinations and selecting driving directions according to the situation ahead [18]. Ben et al. presented an agent-based Cellular Automata (CA) environment modeling method that simulated four different evacuation scenarios and effectively guided crowd evacuation [19]. Was et al. proposed a proxy-based non-homogeneous cellular automaton model and an asynchronous cellular automaton model, enabling people to simulate pedestrian complex decision processes in complex environments [20].

III. Model Establishment

In this section, a static early warning model of crowd aggregation is established, and the crowd gathering state is derived through formulas. In addition, a dynamic spatio-temporal evolution model of the crowd situation is also established, and

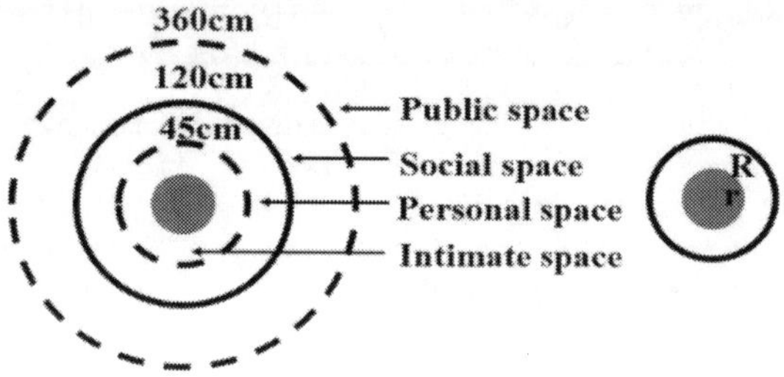

Figure 1. Individual model based on personal space theory.

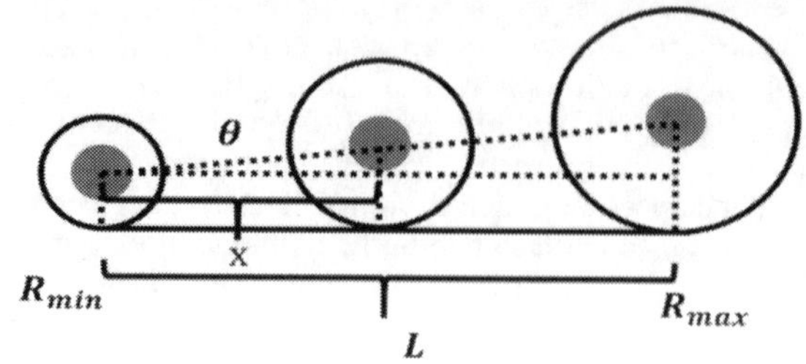

Figure 2. Relationship between personal activity space and distance.

the calculation methods of the crowd density are given from two perspectives: high altitude and low altitude.

A. Static Early Warning Model of Crowd Aggregation

In 1966, Edward Hall proposed the theory of personal space, which distinguishes four personal spatial distances, intimate distance, personal distance, social distance and public distance [21], as shown in Figure 1(a). Personal space theory is a kind of intimacy interpretation that serves the public relations of the public, which only divides the distance of the individual space and generally just applies to individual motion research. However, personal space theory does not directly quantify the relationship between population density and distance, and has great limitations for the application of large crowded places. On the basis of personal space theory, we defined the individual model as a solid circle with radius r, and the personal space is defined as a hollow circle with radius R, as shown in Figure 1(b). In the crowded place, we fitted the relationship between density and distance to analyze the distribution law of population density in large crowds. Firstly, we define the aggregation state T when a crowd gathers in a site, assuming that the crowd is in absolute static state with the most reasonable and safe distribution state, whose optimality depends on the characteristics of the site and the nature of the event. We assume that the determinant is expressed as the attraction of the site, therefore, the site is divided into n attraction points $O_j (j = 1, 2, ..., n)$. Each attraction point will cause the crowd to distribute according to some rules in the range of itself, so the position and size of each individual are different. These aggregates of individuals with different positions and sizes of individual space are called the crowd distribution at the attraction point, which is recorded as $U(O_j)$, and the aggregation state of the site is as follows:

$$T = \sum_{j=1}^{n} U(O_j), \frac{\partial T}{\partial t} = 0 \tag{1}$$

According to the actual situation, we set a plurality of attraction points for the place, and select one attraction point O_1. Then, we set two individual activity ranges closest to and farthest from the attraction point O_1. R_{min} is the radius of the nearest individual activity range from O_1, and R_{max} is the radius of the farthest individual activity range from O_1, as follows the formula calculating the change trend of the personal space radius R:

$$R = \tan\theta * x + A = \frac{R_{max} - R_{min}}{L} * x + A \tag{2}$$

Where θ is the angle between the center line of the two individuals range of activity and the horizontal plane. L is the straight line distance between the center of the farthest individual range of activity and the attraction point. A is the constant of $0.22 \sim 0.25$, representing the radius of the first individual space closest to O_1. x is a variable between 0 and L that changing along with L, as shown in Figure 2.

At this time, the personal activity space has a corresponding relationship with the distance. Assuming that the activity radius of the individual i is R_i, the area occupied by the individual at that place is S_i, and the density ρ_i at that place is $\frac{1}{S_i}$:

$$\rho_i = \frac{1}{S_i} = \frac{1}{\pi {R_i}^2} = \frac{1}{\pi(\tan\theta * x + A)^2} \tag{3}$$

So, we get the corresponding relationship between different size of activity space and the density of the individual's position at this time. Then, we use the least square method to fit the discrete points of different density in different size of activity space, so as to determine the relationship between density and distance. The main idea of the least square method is to solve unknown parameters so that the sum of squares of residual errors can be minimized:

$$E = \sum_{i=1}^{n} (\rho_i - \hat{\rho}_i)^2 \tag{4}$$

The observed value ρ_i is the density of the position of the individual obtained after we calculate the trend of density change. The theoretical value $\hat{\rho}_i$ is the value of the polynomial after we obtain the specific coefficient under the set order. The objective function is also the loss function that is often said in machine learning. Our goal is to obtain the parameters when the objective function is minimized. The final fitting result is the relationship between the distance and the density at the attraction point O_1. After calculating the density at different distances, there is a microscopic individual combination N, which can be regarded as a population aggregation state $U(O_1)$ from a macro perspective:

$$U(O_1) = N = \sum_{i=1}^{n} P_i \tag{5}$$

Among them, P_i is the information set of the location of the individual i and the current personal space size. In the same way, the aggregation state $U(O_2)$ at the second attraction point O_2 is calculated.By analogy, a crowded static early warning model $T = \sum_{j=1}^{n} U(O_j)$ can be obtained.

B. Dynamic Evolution Model of Crowd Situation

The perception of crowd density is divided into high-altitude overall perspective and low-altitude local perspective. Low-altitude camera equipment tends to capture rich human characteristics and perceive local population density more accurately. When it is necessary to perceive the overall crowd situation as a whole, highlighting individual characteristics is not conducive to observing the overall movement trend, so the

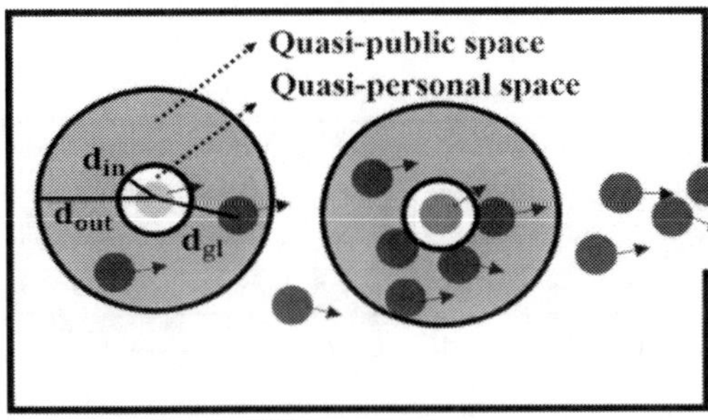

Figure 3. Density judgment of key moving points.

position and movement trend of the crowd at different times can be perceived by using high-altitude camera equipment.

The crowd gathering static early warning model describes the gathering state T of the site. If the crowd distribution V of all the moments t in the activity is described, the dynamic evolution of the crowd situation can be obtained. The static model of the crowd is a certain moment of the dynamic model:$V_t = T$. Since the perception of the crowd situation pays more attention to the group behavior, the characteristics of the person itself are no longer concerned. Therefore, what we need to know is the position evolution and the movement trend of the key moving point Q in the video image at different moments. The point Q can be obtained by extracting the foreground of the moving target from the Gaussian mixture model. Assuming that the mixed gaussian model consists of K Gaussian models, the probability density function is as follows:

$$p(w) = \sum_{k=1}^{K} p(k)p(w|k) = \sum_{k=1}^{K} \pi_k N(w|\pi_k, \sum k) \quad (6)$$

Where $p(w|k) = N(w|\pi_k, \sum k)$ is the probability density function of the gaussian model k, that is, the probability of generating w after the model k selected, $p(k) = \pi_k$ is the weight of the gaussian model k, that is, the prior probability of the model k is selected, and $\sum_{k=1}^{K} \pi_k = 1$. Then, the open operation and morphological denoising are performed on the model results. Finally, the foreground image consist of key moving points is obtain.

In the static model, the individual model represents a human body. In the crowd situation model in this section, the individual model is described to the simulation of the key moving point Q. At this time, the personal space is correspondingly transformed into the motion space between the key moving points, and the personal space distance is redefined as a point. The personal space distance is also redefined as the distance between the set of points $\sum_{i=1}^{n} Q_i$:

$$d_{gl} = \sqrt{(m_g - m_l)^2 + (n_g - n_l)^2}, g \neq l, l \in [1, n-1] \quad (7)$$

d_{gl} denotes the distance between any moving point Q_g and other moving points Q_l, (m_g, n_g), (m_l, n_l) are the position coordinates of the moving point Q_g and the moving point Q_l, respectively.The distance and direction of motion between the points change with time. We specify a personal space for each moving point Q_i, shown as the inner circle in Figure 3. And the public space shown as the outer circle in Figure 3. The number of moving points contained in the space between them is used as the basis for dividing the density:

$$d_{in} < d_{gl} < d_{out} \quad (8)$$

Where d_{in} represents the distance from the center of the circle to the inner circle, and d_{out} represents the distance from the center of the circle to the outer circle.

The perception of local crowd situation depends on the video and image acquired by low-altitude camera with obvious individual characteristics. We use Multi-column Convolution Neural Network (MCNN) model to extract human head features of different sizes [13]. The original image obtains different size of human head features through parallel networks with different sizes of three-column filters. Finally, the obtained features are weighted linearly to obtain the crowd density map. The model uses the maximum pooling layer of 2*2 and the activation function of the linear rectifier function, and integrates the three-column feature map. The loss function uses the optimized Euclidean loss function, which can standardize the density map of the network output:

$$L(\beta) = \frac{1}{2N} \sum_{i=1}^{N} ||F(X_i, \beta) - F_i||_2^2. \quad (9)$$

Here β is the network parameter to be optimized, N is the number of training images, X_i is the input image, F_i is the ground truth density map corresponding to X_i, $F(X_i, \beta)$ is the density map generated by MCNN. Figure 4 shows the structure of our MCNN. The three-column network structure has the same number of convolution layers and functions for each column except that the size of the filter. The purpose is to capture the head features of different sizes. Therefore, the first column is taken as an example. Enter an image of unlimited size, the first layer whose filters with 7*7 size to capture the local human head features. Then, max pooling is applied for each 22 region to reduce the resolution of the upper layer image to $\frac{1}{4}$ of the original image, the number of parameters is reduced, and more useful features are extracted. At the end, the features are weighted and stacked by a 1*1 filter, so that the output results are averaged for density grading processing. The density normalization process mainly depends on the Gaussian kernel function. This paper proposes that the adaptive Gaussian kernel function is slightly different from Zhang[14]:

$$F(x) = \sum_{i=1}^{M} \delta_i * G(x, \sigma_i) \quad (10)$$

Where δ_i represents the impulse function of each head, M is the number of heads in the image. And σ_i denotes the maximum head distance of the adaptation within a certain range (Using the maximum is to make the crowds more dense), $\sigma_i = \alpha max(d_{ij})$. α is the weight value of the adaptive range. In our experiment, it shows that when $\alpha = 0.5$ the crowds intensity is the most consistent with the actual situation.

IV. MODEL APPLICATION

Located near Jinji Lake in Suzhou City in China, the city life square covers an area of 4300 square meters and periodically carries out large-scale fountain projection activities, with a maximum of 35,000 people. Our crowds gathering model was been applied in this square. The data come from the video camera equipment covering the inside and the exits of the square and the construction drawings of the construction of the site. The crowd distribution of the square was been investigated on the spot. The concrete implementation is as follows.

A. Application of Static Early Warning Model

We select the fountain where it is an attraction point $O_1(n = 1)$, then, establish a spatial coordinate system choos-

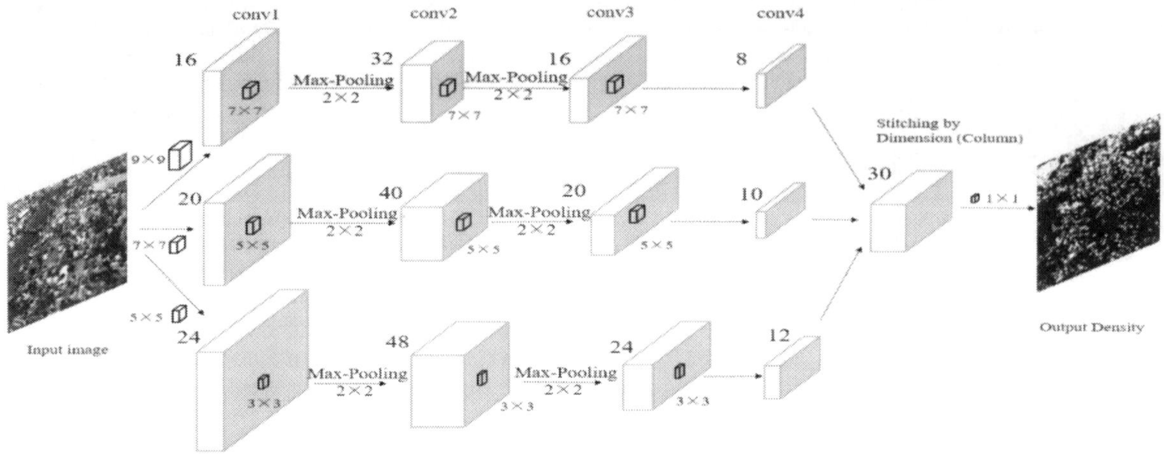

Figure 4. MCNN Network Structure [13].

ing O_1 as the coordinate origin. The radius r of the individual model is determined by the shoulder width of the person standing. according to [22] [23], a solid circle with radius $r = 22cm$ is used as an individual model in this paper. Through field survey and CAD drawing measurement, we set $L = 200m$ in the static early warning model, and take R_{max} and R_{min} as $0.62m$ and $0.25m$ respectively according to the queued waiting state pedestrian service level table [24]. When the least squares method is fitted, we calculate it repeatedly. When the loss E reaches 0.1 at the first time, the fitting effect is the best, and the relationship between the crowd density ρ and the distance d from the attraction point is calculated as:

$$\rho = -1.8782e^{-12}d^5 + 2.3706e^{-9}d^4 - 1.187e^{-6}d^3 + 0.0030768d^2 - 0.045949d + 3.9659 \quad (11)$$

Taking $N = 50000$ different distance corresponding to different density of points cyclic calculation, these point sets N is the crowd aggregation state $U(O_1)$ at the point O_1:

$$U(O_1) = \sum_{i=1}^{n} P_i = \sum_{i=1}^{n} P(d_i, \rho_i) \quad (12)$$

thus establishing a static early warning model of crowd aggregation taking Fountain Square as an example.

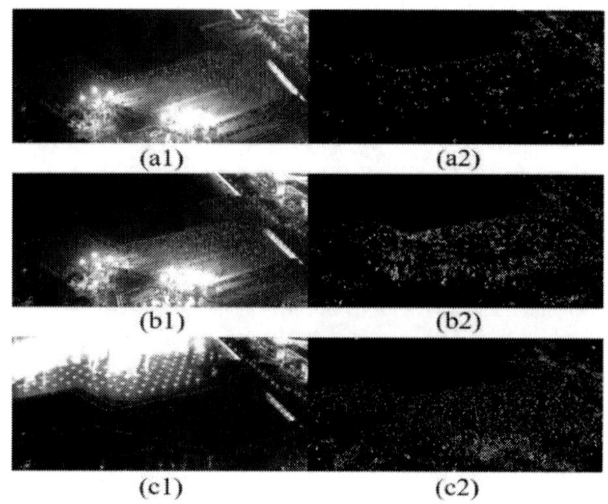

Figure 5. Key moving points map of fountain square in different time period(a1) Low crowd density real-time video (a2) Low crowd density key moving points set (b1) Medium crowd density real-time video (b2) Medium crowd density key moving points set (c1) High crowd density real-time video (c2) High crowd density key moving points set.

B. Application of Dynamic Evolution Model

We intercept the key frames of the video images captured by the aerial camera. We extract the foreground image of the moving target through the Gauss mixture model, and get the set of the key moving points. At low density, we take 18724 moving points, 43779 moving points at medium density, and 61386 moving points at high density, as shown in Figure 5. According to the distance between the moving points, we can judge the density grade at the point whether it is between d_{in} and d_{out}. Here, we select $d_{in} = 1$ and $d_{out} = 8$ to get the density grade of the key moving points, which reflects the crowd situation at that time, as shown in Figure 6 (a1), (b1), (c1). At low density, the distribution of moving points is scattered and the intensity is relatively light. At medium density, the moving points cover the image area in a large area, and some of the point sets are in a highly concentrated state. While at high density, the moving points basically occupy the image area, showing a trend of global high density, reflecting the high crowding in the square at the moment. The distance between people is very short, which leads to people moving slowly and potential safety hazards.

We performed a curve analysis of the population density at the same angle for the three densities. According to the collected data, a density curve is shown, as shown by the red lines in Figure 6 (a2), (b2) and (c2), the horizontal axis represents the distance from the attraction point, and the vertical axis represents the density at that point. Comparing the crowd density change of static early warning model of crowd aggregation (blue line in Figure 6) with that of low density, medium density and high density.We found that, when the crowd density reaches high density, the density line almost exceeds the warning line, which means potential safety hazards could be in the square, as shown in Figure 6 (c2). Under the high density, pedestrians often have inevitable contact with each other. It is impossible to walk horizontally or reversely, and the flow of people is extremely unstable, which is in accordance with the conclusion of Figure 5 (c1), (c2). We carry out dynamic crowd situational awareness of high-

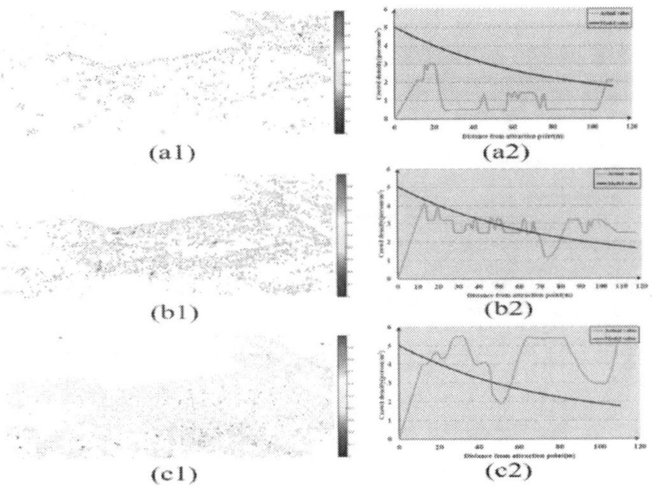

Figure 6. The crowd density curve of the early warning model and the actual population density curve under three states. (a) Early warning curve and low density curve (b) Early warning curve and medium density curve (c) Early warning curve and high density curve.

altitude video, which mainly includes the following three steps: extracting video key frames, extracting foreground images of sports people through Gaussian mixture model, and performing density calculation on all key moving points to obtain density classification of moving points. After the above work is carried out, the perception of the crowd situation can be realized to capture the preference trend of the crowd evacuation. Then, we can formulate the strategy for evacuation of the crowd, which can guide the staff to carry out the evacuation work quickly and effectively. Based on the perception of the crowd situation, we finally get the direction and magnitude of the crowd flow, which provides a reference for our subsequent simulation parameter settings. In addition, we also attempted to analyze the density of low-altitude crowd.

V. Conclusion

In this paper, we discussed the limitations of Hall's personal space theory in the crowded scene. On the basis of this, we explored the quantitative relationship between crowd density and distance, so that the static early warning model for crowd gathering can be established. In contrast, we used the characteristics of overall video images to perceive the temporal and spatial evolution of the crowd situation and established a dynamic model of the crowd situation. The joint analysis of static early warning model and dynamic model can comprehensively perceive the real-time situation of the crowd and improve the public safety of the site. We have successfully applied our models in the Fountain Square of Suzhou City. Through the video images acquired by the high-altitude camera equipment, we perceived the changes in the crowd situation of the site. In future work, we will fuse heterogeneous multi-granularity surveillance videos and supplement the entire situation with local actual number to estimate the number of people in the entire venue.

References

[1] S. Pu, T. Song, Y. Zhang, and D. Xie, "Estimation of crowd density in surveillance scenes based on deep convolutional neural network," Procedia computer science, vol. 111, 2017, pp. 154–159.

[2] D. Helbing, A. Johansson, and H. Z. Al-Abideen, "Dynamics of crowd disasters: An empirical study," Physical review E, vol. 75, no. 4, 2007, p. 046109.

[3] A. Johansson, D. Helbing, H. Z. Al-Abideen, and S. Al-Bosta, "From crowd dynamics to crowd safety: a video-based analysis," Advances in Complex Systems, vol. 11, no. 04, 2008, pp. 497–527.

[4] M. Moussaïd, D. Helbing, and G. Theraulaz, "How simple rules determine pedestrian behavior and crowd disasters," Proceedings of the National Academy of Sciences, vol. 108, no. 17, 2011, pp. 6884–6888.

[5] S. A. M. Saleh, S. A. Suandi, and H. Ibrahim, "Recent survey on crowd density estimation and counting for visual surveillance," Engineering Applications of Artificial Intelligence, vol. 41, 2015, pp. 103–114.

[6] H. Luo et al., "A high-density crowd counting method based on convolutional feature fusion," Applied Sciences, vol. 8, no. 12, 2018, p. 2367.

[7] T. Zhao and R. Nevatia, "Tracking multiple humans in complex situations," IEEE Transactions on Pattern Analysis & Machine Intelligence, no. 9, 2004, pp. 1208–1221.

[8] W. Ge and R. T. Collins, "Crowd density analysis with marked point processes [applications corner]," IEEE Signal Processing Magazine, vol. 27, no. 5, 2010, pp. 107–123.

[9] A. S. Rao, J. Gubbi, S. Marusic, and M. Palaniswami, "Estimation of crowd density by clustering motion cues," The Visual Computer, vol. 31, no. 11, 2015, pp. 1533–1552.

[10] K. Nagao, D. Yanagisawa, and K. Nishinari, "Estimation of crowd density applying wavelet transform and machine learning," Physica A: Statistical Mechanics and its Applications, vol. 510, 2018, pp. 145–163.

[11] V. J. Kok and C. S. Chan, "Granular-based dense crowd density estimation," Multimedia Tools and Applications, vol. 77, no. 15, 2018, pp. 20 227–20 246.

[12] O. Meynberg, S. Cui, and P. Reinartz, "Detection of high-density crowds in aerial images using texture classification," Remote Sensing, vol. 8, no. 6, 2016, p. 470.

[13] Y. Zhang, D. Zhou, S. Chen, S. Gao, and Y. Ma, "Single-image crowd counting via multi-column convolutional neural network," in Proceedings of the IEEE conference on computer vision and pattern recognition, 2016, pp. 589–597.

[14] C. Feliciani and K. Nishinari, "An improved cellular automata model to simulate the behavior of high density crowd and validation by experimental data," Physica A: Statistical Mechanics and its Applications, vol. 451, 2016, pp. 135–148.

[15] J. Ji, L. Lu, Z. Jin, S. Wei, and L. Ni, "A cellular automata model for high-density crowd evacuation using triangle grids," Physica A: Statistical Mechanics and its Applications, vol. 509, 2018, pp. 1034–1045.

[16] D. Helbing and P. Molnar, "Social force model for pedestrian dynamics," Physical review E, vol. 51, no. 5, 1995, p. 4282.

[17] X. Yang, H. Dong, Q. Wang, Y. Chen, and X. Hu, "Guided crowd dynamics via modified social force model," Physica A: Statistical Mechanics and its Applications, vol. 411, 2014, pp. 63–73.

[18] S. Tak, S. Kim, and H. Yeo, "Agent-based pedestrian cell transmission model for evacuation," Transportmetrica A: transport science, vol. 14, no. 5-6, 2018, pp. 484–502.

[19] X. Ben, X. Huang, Z. Zhuang, R. Yan, and S. Xu, "Agent-based approach for crowded pedestrian evacuation simulation," IET Intelligent Transport Systems, vol. 7, no. 1, 2013, pp. 55–67.

[20] J. Was and R. Lubas, "Towards realistic and effective agent-based models of crowd dynamics," Neurocomputing, vol. 146, 2014, pp. 199–209.

[21] E. T. Hall, The Hidden Dimension. Garden City, NY: Doubleday, 1966, vol. 609.

[22] Y.-C. Lin, M.-J. J. Wang, and E. M. Wang, "The comparisons of anthropometric characteristics among four peoples in east asia," Applied Ergonomics, vol. 35, no. 2, 2004, pp. 173–178.

[23] C. C. Gordon et al., "2010 anthropometric survey of us marine corps personnel: methods and summary statistics," Army Natick Soldier Research Development and Engineering Center Ma, Tech. Rep., 2013.

[24] H. C. Manual, "Highway capacity manual," Washington, DC, vol. 2, 2000.

A Multi-Objective Optimization Method on Consumer's Benefit in Peer-to-peer Energy Trading

Mitsue Imahori, Ryo Hase and Norihiko Shinomiya

Graduate School of Engineering
Soka University
Tokyo, Japan 192–8577
Email: shinomi@soka.ac.jp

Abstract—**In recent years, many countries have been promoting the shift from centralized energy systems to distributed ones for clean energy utilization. Direct energy trading among consumers has drawn increasing interest in the development of efficient utilization of distributed energy systems. However, a part of consumers might not be able to receive electricity from their preferred suppliers since some suppliers have limited capacity of supplying electricity. This occasion leads to a decrease in the consumer's benefit. Existing studies are mainly focused on not the equity of prosumer's benefit but the efficiency of resource allocation. Therefore, a mechanism that satisfies not only balance between supply and demand but market participants' preferences is required. In this paper, a multi-objective optimization problem as market mechanism is proposed to improve both the equity of consumer's benefit and the efficiency of resource allocation. For solving the proposed optimization problem, six Evolutionary Algorithms (EAs) are selected. Simulation results show that the selected EAs can be classified into two types: (i) algorithms optimizing both the efficiency of resource allocation and the equity of consumer's benefit and (ii) algorithms optimizing only one of the two objectives.**

Keywords–Peer-to-Peer Energy Trading; Evolutionary Algorithm; Multi-objective Optimization Problem; Graph Theory.

I. Introduction

Many countries have been encouraging people to utilize distributed energy systems such as solar and wind power generations for environmental issues. Existing energy systems have been relying on fossil fuels heavily because this kind of energy systems can supply electricity to a great number of consumers with fewer electric outage. However, such energy systems emit a large amount of greenhouse gas, which leads to a factor contributing to global warming. Therefore, many countries have legislated policy to enhance the rate of renewable energy utilization.

One of the efforts of governments in many countries is to enact Feed-In Tariff (FIT), which aims at spreading renewable energy systems widely to general households. Consumers who own energy generators are called prosumers [1] because they do not only consume electricity but also produce it. FIT guarantees that public utilities purchase excess electricity from consumers at a fixed rate in a certain period. FIT leads consumers to be able to have the outlook for the return on installation costs of renewable energy systems. Therefore, renewable energy systems have drawn increasing interest in general households, and the number of prosumers has been increasing year by year.

For efficient excess electricity utilization, energy market frameworks have been proposed by governments in many countries. For example in Japan, one of the methods is Virtual Power Plant (VPP) that aggregates capacities of heterogeneous distributed energy resources. Another example is Demand Response (DR) which is a change in consumption of consumers to match demand for electricity with supply. In VPP and DR, there are aggregators who join a local energy market as third party to manage prosumer's energy resources. However, in these methods, transparency of trading is unclear, and an intermediate margin is incurred due to a third party such as an aggregator.

In order to cope with the issues described above, direct energy trading among consumers and prosumers that is regarded as Peer-to-Peer (P2P) energy trading has been gathering attention. Fig. 1 represents present energy trading, and Fig. 2 shows P2P energy trading. As shown in Fig. 1, consumers can trade electricity with the only one public utility in present energy trading. On the other hand, as shown in Fig. 2, consumers can trade electricity with not only the public utility but other consumers in P2P energy trading. Energy trading without a third party is expected to increase transparency of trading and reduce electricity rates. P2P energy trading would make consumers motivated to exchange electricity with others, and efficient electricity utilization in a local energy market will be realized. Nowadays, the feasibility of P2P energy trading will improve with the advent of blockchain technology.

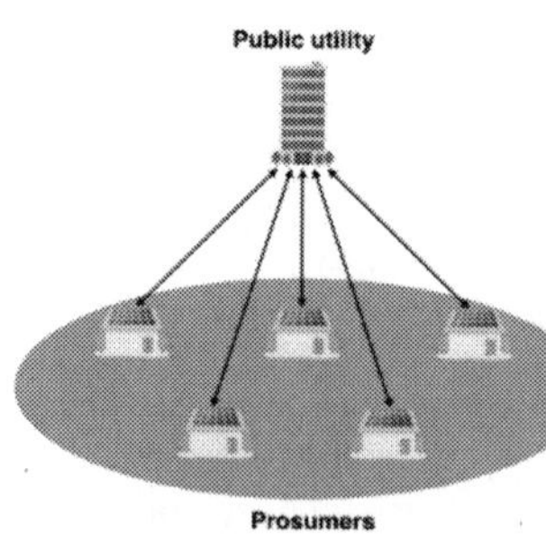

Fig 1. Present energy trading.

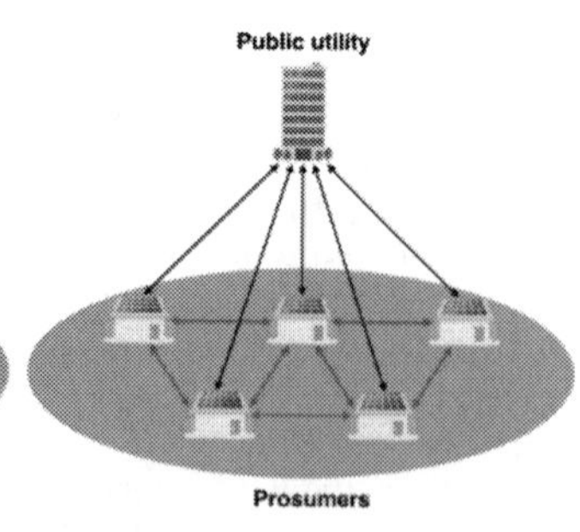

Fig 2. Peer-to-peer energy trading.

However, if P2P energy trading is implemented in practical markets, a couple of issues might occur due to market constraints. In P2P energy trading, candidates for consumer's trading partner will be diversified, and each consumer will have preferences for market participants. Consumers will decide their trading partners based on their preferences. There is a special constraint that must meet supply and demand for electricity in energy markets. If each market participant acts to maximize their benefit in markets and decides their trading partner arbitrarily, balance between supply and demand for electricity might collapse because of breaking the market constraints. Furthermore, if each market participant decides their trading partners under the market constraints, some consumers might not be able to trade electricity with their desirable partners since prosumers have limited capacity of supplying electricity. These occasions lead to a decrease in the consumer's benefit. Therefore, a mechanism that satisfies not only balance between supply and demand but market participant's preference is required.

For P2P energy trading realization, many studies have been conducted to consider P2P trading models. Jiawen *et al.* propose an auction mechanism that determines optimal electricity rates and the amount of electricity traded between sellers and buyers in an electric vehicle market in [2]. In [3], Muhammad *et al.* present a smart home model for minimizing the total of payment to the public utility and eliminating inequalities of energy. Pourya *et al.* formulate an economic dispatch problem for reducing operation costs in a community microgrid in [4]. Yue *et al.* evaluate some P2P energy sharing mechanisms based on multi-agent simulation frameworks that might bring both economic and technical benefit in [5]. Chao *et al.* present a two-stage aggregated control for maximizing economic benefit of each prosumer in [6]. In [7], Wayes *et al.* present a price discrimination method that is able to conduct envy-free energy trading and to maximize the total of consumer's benefit. These studies described above analyze not the equity of consumer's benefit but only the efficiency of resource allocation in P2P trading markets.

Therefore, our study proposes a P2P energy trading model and analyzes trading focusing on each consumer's benefit besides an overall market. In P2P trading, consumer's production and demand vary over time, and their benefit is anticipated changing complicatedly. Our model is denoted by Time-Varying Graph (TVG) [8] to represent time-varying consumer's behavior. Furthermore, a multi-objective optimization problem as market mechanism is formulated to investigate benefit of each consumer. Since P2P energy trading has not been applied to a practical market, electricity trading should be investigated more carefully.

This paper is structured as follows. Section II explains the definitions of our energy trading model with a time-varying graph. Section III formulates a multi-objective optimization problem and demonstrates the simulation results. Section IV concludes this paper and expresses future works.

II. Model Representation

This section introduces our P2P energy trading model by utilizing notation of graph theory. An optimization problem is formulated to investigate P2P energy trading.

A. P2P energy trading model as graphs

Our electricity market model is composed of two kinds of participants that are a public utility and consumers. The set of all participants is expressed by V. Public utility is denoted by $v_p \in V$. Since energy trading among only consumers will not be able to provide for all demand, it is assumed that there is a public utility in our model for covering all electricity deficit and excess electricity. Consumer is represented by $v_i \in V(i = 1, 2, \ldots, |N|)$ and varies its behavior between seller and buyer according to time. If a consumer has excess electricity, the consumer can be seller. On the other hand, if a consumer runs out of generated electricity, the consumer can be buyer. Some consumers might not have own energy generators, and their production should be set to zero in this case. $V_S \subset V$ indicates the set of consumers who are sellers, and $V_B \subset V$ expresses the set of consumers who are buyers.

Consumer v_i changes its behavior depending on its production and consumption of electricity in P2P trading markets. Consumers must trade electricity during time span $\mathcal{T}$. Consumer's production and consumption at each time $t \in \mathcal{T}$ are represented by $p_i^t \in \mathbb{R}$ and $c_i^t \in \mathbb{R}$ respectively. If $p_i^t > c_i^t$, v_i will be seller and can supply electricity to other participants. Conversely, if $p_i^t < c_i^t$, v_i will be buyer and can purchase electricity from other participants. Furthermore, if $p_i^t = c_i^t$, v_i will be neither seller or buyer and does nothing in markets at t.

In order to model a P2P trading market considering time-varying consumer's behavior, TVG is utilized. A P2P trading model at each time is represented by TVG that consists of four types of vertices: the white vertices behaving as sellers, the black vertices behaving as buyers, the gray vertex doing nothing in the markets, and the blue vertices expressing public utilities. The set of arcs is denoted by A, and each arc of TVG at t is represented by $(v_i, v_j) \in A^t$. Arc (v_i, v_j) expresses the relationship where v_j can purchase electricity with v_i. Each arc must connect two vertices. The direction of the arrows represents electricity flow. TVG in Fig. 3 is expressed as $\mathcal{G} = (V, A, \mathcal{T})$. By using this model, consumer's benefit can be investigated in detail at each time.

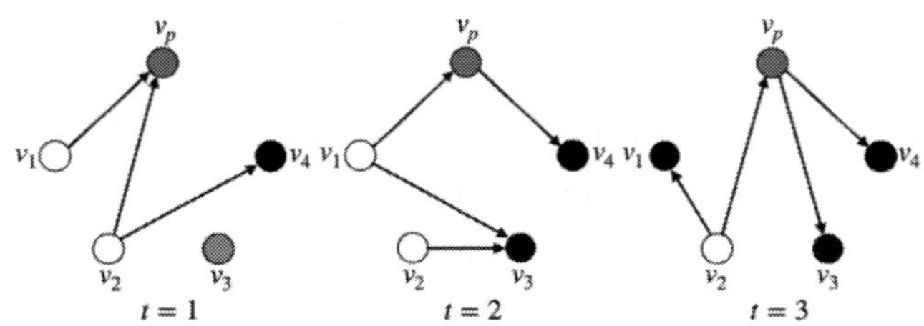

Fig 3. Time-Varying Graph $\mathcal{G}$.

An underlying graph indicates relationships among market participants where they can trade electricity with each other over a trading period as a sort of footprints of TVG. Fig. 4 that consists of the blue vertices expressing a public utility and the orange vertices representing consumers is represented by an underlying graph of $\mathcal{G}$ in Fig. 3. The set of edges is denoted by E, and each edge of the underlying graph is represented by $(v_i, v_j) \in E$. Edge (v_i, v_j) denotes the relationship where v_j can purchase electricity from v_i. Underlying graph in Fig.

4 is expressed by $G = (V, E)$. Since an underlying graph is finalized by aggregating TVG, the cumulative benefit of each consumer can be analyzed in this model.

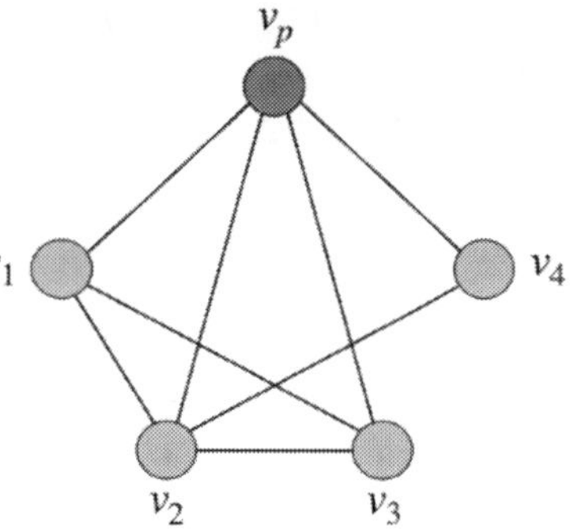

Fig 4. An underlying graph G.

B. Constraints of trading volume

Each consumer has capacity of supplying and purchasing electricity depending on its production and consumption. The amount of electricity traded between v_i and v_j is represented by $x\colon (V_S \cup \{v_p\}) \times (V_B \cup \{v_p\}) \to \mathbb{R}$, and x is called trading volume. Each arc $(v_i, v_j) \in A^t$ has capacity where v_i can supply electricity to v_j up to the maximum trading volume. Capacity of $(v_i, v_j) \in A^t$ is denoted by the function cap : $(V_S \cup \{v_p\}) \times (V_B \cup \{v_p\}) \times \mathcal{T} \to \mathbb{R}$. The trading volume on each arc must satisfy the following constraints:

$$0 \leq x^t(v_i, v_j) \leq cap^t(v_i, v_j) \quad (v_i \in V_S, v_j \in V_B, t \in \mathcal{T}), \tag{1}$$

$$0 \leq x^t(v_i, v_p) \leq cap^t(v_i, v_p) \quad (v_i \in V_S, t \in \mathcal{T}), \tag{2}$$

$$0 \leq x^t(v_p, v_j) \leq cap^t(v_p, v_j) \quad (v_j \in V_B, t \in \mathcal{T}). \tag{3}$$

Funcion cap is calculated by different formulae depending on trading pairs. Excess electricity of seller v_i is defined as $p_i^t - c_i^t$, and electricity deficit of buyer v_j is defined as $c_j^t - p_j^t$. If both v_i and v_j are prosumers, capacity of (v_i, v_j) at t is set as

$$cap^t(v_i, v_j) = \min\left((p_i^t - c_i^t), (c_j^t - p_j^t)\right).$$

Since a public utility covers all consumer's electricity deficit, it is assumed that the public utility can supply electricity to all consumers. Therefore, capacity of (v_p, v_j) at t is defined as

$$cap^t(v_p, v_j) = c_j^t - p_j^t.$$

Moreover, since the public utility covers all consumer's excess electricity, it is assumed that the public utility can purchase electricity from all consumers. Therefore, capacity of (v_i, v_p) at t is defined as

$$cap^t(v_i, v_p) = p_i^t - c_i^t.$$

Sellers must sell electricity which is equal to the amount of own excess electricity to others. Buyers must purchase electricity which is equal to the amount of own electricity deficit from others. The above constraints are expressed by

$$\sum_{v_j \in V_B \cup \{v_p\}} x^t(v_i, v_j) = p_i^t - c_i^t \quad (v_i \in V_S, t \in \mathcal{T}), \tag{4}$$

$$\sum_{v_i \in V_S \cup \{v_p\}} x^t(v_i, v_j) = c_j^t - p_j^t \quad (v_j \in V_B, t \in \mathcal{T}). \tag{5}$$

C. Rate

Consumers behaving as seller and a public utility have rates when dealing with their electricity. Seller $v_i \in V_S$ offers the unit of electricity with rate $r_i \in \mathbb{R}$ to buyers $v_i \in V_B$. When v_i supplies electricity $x^t(v_i, v_j)$ to v_j, v_j must purchase electricity at $x^t(v_i, v_j) \cdot r_i$ from v_i. Public utility v_p offers the unit of electricity to buyers with rate $r_s \in \mathbb{R}$, where it is assumed that $r_s \geq r_i$. When v_p supplies electricity $x^t(v_p, v_j)$ to v_j, v_j must purchase electricity at $x^t(v_p, v_j) \cdot r_s$ from v_p. Public utility v_p purchases electricity at rate $r_b \in \mathbb{R}$ from sellers, where it is assumed that $r_i \geq r_b$. When v_i supplies electricity $x^t(v_i, v_p)$ to v_p, v_p must purchase electricity at $x^t(v_i, v_p) \cdot r_b$ from v_i.

D. Reservation price

Each consumer has a reservation price in energy trading. The reservation price of buyers is the maximum price where buyers can purchase electricity from others. Conversely, the reservation price of sellers is the minimum price where sellers can supply electricity to others. The reservation prices of consumers are represented by the function $\omega\colon V \times \mathcal{T} \to \mathbb{R}$. ω is calculated from different formulae depending on consumer's behavior. Thus, the reservation prices are expressed by the following formulae:

$$\omega^t(v_i) = \begin{cases} (p_i^t - c_i^t) \cdot r_b & (p_i^t > c_i^t), \\ (c_i^t - p_i^t) \cdot r_s & (p_i^t < c_i^t). \end{cases}$$

Since each consumer must deal electricity with the only public utility in present electricity trading, $\omega^t(v_i)$ is set as a price offered by the public utility in this paper.

E. Consumer's benefit

Consumers can benefit from trading when they trade electricity with more favorable partners than current ones. Consumer's benefit is represented by the function $\pi\colon V \to \mathbb{R}$. π is also calculated from different formulae depending on consumer's behavior. Seller's benefit is defined as the difference between the total income and the reservation price of sellers. Consumer's income is represented by the function $\zeta\colon V_s \times V_b \times \mathcal{T} \to \mathbb{R}$. The total of each seller's income is defined as

$$\zeta^t(v_i) = \sum_{v_j \in V_B} x^t(v_i, v_j) \cdot r_i + x^t(v_p, v_i) \cdot r_s.$$

If a consumer behaves as seller, consumer's benefit is defined as

$$\pi^t(v_i) = \zeta^t(v_i) - \omega^t(v_i).$$

Conversely, buyer's benefit is defined as the difference between the reservation price of buyers and the total of expenditure. Consumer's expenditure is represented by the function $\eta\colon V_s \times V_b \times \mathcal{T} \to \mathbb{R}$. The total of buyer's expenditure is defined as

$$\eta^t(v_j) = \sum_{v_i \in V_S} x^t(v_i, v_j) \cdot r_i + x^t(v_p, v_j) \cdot r_s.$$

If a consumer behaves as buyer, buyer's benefit is defined as

$$\pi^t(v_j) = \omega^t(v_j) - \eta^t(v_j).$$

Since all of the consumers must not suffer from monetary deficits caused by electricity trading in our model, it is assumed that $\pi^t(v_i) \geq 0$, $\pi^t(v_j) \geq 0$. This research focuses on P2P trading in one local energy market, that is, a public utility will be negligibly affected by energy trading. Therefore, public utility's benefit is not considered.

F. Problem formulation

In order to investigate consumer's benefit, a multi-objective optimization problem is formulated. One of the objectives is to maximize the total of consumer's benefit. The other objective is to minimize the standard deviation of consumer's benefit. This problem is expected to obtain solutions with the high efficiency of resource allocation and the high equity of prosumer's benefit. The problem is defined as follows.

$$\text{maximize} \quad \sum_{v_i \in V_S \cup V_B} \pi^t(v_i).$$

$$\text{minimize} \quad \sqrt{\frac{\sum_{v_i \in V_S \cup V_B} (\overline{\pi} - \pi^t(v_i))^2}{|N|}}.$$

$$\text{subject to} \quad (1), (2), (3), (4), \text{and } (5),$$

where the objective functions are optimized at each time t.

Constraints (1), (2), and (3) indicate that the amount of electricity traded between participants on each arc is less than or equal to capacity of each arc. These constraints also show that the amount of electricity traded between participants is not a negative value. Constraint (4) represents that the total of seller's trading volume is equal to the amount of own excess electricity, and constraint (5) expresses that the total of buyer's trading volume is equal to the amount of own electricity deficit.

III. EXPERIMENTAL RESULTS

To obtain solutions optimized by the multi-objective optimization problem, a simulator is developed with Platypus [9] that is a framework for evolutionary computing in Python. The following six selected Evolutionary Algorithms (EAs) as metaheuristics methods are utilized in our simulation.

- Non-dominated Sorting Genetic Algorithms-I I (NSGA-II)
- Generalized Differential Evolution-III (GDE3)
- Optimized MultiObjective Particle Swarm Optimization (OMOPSO)
- Speed-constrained Multiobjective Particle Swarm Optimization (SMPSO)
- Strength Pareto Evolutionary Algorithm-II (SPEA2)
- ϵ-MultiObjective Evolutionary Algorithm (ϵ-MOEA)

The reason for utilizing metaheuristics algorithms is that they are expected to be able to apply for an expanded market with a large number of participants.

A. Conditions

In our simulation, parameters were determined in reference to the electricity market in Japan. The public utility supplies electricity to consumers at 29.05 yen per kWh and purchases electricity from consumers at 8.05 yen per kWh. Consumers supply electricity to other consumers at 18.55 yen per kWh, it comes from the average between the public utility's offering rate and purchasing rate. Seller's production p_i and consumption c_i are set to 549 Wh and 502 Wh respectively. Buyer's production p_i and consumption c_i are set to 455 Wh and 502 Wh respectively. The number of iterations is set to 1,000. Since the optimization problem was solved every one hour for deciding trading partners, trading for 1000 hours was determined in the experiments. In each round of simulations, the number of samples is set to 10000, and the population is set to 100. For OMOPSO and ϵ-MOEA, ϵ is set to 0.05.

With the assumed market, a simulation was conducted with each of the following four patterns:

- 3 sellers and 0 buyer (Pattern 1)
- 2 sellers and 1 buyer (Pattern 2)
- 1 seller and 2 buyers (Pattern 3)
- 0 seller and 3 buyers (Pattern 4)

B. Results and discussion

In Pattern 1 and Pattern 4, there is only one kind of solutions that both the total of consumer's benefit and the standard deviation are zero in all selected EAs. This paper introduces only the results of Pattern 2 because the results of Pattern 3 have a tendency similar to Pattern 2. Since EAs obtained Pareto solutions, this research randomly extracted one of the Pareto solutions at each time.

Fig. 5 depicts the solutions obtained by NSGA-II in Pattern 2. The results of SMPSO, SPEA2 and ϵ-MOEA have a tendency similar to NSGA-II. In Fig. 5, the horizontal axis depicts the total of consumer's benefit, and the vertical axis shows the standard deviation of consumer's benefit. Simulation results show that NSGA-II discovered various kinds of solutions under the same conditions. Figs. 6 and 7 show each of the two objective functions at each time in Fig. 5. In Fig. 6, the horizontal axis depicts t, and the vertical axis shows the total of consumer's benefit. In Fig. 7, the horizontal axis depicts t, and the vertical axis shows the standard deviation of consumer's benefit. These results show that the solutions are dense toward the optimal area, and NSGA-II tended to find solutions on the Pareto front. As shown from the results, NSGA-II facilitates deciding ideal trading depending on methods to select solutions.

Fig. 8 represents the solutions obtained by OMOPSO in Pattern 2. The results of GDE3 have a tendency similar to OMOPSO. The horizontal and vertical axes in Fig. 8 depict the same as Fig. 5. Simulation results show that OMOPSO found solutions optimized for only one of the two objective functions in most cases. Figs. 9 and 10 show each of the two objective functions at each time in Fig. 8. The horizontal and vertical axes in Fig. 9 depict the same as Fig. 6, and the horizontal and vertical axes in Fig. 10 represent the same as Fig. 7. As shown in Fig. 9, the solutions are dense in the upper part and the lower part of the figure. The solutions in the upper part show the maximum total of consumer's benefit. On the other hand, the solutions in the lower part show that all consumers could not obtain benefit at that time. Fig. 10 also shows that the solutions are dense in the upper part and the lower part of the figure. The solutions in the lower part show that the variation in consumer's benefit is zero, that is, they are the best solutions in terms of the equity of consumer's benefit. On the other hand, the solutions in the upper part show that consumer's benefit with the low equity is obtained. As shown from the results, when only one objective function is optimized, the other objective function is likely to be inferior in this algorithm.

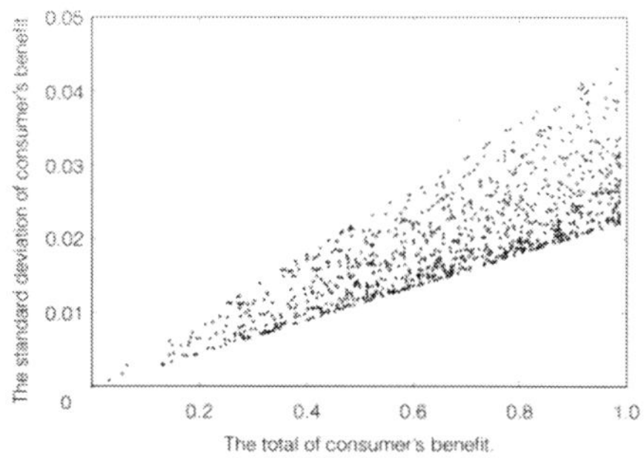

Fig 5. Solutions obtained by NSGA-II in Pattern 2.

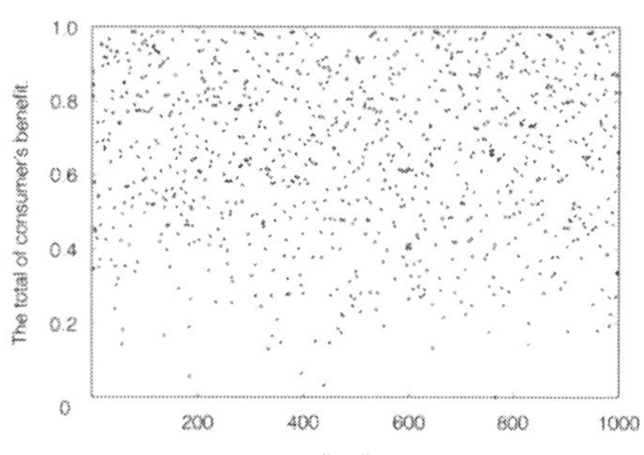

Fig 6. Total of consumer's benefit obtained by NSGA-II.

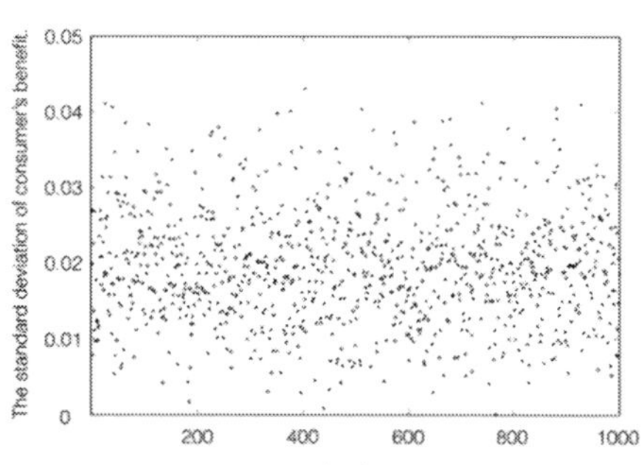

Fig 7. Standard deviation obtained by NSGA-II.

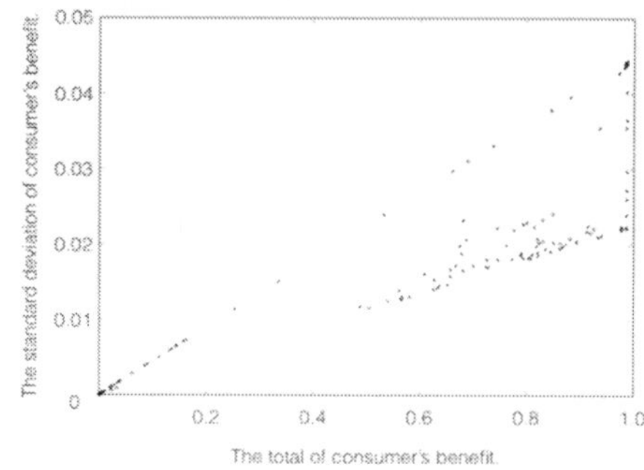

Fig 8. Solutions obtained by OMOPSO in Pattern 2.

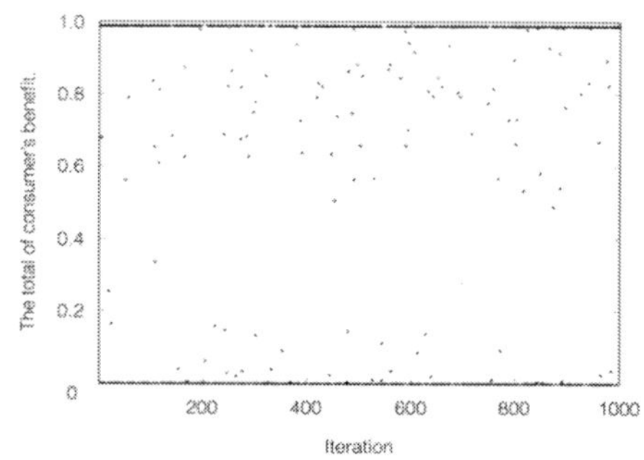

Fig 9. Total of consumer's benefit obtained by OMOPSO.

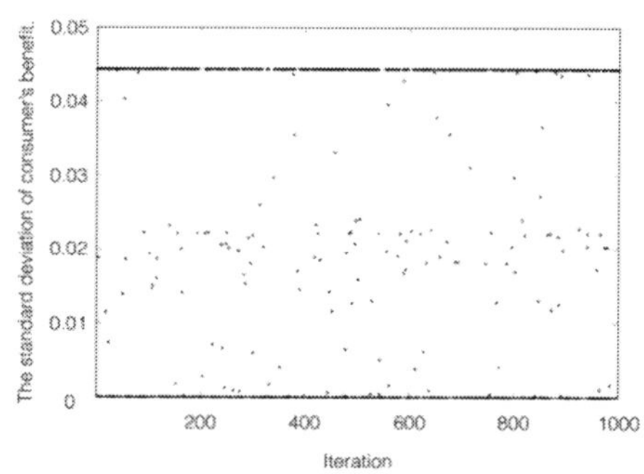

Fig 10. Standard deviation obtained by OMOPSO.

IV. CONCLUSION AND FUTURE WORK

This research proposed the P2P trading model with time-varying consumer's behavior and the multi-objective optimization problem was formulated to investigate consumer's benefit. Simulation results show that OMOPSO and GDE3 tended to find solutions optimized for only one of the two objective functions, and the other algorithms such as NSGA-I I, SMPSO, SPEA2 and ϵ-MOEA tended to discover solutions dense on the Pareto front. As shown from the results, NSGA-II, SMPSO, SPEA2 and ϵ-MOEA facilitate deciding ideal trading depending on methods to select solutions. As future work, a method to select solutions obtained by the multi-objective optimization problem should be considered to allocate energy that consumers can obtain benefit equitably.

REFERENCES

[1] A. Toffler and H. Toffler, "Revolutionary Wealth," Knopf, 2006.

[2] J. Kang, R. Yu, X. Huang, S. Maharjan, Y. Zhang, and E. Hossain, "Enabling Localized Peer-to-Peer Electricity Trading Among Plug-in Hybrid Electric Vehicles Using Consortium Blockchains," IEEE Transactions on Industrial Informatics, IEEE, vol.13, pp. 3154-3164, 2017.

[3] M. R. Alam, M. St-Hilaire, and T. Kunz, "An optimal P2P energy trading model for smart homes in the smart grid," Energy Efficiency, Springer, vol.10, pp. 1475-1493, 2017.

[4] P. Shamsi, H. Xie, A. Longe, and J. Joo, "Economic Dispatch for an Agent-Based Community Microgrid," IEEE, vol. 7, pp. 2317 - 2324, 2016.

[5] Y. Zhou, J. Wu, and C. Long, "Evaluation of peer-to-peer energy sharing mechanisms based on a multiagent simulation framework," Applied Energy, ELSEVIER, pp.993-1022, 2018.

[6] C. Long, J. Wu, C. Zhang, L. Thomas, M. Cheng, and Nick Jenkins, "Peer-to-Peer Energy Trading in a Community Microgrid," IEEE Power & Energy Society General Meeting, 2017.

[7] W. Tushar, C. Yuen, D. B. Smith and H. V. Poor, "Price Discrimination for Energy Trading in Smart Grid: A Game Theoretic Approach," IEEE Transactions on Smart Grid, vol. 8, no. 4, pp. 1790-1801, 2017.

[8] A. Casteigts, P. Flocchini, W. Quattrociocchi, and N. Santoro, "Time-Varying Graphs and Dynamic Networks," Ad-hoc, Mobile, and Wireless Networks, International Conference on Ad-Hoc Networks and Wireless, Springer, pp.346-359, 2011.

[9] "Platypus - Multiobjective Optimization in Python," https://platypus.readthedocs.io/en/latest/ (Last visited: October. 24, 2019)

An Innovative Memristor-Based Near Field Communication Topology Adopted as Security Key

Colin Sokol Kuka
Department of Electronic Engineering
University of York
Heslington
York YO10 5EZ
sk1759@york.ac.uk

Mohammed Alkahtani
and Gor Poliposyan
University of Liverpool
Liverpool L69 3BX
m.alkahtani@liverpool.ac.uk
Gor.Poliposyan@liverpool.ac.uk

Muflah Alahammad
University of Cranfield
Bedford MK43 0AL
m.s.alhammad@cranfield.ac.uk

***Abstract*—In recent years, the security of power systems has become a growing challenge resulting from the expansion of the use of wireless power and data transmission. This paper introduces a new circuit topology for Near Field Communication (NFC) Topology which are based on the Wireless Power and Data Transfer (WPDT) systems. Traditional WPDT circuits are based on inverters to create an oscillation for the transmitter coil. By adopting switches, the traditional WPDT circuitry has intrinsic sources of power loss and requires an extra switching time control circuit for the correct commutation. In addition, these systems have low data cryptography capabilities. Therefore, a new WPDT system has been developed which utilises memristors without adopting switches. In addition, this topology is as advantageous it is possible to adopt chaotic encryption for NFC security. The simulation results and tests prove the functionality of the WPDT based on Memristor and their quality of data generation and storage. The major application for this type of circuitry is the NFC digital code for the opening of the high security block.**

Keywords–Decryption, Digital key, Encryption, High Security, Memristor, Near Field Communication (NFC), Wireless Power and Data Transfer, Security Lock;

I. INTRODUCTION

The growing request for wireless technology has quickly attracted a lot of attention in the investigation of Wireless Power and Data Transfer (WPDT) systems for different uses. Unlike RF transmission, the operating principle of WPDT is based on the resonance of magnetic and electric fields by means of an alternating current in the LC circuit. This AC power is created by switches activated in external control system. For short-range tasks such as a gap of few centimetres, the working frequency of the resonant circuit is generally in the range from 10 kHz to a few MHz [1]. Typically, the power dissipation in the inverter grows with the operating frequency. As the air gap increases, less connection of the magnetic flux is caught by the receiver winding [2], [3]. Most of the research results in WPT systems focus on effective transfer mode, operating principles and circuit topology [4], [5], [6].

In the near future, the inductive WPDT connection will gradually eliminate charging and communication cables as power and data can be integrated simultaneously [7]. On the other hand, it inevitably entails the hazards of theft or loss of power and data. While a selective WPDT technology can achieve a power transmission oriented to specific receivers through multiple receivers [8], [9], illegal receivers can track and block the operating frequency to steal power and data.

In this work, we present a new WPDT topology with advanced security capabilities. We use the memristor to create LC resonance oscillation instead of traditional switches and therefore less power dissipation. Also, there is no need to add an external circuit to operate the switches, and there will be no timing problems. In addition, thanks to the unique non-linearity and memory characteristics of the memristor, it is possible to adopt a mutual authentication key based on the last state and its subsequent encryption and decryption.

A. *Memristor*

The memristor is a circuit element based on the electrical charge q and the magnetic flux φ constitutive relationship theorized by Prof. Leon Chua [10]. This component (short for memory resistor) was manufactured for the first time by Hewlett Packard laboratories [11]. This device has a pinched $I - V$ hysteresis cycle with switching mechanism and has the ability to remember its last state [12], [13]. Details on the history, device, manufacturing and characterization of the memristor are available in the following references [14], [15], [16]. Memristors with their non-linearities are properly integrated into existing linear or non-linear electronic circuits to create several new chaotic circuits [17]. Dynamic behaviors, such as chaos and hyper-chaos [18], [19], coexisting multiple attractors [20], [21], hyper-chaotic multi-wing [22], [23] and hidden attractors [24], [25], [26] have been studied and analyzed by numerical simulations and hardware experiments.

In this work, we therefore propose a memoristor-based architecture for WPT systems. The system has the quality of transmitting power and data wirelessly without using any switch and driver circuitry. In addition, the system is not predictable by the algorithm and therefore has the ability to achieve the highest level of encryption due to the last state of the memristor that cannot be predicted and measured. The rest of the document is organized as follows. The main functionality and encryption and decryption capabilities are shown in the next paragraph. In the section III, there is an analysis of the WPT based on memristor and its stability. System functionality and simulation results are presented in the section IV. Finally, the section V concludes the document.

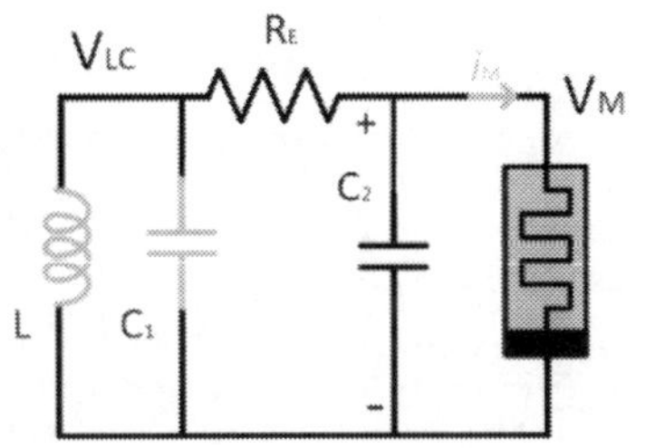

Figure 1. Memsistive circuit developed by L. Chua[10].

II. Wireless Power Transfer and Memristor

A special type of WPT system very sensitive to the problem of cryptography is the Near Field Communication (NFC) which is widely used in contactless credit cards, smartphones and digital keys. NFC is a low-bandwidth, two-way wireless communication technology that utilises electromagnetic induction to transmit information and allows data to be exchanged between devices separated by up to 4 inches [27]. Access cards and digital keys have internal user data encrypted by software and stored in the device. This encryption is traditionally based on the Hash function [28], [29]. This type of algorithm is well known and is widely available on the Internet. For high security applications, this important data must be protected by an internal electronic device. In this work, we introduce an NFC system based on a memory circuit capable of producing chaotic waveforms. There are three great benefits of memristors, which are used in this WPT application:

- Provides less heat than transistors or switches.
- Able to store charge and remember its last state.
- Ability to develop chaotic behaviour.

In this way, the WPT system with memristor does not require external circuits to drive the times and is able to create highly encrypted protection. It is not based on an algorithm that can be hacked. The generated waveform is chaotic and is based on the last state of the state variables. Each time the system reads from the memristor, it will take the internal state of the memristor to a different point of stability, which is completely chaotic and unrelated to the previous one.

In literature, there is no such system. The cryptography proposed in the references [30], [31] is built on the change in transmission frequency that makes other receivers out of resonance. Causal variation of the capacitor array according to the algorithm creates the frequency and correspondence with the receiver for maximum power output. Then, the transmitted power can be packed with different frequencies and delivered to the receiver in a specific time interval [32], [33], [34]. Nevertheless, these types of switched capacitor cryptography are affected by discrete algorithm adjustment, finite selections and are easy to clone. In comparison, the memristor has been used efficiently in imaging and communication encryption [35], [36] providing the highest level of encryption achieved. In a chaotic model of memristor-based cryptography, circuit chaos is critical to deciding on chaotic encryption and decryption. For example, a user key, which is defined as the initial values caused the chaos of the memristor circuit, has a chaotic generation of sequences. From this sequence, encryption and decryption is developed. Therefore, it is possible to combine WTP technology and the chaotic memristor-based circuit together.

Figure 2. Commercial product of a security safe lock with a NFC system opening key. Image collected from source [37].

TABLE I. Parameters of the system proposed.

Parameter	Transmitter	Receiver	Value
C_1	C_{MT}	C_{MR}	6.8 nF
C_2	C_T	C_R	68 nF
R_E	R_T	R_R	2.18 kΩ
L	L_T	L_R	8 mH
M			4 mH

A. *Typical Functionality*

Memristor-based chaotic cryptography system model consists of two parts shown in Fig. 3 and 4, which are two symmetrical Chua's circuits, Transmitter and Receiver respectively. In a typical Chua circuit, the initial condition is applied on the Capacitor C_T from external digital source. Therefore, in the $L_T C_T$ and $L_R C_R$ there is a connection to A/D or D/A converters. According to the cryptosystem model shown in Fig. 3, the process of chaotic encryption key for opening safety data is described as follows:

1) The high security lock has a database of customers and each lock has in the internal memory the ID of the customer.
2) The digital key or Access Card has internal ID encrypted by the last Memristor chaotic status.
3) At the attempt to open the safe, the lock and digital key (Receiver) are connected to each other. Both Memristors will develop a chaotic behaviour.
4) The chaotic behaviour generated in the transmitter circuit depends from the receiver status because it induces a voltage in the transmitter coil and consequently giving a new initial condition V_{IN}. In this way, the safe security lock digital part can immediately recognise the authenticity of the user decrypting the data received.
5) If the Memristor status of the digital key is the same of the last status check, the digital part can convert data. Otherwise, the receiver will bring the transmitter Memristor in an unknown variables status, hence not allowing to open the lock.

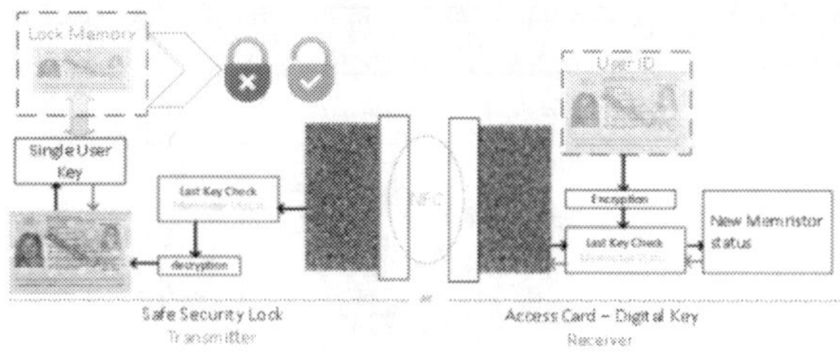

Figure 3. The crypto-system model: on the left the transmitter lock and the receiver in the Access Card Key.

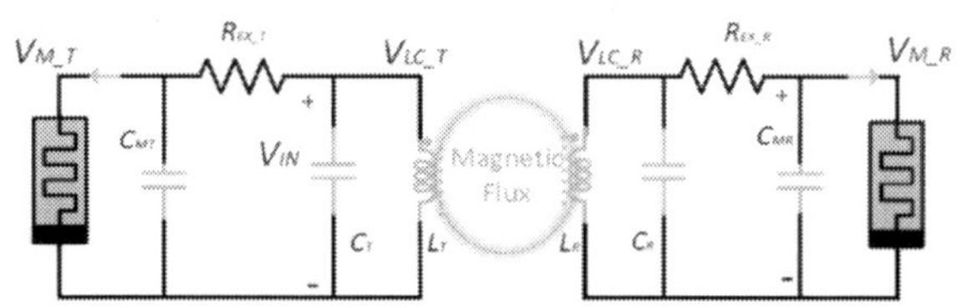

Figure 4. The wireless power and data transfer system built with Memristors.

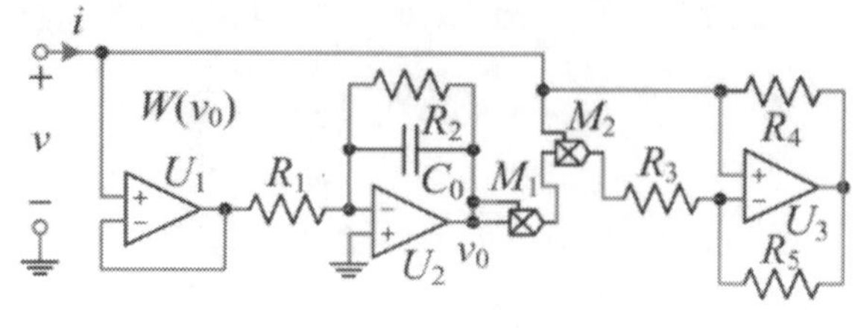

Figure 5. Non-ideal active voltage-controlled memristor equivalent realisation. This circuit is active and only C_0 has charge storing qualities. The real memristor has similar behaviour and possesses all the qualities mentioned in the paper but it not available in any simulation library.

TABLE II. MEMRISTOR MODEL INTERNAL VALUES.

Memristor equivalent			
Parameter	Value	Parameter	Value
R_1	4 kΩ	R_5	2 kΩ
R_2	10 kΩ	C_0	1 nF
R_3	1.4 kΩ	g_1	1
R_4	2 kΩ	g_2	0.1

6) When the WPT system has reached an End Of File, both digital parts will disconnect the Memristor storing their last status.

Moreover, any forgery attempt to the digital key or smartphone will leave an indelible mark as it will bring the memristor internal status in unexpected value for the authentication key in safe security lock. There is no possibility to come back. It is true that the electronic system can be cloned but the internal value of the memristor can never be predicted and there is not an algorithm that could predict this value.

III. Stability and Chaotic Behaviour

In this Section, we analyse the principles of inductive coupling and Memristor state valiable in order to integrate them for the developed Memristor-based Wireless Power and Data Transfer system.

A. Wireless Power Transmission

The WPT system built with memristors is shown in Fig. 4. The memristive Chua's circuit introduced in 1 has been improved as the inductor is a mutual inductance and C_R is the compensation capacitor. As depicted in Fig. 4, the system is completely symmetric as two copies of the Chua circuit. The latter circuit creates an oscillation which can bring to equilibrium, chaos or unstability. In reference of memristive Chua's circuit, it has been considered the parameters' values shown in Table I. As notices, the inductors values L_T and L_R are 8 mH which is lower of the usual values in Chua memristive circuits around 12 mH. It is possible to use a lower value because of mutual induction. The current flowing in L_T or the transmitter coil sets up a magnetic field around itself with some of these magnetic field lines passing through the receiver coil L_R giving us mutual inductance. When the inductances of the two coils are the same and equal, L_T is equal to L_R, the mutual inductance that exists between the two coils will equal the value of one single coil as the square root of two equal values is the same as one single value as shown:

$$M = k\sqrt{L_T L_R} = kL \tag{1}$$

where k is the coupling coefficient expressed as a fractional number between 0 and 1, where 0 indicates zero or no inductive coupling, and 1 indicating full or maximum inductive coupling. In our application, the coupling coefficient is an range between 0.4 to 0.6. A lower value of coupling is not enough to start chaotic behaviour and to change the status of the memristor. One coil induces a voltage in an adjacent coil, therefore the transmitter L_T induces a voltage v_R^{in} in the receiver, and viceversa.

$$\begin{cases} v_R^{in} = L_R \frac{dL_R}{dt} + M \frac{dL_T}{dt} \\ v_T^{in} = L_T \frac{dL_T}{dt} + M \frac{dL_R}{dt} \end{cases} \tag{2}$$

Using this relationships, it is possible to adopt lower inductances than the Chua's circuit and the symmetry of the circuitry allows to transmit the chaotic behaviour. This chaotic behaviour is necessary for the encryption. The transmitter and receiver will resonate at the same frequency :

$$f_0 = \frac{1}{2\pi\sqrt{LC_2}} \tag{3}$$

which adopting the values reported in II gives 6.8 kHz. It is important to notice that this application it is not necessary to achieve high efficiency. The receiver needs just enough power to start its own oscillation and the chaotic behaviour necessary for the encryption.

B. Memristor state variables

Therefore, it is important to show that the system has no variation compared to the Chua memristive circuit and is therefore stable. Either side of the system must be capable of engaging in chaotic behaviour whenever they are in close proximity to each other. The behaviour of the circuit derives from the classic third order Chua circuit replacing it with the non-ideal voltage controlled active memristor shown in Fig. 5. The latter is composed by a buffer U_1, an integrator

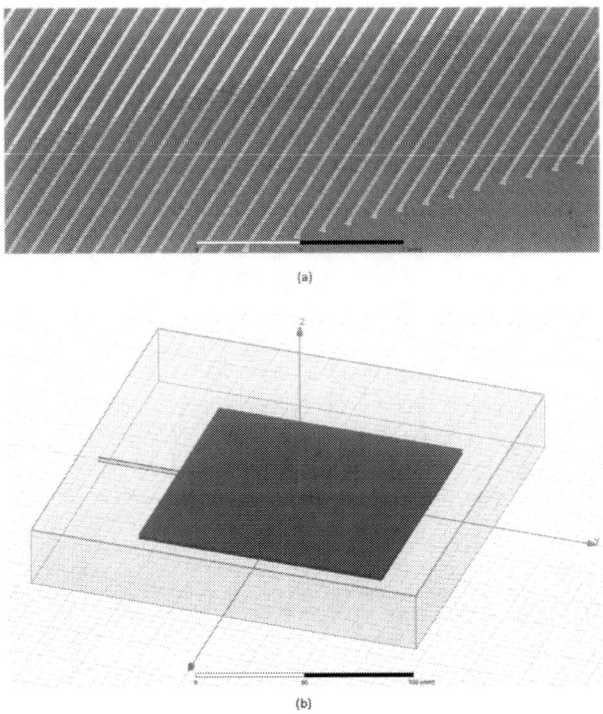

Figure 6. (a) Magnification of the 8 mH coils. Structure of the receiver (brown) and transmitter (purple) in the ANSYS analysis.

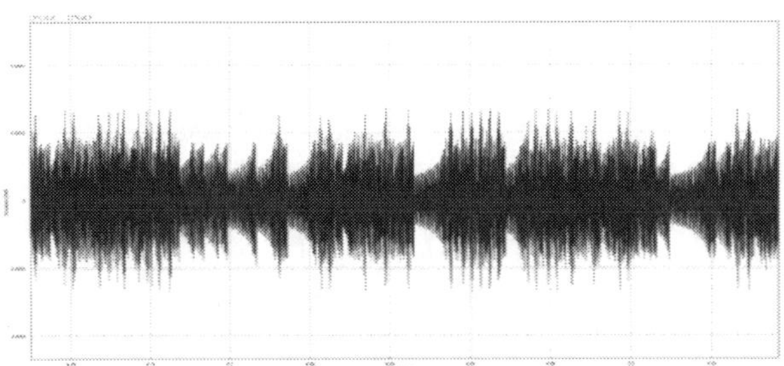

Figure 7. The power transmitted (blue) and received (red) are around 2 mW and they have also a chaotic behaviour.

U_2 connected two resistors R_1, R_2, the capacitor C_0, the multipliers M_1 and M_2 and a current inverter U_3 connected to the resistors R_3, R_4 and R_5. This model is characterised by two equations:

$$i_M = (-G_a + G_b \cdot v_0^2)v_M \tag{4}$$

$$\frac{dv_0}{dt} = -\frac{v_M}{R_1C_0} - \frac{v_0}{R_2C_0} \tag{5}$$

where i_M is the current flowing in the memristor, v_M is the voltage on the memristor and v_0 the voltage on its internal capacitor C_0. In addition, the scale factors of the multipliers M_1 and M_2 are indicated as g_1 and g_2 in order to have $G_a = \frac{1}{R_3}$ and $G_b = \frac{g_1g_2}{R_3}$. These relationships give the memristor input-output characteristic and the pinched $I - V$ relationship [21].

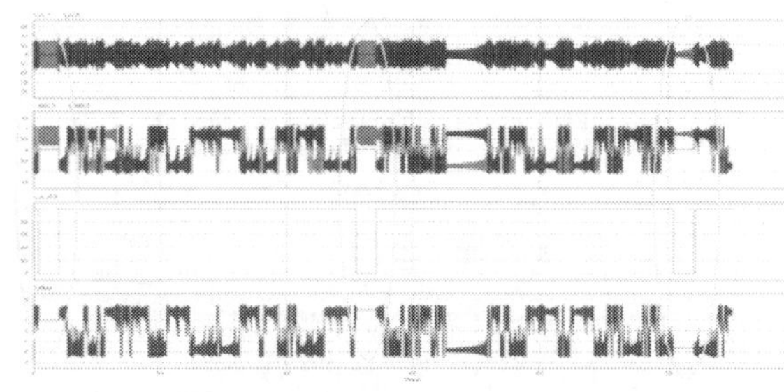

Figure 8. Time step of the chaotic behaviour when the receiver is disconnected (highlighted in yellow): the LC and memristor voltage V_{LC} and V_M in receiver and transmitter, respectively in blue and red. At the disconnection (in the 3rd graph), the receiver memristor holds its last status shown in the 4rd graph.

IV. SYSTEM PERFORMANCE RESULTS

To assess the design, stability and performance of the proposed memristor based WPT system, finite element analysis (FEA) and system simulation are performed. Initially, it has been designed the coils using ANSYS Maxwell v19 as it is is one of the challenging part of this design. It is possible design the size of the coil in the actual size of a passport 88 x 125 mm. In order to achieve the mutual inductance of 6.4 mH, simulation results has shown that is necessary a gap of 2 mm (air, plastic or any material with relative permeability $\mu_R = 1$) between coils. As shown in the simulation design in Fig. 6a the spiral of the inductors has a thickness of 0.1 mm merely visible in a larger scale as Fig. 6b. In purple is the transmitter coil and the brown is the receiver one. By using PSIM simulations, it is possible to plot the power transferred and the system to working power as shown in Fig. 7. When the receiver has finished the communication, it will stop the oscillation in blu in the first two graphs of Fig. 8, and it will keep it last status in the 4th graph for a certain period of disconnection circled in yellow in Fig. 8. Just for illustration, the disconnection is periodic and we have shown only three times.

A. *Experiment*

The system has been build with the advanced software NI multisim 14.2 with commercial devices and Labview functionality. The coils are designed as coupled inductors with the a variable coupling factor. In order to start the chaotic behaviour memristors develop the chaotic waveform following the Chua's memristive circuit. The key design specifications and parameters are listed in Table I and II. The whole system has been verified showing a chaotic temporal behaviour as plot in Fig. 9. The time plot can only partially give an understanding of the chaotic behaviour, therefore the system has been plot with an oscilloscope in X-Y mode. The results are the phase portraits of the chaotic attractors fully synchronised between the transmitter (left) and the receiver (right) in a time representation in milliseconds (10 ms/div). as shown in Fig. 10. The two circuits can generate multistability and have the same behaviours because they have the same circuit parameters. Thus, the initial conditions can be used as a chaotic key sequence in encryption and decryption which is transmitted in a synchronisation process.

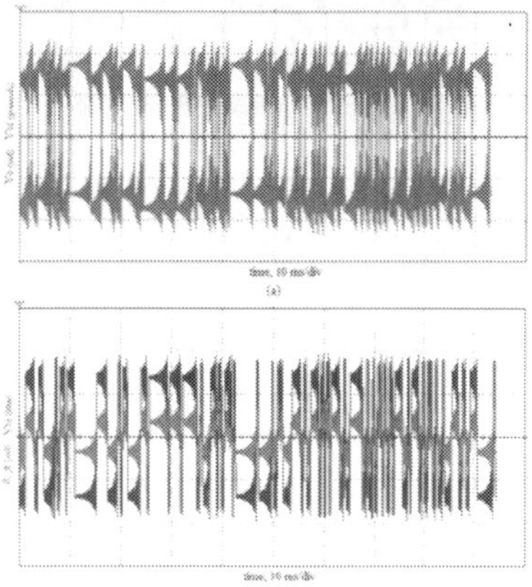

Figure 9. Time step of the chaotic behaviour in the receiver: the memristor voltage V_M in greenish and internal status V_0 in red(a) and coil current i_L in red and memristor voltage V_M in blue (b).

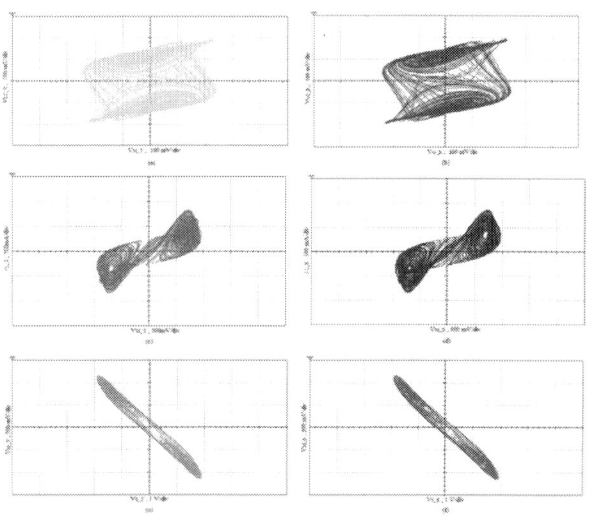

Figure 10. Synchronisation of the phase portraits of a chaotic attractor: voltage in the inductor V_{LC} referred to the memristor voltage V_M in the receiver (a) and transmitter (b) coil; current in the inductor i_L referred to the memristor voltage V_M in the receiver (c) and transmitter (d) coil; the memristor voltage V_M referred to its internal voltage status V_0 in the receiver (e) and transmitter (f).

V. Conclusions

In the future, security on power systems will play a critical role in all electronic devices. This is the main consequence of the elimination of wires and the deployment of wireless power and data transmission. This growing challenge is met with the extreme use of software and algorithms leading to data encryption and decryption. Unfortunately, once the type of algorithm is known, it is often violated because it is based in the programming code. An advanced circuit topology for wireless power and data transmission using the memory circuit has been introduced in this article. Traditional WPT circuits are based on inverters in order to generate an oscillation for the transmitter coils. By adopting switches, the system has intrinsic energy dissipation sources and requires an additional control circuit for the correct switching time. The memristor is able to create a chaotic oscillation without adopting switches. The oscillation makes the system transmit power and chaotic behaviour is very advantageous for high security encryption. The functionality of the system has been experimented and verified. In future works, the system will be experimented with data transmission performance and improved cryptography capabilities.

References

[1] I. Yoon and H. Ling, "Investigation of near-field wireless power transfer under multiple transmitters," IEEE Antennas and Wireless Propagation Letters, vol. 10, 2011, pp. 662–665.

[2] V. Vijayakumaran Nair and J. R. Choi, "An efficiency enhancement technique for a wireless power transmission system based on a multiple coil switching technique," Energies, vol. 9, no. 3, 2016. [Online]. Available: https://www.mdpi.com/1996-1073/9/3/156

[3] S. Kuka, K. Ni, and M. Alkahtani, "A review of methods and challenges for improvement in efficiency and distance for wireless power transfer applications," Power Electronics and Drives, 2019.

[4] Z. Wang, X. Wei, and H. Dai, "Principle elaboration and system structure validation of wireless power transfer via strongly coupled magnetic resonances," in 2013 IEEE Vehicle Power and Propulsion Conference (VPPC). IEEE, 2013, pp. 1–6.

[5] R. Jay and S. Palermo, "Resonant coupling analysis for a two-coil wireless power transfer system," in 2014 IEEE Dallas Circuits and Systems Conference (DCAS). IEEE, 2014, pp. 1–4.

[6] T. C. Beh, T. Imura, M. Kato, and Y. Hori, "Basic study of improving efficiency of wireless power transfer via magnetic resonance coupling based on impedance matching," in 2010 IEEE International Symposium on Industrial Electronics. IEEE, 2010, pp. 2011–2016.

[7] J. Wu, C. Zhao, Z. Lin, J. Du, Y. Hu, and X. He, "Wireless power and data transfer via a common inductive link using frequency division multiplexing," IEEE Transactions on Industrial Electronics, vol. 62, no. 12, Dec 2015, pp. 7810–7820.

[8] C. Jiang, K. Chau, C. Liu, and W. Han, "Wireless dc motor drives with selectability and controllability," Energies, vol. 10, no. 1, 2017. [Online]. Available: https://www.mdpi.com/1996-1073/10/1/49

[9] Y. Zhang, T. Lu, Z. Zhao, F. He, K. Chen, and L. Yuan, "Selective wireless power transfer to multiple loads using receivers of different resonant frequencies," IEEE Transactions on Power Electronics, vol. 30, no. 11, Nov 2015, pp. 6001–6005.

[10] L. Chua, "Memristor-the missing circuit element," IEEE Transactions on circuit theory, vol. 18, no. 5, 1971, pp. 507–519.

[11] R. Stanley Williams, "How we found the missing memristor," in Chaos, CNN, Memristors and Beyond: A Festschrift for Leon Chua With DVD-ROM, composed by Eleonora Bilotta. World Scientific, 2013, pp. 483–489.

[12] O. A. Olumodeji, A. P. Bramanti, M. Gottardi, and S. Iannotta, "A memristor-based pixel implementing light-to-resistance conversion," Optical Engineering, vol. 55, no. 2, 2016, p. 020501.

[13] O. A. Olumodeji, A. P. Bramanti, and M. Gottardi, "A memristive pixel architecture for real-time tracking," IEEE Sensors Journal, vol. 16, no. 22, 2016, pp. 7911–7918.

[14] D. B. Strukov, G. S. Snider, D. R. Stewart, and R. S. Williams, "The missing memristor found," nature, vol. 453, no. 7191, 2008, p. 80.

[15] D. Lin, L. Chua, and S.-Y. Hui, "The first man-made memristor: Circa 1801 [scanning our past]," Proceedings of the IEEE, vol. 103, no. 1, 2014, pp. 131–136.

[16] L. O. Chua and S. M. Kang, "Memristive devices and systems," Proceedings of the IEEE, vol. 64, no. 2, 1976, pp. 209–223.

[17] B. Bao, T. Jiang, Q. Xu, M. Chen, H. Wu, and Y. Hu, "Coexisting infinitely many attractors in active band-pass filter-based memristive circuit," Nonlinear Dynamics, vol. 86, no. 3, 2016, pp. 1711–1723.

[18] I. Petras, "Fractional-order memristor-based chua's circuit," IEEE Transactions on Circuits and Systems II: Express Briefs, vol. 57, no. 12, 2010, pp. 975–979.

[19] A. L. Fitch, D. Yu, H. H. Iu, and V. Sreeram, "Hyperchaos in a memristor-based modified canonical chua's circuit," International Journal of Bifurcation and Chaos, vol. 22, no. 06, 2012, p. 1250133.

[20] J. Kengne, Z. Njitacke Tabekoueng, V. Kamdoum Tamba, and A. Nguomkam Negou, "Periodicity, chaos, and multiple attractors in a memristor-based shinriki's circuit," Chaos: An Interdisciplinary Journal of Nonlinear Science, vol. 25, no. 10, 2015, p. 103126.

[21] Q. Xu, Y. Lin, B. Bao, and M. Chen, "Multiple attractors in a non-ideal active voltage-controlled memristor based chua's circuit," Chaos, Solitons & Fractals, vol. 83, 2016, pp. 186–200.

[22] J. Ma, Z. Chen, Z. Wang, and Q. Zhang, "A four-wing hyper-chaotic attractor generated from a 4-d memristive system with a line equilibrium," Nonlinear Dynamics, vol. 81, no. 3, Aug 2015, pp. 1275–1288. [Online]. Available: https://doi.org/10.1007/s11071-015-2067-4

[23] L. Zhou, C. Wang, and L. Zhou, "Generating hyperchaotic multi-wing attractor in a 4d memristive circuit," Nonlinear Dynamics, vol. 85, no. 4, 2016, pp. 2653–2663.

[24] B. Bao, H. Bao, N. Wang, M. Chen, and Q. Xu, "Hidden extreme multistability in memristive hyperchaotic system," Chaos, Solitons & Fractals, vol. 94, 2017, pp. 102–111.

[25] H. Bao, N. Wang, H. Wu, Z. Song, and B. Bao, "Bi-stability in an improved memristor-based third-order wien-bridge oscillator," IETE Technical Review, vol. 36, no. 2, 2019, pp. 109–116.

[26] H. Bao, N. Wang, B. Bao, M. Chen, P. Jin, and G. Wang, "Initial condition-dependent dynamics and transient period in memristor-based hypogenetic jerk system with four line equilibria," Communications in Nonlinear Science and Numerical Simulation, vol. 57, 2018, pp. 264–275.

[27] A. Alzahrani, A. Alqhtani, H. Elmiligi, F. Gebali, and M. S. Yasein, "Nfc security analysis and vulnerabilities in healthcare applications," in 2013 IEEE Pacific Rim Conference on Communications, Computers and Signal Processing (PACRIM), Aug 2013, pp. 302–305.

[28] N. Ramya, U. Sandhya, and L. Gayathri, "Biometric authentication to ensure security in epassports," in 2018 International Conference on Communication, Computing and Internet of Things (IC3IoT), Feb 2018, pp. 342–346.

[29] F. Hamad, J. Zraqou, A. Maaita, and A. A. Taleb, "A secure authentication system for epassport detection and verification," in 2015 European Intelligence and Security Informatics Conference, Sep. 2015, pp. 173–176.

[30] W. Liu, K. T. Chau, C. H. T. Lee, C. Jiang, and W. Han, "A switched-capacitorless energy-encrypted transmitter for roadway-charging electric vehicles," IEEE Transactions on Magnetics, vol. 54, no. 11, Nov 2018, pp. 1–6.

[31] Z. Zhang, K. T. Chau, C. Qiu, and C. Liu, "Energy encryption for wireless power transfer," IEEE Transactions on Power Electronics, vol. 30, no. 9, Sep. 2015, pp. 5237–5246.

[32] Z. Zhang, K. Chau, C. Liu, C. Qiu, and F. Lin, "An efficient wireless power transfer system with security considerations for electric vehicle applications," Journal of Applied Physics, vol. 115, no. 17, 2014, p. 17A328.

[33] M. Sadzali, A. Ali, M. Azizan, and M. Albreem, "The security energy encryption in wireless power transfer," in AIP Conference Proceedings, vol. 1885, no. 1. AIP Publishing, 2017, p. 020242.

[34] E. Ahene, M. Ofori-Oduro, and B. Agyemang, "Secure energy encryption for wireless power transfer," in 2017 IEEE 7th International Advance Computing Conference (IACC), Jan 2017, pp. 199–204.

[35] F. Yang, J. Mou, K. Sun, Y. Cao, and J. Jin, "Color image compression-encryption algorithm based on fractional-order memristor chaotic circuit," IEEE Access, vol. 7, 2019, pp. 58 751–58 763.

[36] H. Abunahla, D. Shehada, C. Y. Yeun, C. J. OKelly, M. A. Jaoude, and B. Mohammad, "Novel microscale memristor with uniqueness property for securing communications," in 2016 IEEE 59th International Midwest Symposium on Circuits and Systems (MWSCAS), Oct 2016, pp. 1–4.

[37] Aliexpress. Nfc door lock. [Online]. Available: http://aliexpress.com

Strategic Engineering as Closed Loop Approach to Address Complex Systems

Agostino G. Bruzzone
Simulation Team, Genoa University
Genoa, Italy
agostino.bruzzone@simulationteam.com
www.simulationteam.com

Marina Massei
DIME, Genoa University
Genoa, Italy
massei@itim.unige.it
www.itim.unige.it/strategos

Kirill Sinelshchikov
Simulation Team
Genoa, Italy
kirill@simulationteam.com
www.simulationteam.com

Abstract— **The innovative discipline defined as Strategic Engineering develops architectures dealing with Decision Making in Complex Systems. The paper proposes how to create a closed loop that combines Modeling & Simulation (M&S), Data Analytics and Artificial Intelligence (AI) to filter and elaborate Big Data, extract information, forecast impacts of decisions by Simulation and collect back the actual results to correct the models. In this sense, even the development and implementation processes should rely on special scientists and engineers able to address the complex problems by solid foundations in M&S and AI. Several real cases are proposed in the paper as example to show the potential of this approach and to validate the methodology.**

Keywords- Strategic Engineering; Modeling; Simulation; Artificial Intelligence; Data Analytics; Strategic Management,; Strategic Planning; Decision Making.

I. INTRODUCTION

Since many years, the Decision Makers have to address complex problems with many different factors and strongly correlated where there is just a limited number of degrees of freedom available to them and where the quality of the decisions are related to multiple opposite target functions [1][2]. Nowadays this situation is even more critical due to several factors including globalization, increased speed and dynamics of Businesses and International Affairs, New Players and more Interconnected world [3].

Indeed, looking around over the world, from Geo Politics to Business, from logistics to marketing, it emerges that these kinds of problems are turning very common and challenging, while the environment turn to be more and more time sensitive [4][5][6][7][8][9]. The second effects of the decisions as well as the high level of interconnectivity makes it hard to evaluate all consequences and it emerge the necessity to rely on a solid and strong methodological approach based on quantitative techniques [10]. From this point of view, a new emerging discipline, named "Strategic Engineering", represents a step forward able to use the state of art of current technologies to address Strategic Decision Making into an innovative way.

This paper proposes the foundations of Strategic Engineering as well as case studies where it could be effectively used to provide a strategic advantage in decision making; in addition the paper highlights that the approach should be part of a structured advance in the field of decision making that include educational programs and initiatives for young scientist and engineers as well as for executives and managers. The presentation of STRATEGOS, the 1st Master of Science in Strategic Engineering in Italy and among first ones in the world, represents an important initiative that provides new capabilities to this context, developed in strong connection with major International Institutions as well as multinational companies.

II. THE INNOVATIVE APPROACH LOOKING TO RELIABLE TECHNIQUES IN A NEW WAY

Nowadays, in reference to complex problems, it is quite popular to quote the sentence that "Explanations exist; they have existed for all time; there is always a well-known solution to every human problem — neat, plausible, and wrong" Mencken [11]; without disrespect for this journalist, turning popular after 1 century, the authors have a different point of view, we feel that this popularity emerges due to the simplistic approach of current politicians while complex problems could have many different solutions: elegant solutions, simple solutions, complex solutions as well as no solutions [10]. Thinking back to 66 million years ago, during Cretaceous–Paleogene boundary, the impact of an "asteroid" creating the Chicxulub crater, 150km radius and 20km deep, had a huge impact on the Earth climate: this was a problem that at that time (probably even nowadays) has no solution at least for the living animals over the planet [12]. Moving forward at IV century BC, the Gordian Knot appeared impossible to be untied, therefore Plutarch states that Alexander solved it simply by a single stroke of his sword.

In any case, simple or complex solutions are not always easy to implement and/or to identify; for sure to find them and to identify right decisions to deal with them is fundamental to acquire data, develop knowledge and understanding, evaluate consequence and to apply the solutions while keeping control of the situation to correct it and achieve desired results. This paper keeps out of generic discussions and provides a description of how Strategic Engineering applies modern techniques to face these challenges. Strategic Engineering is a combined use of Modeling and Simulation (M&S), Artificial Intelligence (AI) and Data Analytics devoted to support Strategic Decision Making. Indeed modeling & simulation arisen since '50, to address especially rocket science and supersonic plane engineering, therefore industrial applications emerged within the same decade [13]; so this approach is still pretty advanced even today therefore its base dates back over ½ century. In similar way AI (Artificial Intelligence) origins are quite old and even Turing's developments emerged on '30 and '40 [14]. Data Analytics dates back even to much older times, being used in terms of "moving average" since Roman times to forecast demand of wines and other goods from worldwide.

Indeed, it is important to outline that these methodologies are consolidated, but their combined use is pretty innovative and could rely on new enabling technologies and conditions such as digitalization of companies, social networks, Internet of Things (IoT), Cloud Computing Capabilities, etc.

These methods have today additional capabilities not only for the advances in software, hardware, algorithms and methods, but also for the possibility to use them in closed loop, collecting effects of decisions from the reality and using as input in machine learning and self tuning components as proposed in Fig 1.

III. APPLYING STRATEGIC ENGINEERING

In the following the authors propose some case studies as example of the capabilities offered by applying Strategic Engineering

A. *Threat Networks and Critical Infrastructure Protection*

The Homeland Security issues represent pretty challenging environments, addressing multiple layers and risks related to strategic assets. In this sense, the Critical Infrastructures such as power grid, transportations, and data networks are assets that are targets to threat network and the development of new solutions to reduce their vulnerabilities. The solutions could be pretty wide in sense of approach: from technological solutions, usually as integrated systems, up to policies & doctrines as well as training and institution of ad hoc special teams. To develop these solutions it could be used also a wide spectrum of approach, from penetration tests (cyber or physical or combined), to training and table top exercise. Obviously to face these issues by a comprehensive approach it turns necessary to create synthetic worlds reproducing each different layer as well as their interactions to conduct virtual experiences and exercise [15]. Among these problems, a new popular issue is related to Hybrid Warfare that combines cyber & physical attacks, economics, diplomacy and International Relations with use of Strategic Communications (STRATCOM) and Information Operations (Info Ops) affect public opinion and force opponents to specific decisions [6][16][17].

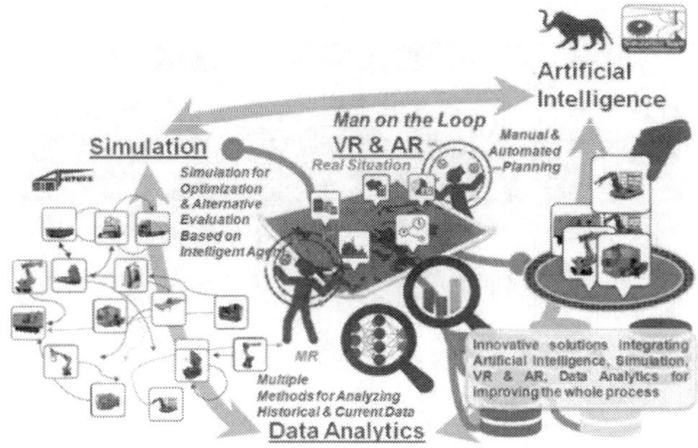

Figure 1. Closed loop use of AI, Simulation and Data Analytics to support decisions

In Hybrid Warfare the attack to critical infrastructures could represent an effective way to obtain results and influence population [18][19], so it is interesting to create models able to reproduce the behavior of people, the social media and collect information from the field to evaluate if the consequences of decisions are properly evaluated by the modes. At the same time, this approach could be used to refine the models and to introduce Machine Learning capabilities. The Solution named "Threat network simulation for Reactive eXperience" (T-REX) was developed in this way and demonstrated in 2015 the capability to reproduce cyber physical attacks by Unmanned Aerial Vehicles (UAV) to a Critical Infrastructure serving 5 towns over a desert area, including Tank Farm, Refinery, Oil Terminal, Port, Power Plant and Desalination Facility (see Fig 2); it is interesting to state that a similar attack was conducted against the biggest world refinery along 2019 in similar way [20].

B. *System of Systems Engineering applied to AWACS*

The renew of Airborne Warning and Control System (AWACS) is an actual issue that deals with the development of a new solutions to a complex problem that is still relying on old technologies on both West and East.

Up to now, big former commercial or transport planes have been adapted to carry large radar shaped as a mushroom (the radome) to discover on very long-range aerial and surface targets with good resolution as well as to support intensive and secure communications; classical examples are Boeing E-3C and Beriev A-50. Nowadays these solutions are very expensive, hard to maintain, to upgrade and operate. In addition, there are potential solutions, available today for instance based on use of autonomous vehicles that could reduce costs as well as vulnerability of the overall system through redundancy. New solutions could even increase coverage and responsiveness. In facts without human crew aircrafts could result lighter, more compact, reduce their consumptions and increase autonomy; obviously the new radar and communication technologies are now using different paradigms and could be more compact and integrated.

Figure 2. Vulnerability Reduction on Critical Infrastructures by using Strategic Engineering and Simulation

Therefore to find a reliable solution in this sense requires to consider many aspects such as the threats and the future scenario to face, the costs and reliability issues, the technological aspects on the platform, the technological aspects on radar solution, the operational modes and strategies, etc.

Even Key Performance Indicators (KPIs) are including many different target functions that are often conflicting as the case of costs versus vulnerability; to properly find optimal solution the authors developed the "Multiple Interoperable Systems for joint Control of Hybrid threats through Intelligent Extended Fusion" (MISCHIEF) that is focusing on defense and homeland security with special attention to aerial threats and include a simple modeling of complex SoS (System of Systems); this solutions create a complex scenario and simulation models to be used for supporting table top exercises as well as engineering analysis considering electronic systems, power engineering, multiple platforms, operational modes as well as ground installations (e.g. airstrips and bases for the new AWACS).

MISCHIEF was developed by Simulation Team as a Serious Game based on Modeling, interoperable Simulation and Serious Game (MS2G) to be intuitive and immersive [21]. In this context, the different engineering solutions are strongly interconnected with the procedures adopted to employ these new assets. The case proposed is a good example on System of Systems Engineering (SoSE) and is available to support evaluation of new hypothetical airborne surveillance systems considering several data such as platform type, maximum speed, autonomy sensor ranges, resolution, power consumptions, reliability and availability, etc.

C. *Improving Industrial Plants: Increasing Line Productivity, Reliability and Safety*

In modern factories and production plants, the evolution related to Industry 4.0 paradigm is enabling new advances. The proposed case is related to the Project named "Wearable Augmented Reality for Employee safety in Manufacturing sYStems" (W-ARTEMYS) where use of Extended Reality (XR) combining Virtual and Augmented Reality (VR & AR) is able improve safety and productivity in plants. This project allows to provide wearable solutions that rely on simple tablets or smartphones as well as on headsets and Hololens™ [22]. Therefore this is just the basis to create Strategic Engineering supports that acquiring all the information provided naturally and intuitively by operators and supervisors along production line and correlating them by Machine Learning could provide the based to create Intelligent Solutions suggesting how to react to alerts and how to improve quality and productivity, maintaining very high level of reliability and safety. The project is applied to hollow glass production lines, but is ongoing in parallel with other related initiatives over beverage bottling lines and frozen good industries.

IV. STRATEGOS AS NECESSITY

It is evident that in addition to developing new models, algorithms and even more combining these elements as integrated closed loop solution for supporting decision making, it is necessary to develop engineers and scientists with a new forma mentis relying on Strategic Engineering approach. From this point of view around the world, several new initiatives are arising such as STRATEGOS in Genoa University [10]. STRATEGOS is a new Master of Science on Strategic Engineering organized in joint cooperation among different Faculties (Engineering, Economics, International Affairs), Institutions (e.g. NATO M&S Center of Excellence, James Cook University Singapore Campus) and Companies (e.g. Accenture, Hitachi, Leonardo, Thales, MBDA, Rina, Seastema, Antycip Simulation, SIM4Future, Rulex etc.). MSc STRATEGOS is a two year International Program [23] that is based on 3 semesters of Lectures, Exercises and Labs plus a Semester of Internship working on a Strategic Engineering Project. The Program is active since 2019 and it has been presented in Tucson, Logrono, Milan, Berlin, Rome, Singapore, Beijing, Wroclaw, Taranto to create an effective network on this subject. STRATEGOS, as new Educational Solution, addresses both young engineering preparation as well as executive and manager upgrades; indeed this is possible through the development of the STRATEGOS Courses side by side with STRATEGOS Workshops addressing specific topics and open to experts from Companies and Institutions. Up to now, STRATEGOS includes already over 70 Workshops and obtained very interesting results in terms of attendance and quality reports.

It is evident that the success in diffusing and applying Strategic Engineering relies on the capability to interact with Top Level Decision Makers, so the new engineers as well as the manager, should learn these approach as well as the capability to collect from the top the needs and expectations as well as to guarantee trustiness on new solutions and their effective use.

V. CONCLUSIONS

The Strategic Engineering is a new approach that emphasizes the combination of AI, M&S and Data Analytics in closed loop getting benefits from the digitalization of the modern world; in this way this approach results much more efficient than in any past similar tentative and allows to filter, elaborate Big Data as well as to guarantee a continuous evolution and tuning of developed models based on machine learning support. It is evident that this approach provides great opportunities in a wide spectrum of application and this paper proposes different cases that support both Defense and Homeland Security as well as Industrial Plants and new complex System of Systems Engineering. It is currently emerging a big need to develop such applications and to encapsulate them within the Decision Making Processes, due to these reasons the development of Educational Programs for young engineers and scientists as well as Continuous Education for Executive and Managers is crucial for guarantee success. Future competitiveness is expected to strongly rely on the use of these innovative Solutions and in their integration with different systems and processes.

REFERENCES

[1] K.M. Eisenhardt and M.J. Zbaracki, "Strategic decision making". Strategic management journal, 13(S2) 1992, pp. 17-37.

[2] T.L. Saaty, "Decision making for leaders". IEEE Transactions on Systems, Man, and Cybernetics, 1985 (3), pp. 450-452.

[3] B. Wooldridge and B. Cowden, "Strategic decision-making in Business". In Oxford Research Encyclopedia of Business and Management, 2020.

[4] A.G. Bruzzone, M. Massei, A. Tremori, S. Poggi, L. Nicoletti and C. Baisini, "Simulation as enabling technologies for agile thinking: training and education aids for decision makers". International Journal of Simulation and Process Modelling 2014, 9, 9(1-2), pp.113-127.

[5] H. Garg, "Some methods for strategic decision - making problems with immediate probabilities in Pythagorean fuzzy environment" International Journal of Intelligent Systems, 33(4) 2018, pp. 687-712.

[6] V. Gerasimov, "The value of science is in the foresight: new challenges demand rethinking the forms and methods of carrying out combat operations ", Military Review, January-February 2016

[7] J.K. Levy, "Multiple criteria decision making and decision support systems for flood risk management". Stochastic Environmental Research and Risk Assessment, 19(6), 2005, pp. 438-447.

[8] A. Özdağoğlu, " A multi-criteria decision-making methodology on the selection of facility location: fuzzy ANP". The International Journal of Advanced Manufacturing Technology, 59(5-8), 787-803. 2012

[9] F. Xiao, "A novel multi-criteria decision making method for assessing health-care waste treatment technologies based on D numbers". Engineering Applications of Artificial Intelligence, 71, 2018, pp. 216-225.

[10] A.G. Bruzzone, "MS2G as pillar for developing strategic engineering as a new discipline for complex problem solving", Keynote Speech at the International Multidisciplinary Modelling & Simulation Multiconference, Budapest, September 2018

[11] H.L. Mencken, "The divine afflatus". New York Evening Mail (16 Nov 1917)

[12] P. Schulte, L. Alegret, I. Arenillas, J.A. Arz, P.J. Barton, P.R. Bown, T.J. Bralower, G.L. Christeson, P. Claeys, C.S. Cockell and G.S. Collins, "The Chicxulub asteroid impact and mass extinction at the Cretaceous-Paleogene boundary", Science 327, No 5970, 2010, pp. 1214–1218.

[13] J. McLeod and S. McLeod, "Simulation of the society", Simulation, 43(6), pp. 320-323

[14] A.M. Turing, "Intelligent machinery", Technical Report of National Physical Laboratory, UK, 1948

[15] A.G. Bruzzone and M. Massei, "Simulation-based military training", . In Guide to Simulation-Based Disciplines 2017, pp. 315-361. Springer, Cham.

[16] V. Gerasimov, "The value of science is in the foresight ", jounral Voyenno-Promysh-lennyy Kurier online , February 26, 2013, (original version in Russian)

[17] E. Cayirci, A.G. Bruzzone, F. Longo and H. Gunneriusson, "A model to describe hybrid conflict environments". Proc. of 13th International Multidisciplanary Modeling & Simulation Multiconference (I3M 2016), 26-28 September 2016, Larnaca, Cyprus (pp. 52-60)

[18] P. Di Bella, "Present and futures scenarios and challenges for M&S terms of human behavior modeling", Invited Speech at I3M2015, Bergeggi, Italy, September 2015

[19] A.G. Bruzzone, M. Massei, R. Di Matteo and I. Vianello, "Innovative modelling of social networks for reproducing complex scenarios", Proc. of I3M, Barcelona, Spain, September 2017.

[20] J. Defterios and V. Cavaliere, "Coordinated strikes knock out half of Saudi oil capacity, more than 5 million barrels a day", CNN Business, 1000 GMT, September 15, 2019

[21] A.G. Bruzzone, M. Massei, G.L. Maglione, K. Sinelshchikov and R. Di Matteo, "A strategic serious game addressing system of systems engineering", Proc. of MAS, Barcelona, September 2017, pp. 214-219.

[22] A.G. Bruzzone, M. Massei, K. Sinelshchikov, F. Longo, M. Agresta, L. Di Donato and C. Di Francesco, "Wearable mixed reality solutions for industrial plants and production lines", Proc. of the Int. Conference on Modeling and Applied Simulation 2019, pp. 181-185.

[23] www.itim.unige.it/strategos

Data-driven Approach for Accurate Estimation and Validation of Ego-Vehicle Speed

Adina Aniculaesei*, Meng Zhang* and Andreas Rausch*
*Institute of Software and Systems Engineering
TU Clausthal, 38678 Clausthal-Zellerfeld, Germany
Email: {adina.aniculaesei, meng.zhang, andreas.rausch}@tu-clausthal.de

***Abstract*—This paper proposes a data-oriented approach for the accurate estimation of the ego-vehicle speed. The approach combines long-term estimation with short-term estimation mechanisms to produce an accurate estimation of vehicle's tire circumference. The long-term estimation method approximates a standard value for the tire circumference on the basis of the vehicle configuration. In turn, the short-term estimation computes an estimation error for the tire circumference based on Global Positioning System (GPS) sensor data. The ego-vehicle speed is then computed on the basis of the estimated tire circumference and the current wheel speed measurement. In this approach, several error sources are considered: the GPS data, the road gradient and the rounding off of the estimated vehicle speed. The approach is validated on two real-world test data batches against the European New Car Assessment Programme (Euro NCAP) safety requirements. The results of the experimental validation demonstrate that the proposed vehicle speed estimation algorithm performs within the limits of the Euro NCAP requirements.**

Keywords–data-based multiresolutional learning; precise parameter estimation; automotive; ego-vehicle speed estimation; Euro NCAP requirements.

I. Introduction

Reactive systems and requirements defined upon them are getting increasingly complex. These systems, used to build a variety of applications, such as multimedia devices or avionic systems, exhibit stochastic behaviour and also operate under real-time constraints and constraints on other resources [1]. Ensuring the correct functioning of these systems is of paramount importance, especially for those systems deployed in safety-critical applications.

Through their continuous interaction with their operation environment, reactive systems are subject to a variety of external stimuli. Often reactive systems are required to perform parameter estimation based on the large amount of data received from the environment. Ideally, the input data is structured, independent and identically distributed. Furthermore, the system can access the data at any time and without any concerns for the required processing time or the storage space. Losing et al. [2] observe that real-world applications produce data in a streaming fashion at an increasing rate, requiring processing on a large-scale and in real-time, as well as continuous learning.

Reactive systems work often not only with input data perceived directly by the sensors from the system environment. Instead, such systems keep an internal state and preserve values of the state variables over several iterations. Architectures, which enable reactive systems the storage of data on a long-term basis but also offer the ability to react to current input coming from the environment, present a particular advantage. Such an architecture would resemble the human memory model, as indicated by Atkinson and Shiffrin [3] and Losing et al. [2].

In the automotive domain, every aspect of driving is supported to a larger or lesser degree by complex software systems. Such systems enhance the driving experience and increase the vehicle safety. A basic functionality introduced in automobiles at the begining of the 20th century is the speedometer, which gains even more attention, especially in the context of Advanced Driving Assisstance Systems (ADAS) and autonomous driving. Car speedometers are reactive systems, which are confronted with the data-related problems mentioned previously.

The job of the speedometer is to indicate the instanteneous speed of the car in miles per hour, kilometers per hour, or both. The speed displayed on the speedometer is however not the actual speed of the vehicle, but an estimation of it. Thus, vehicle speedometers are not 100% accurate.

Car manufactureres build speedometers so that the estimated vehicle speed falls within a narrow range [4]. This range is usually specified through compulsory regulations. Consider for example the european laws [5], which impose the requirement in (1):

$$0 \leq v_{display} - v_{real} \leq 0.1 \cdot v_{real} + 4 \ \frac{km}{h} \tag{1}$$

under the precondition that

$$40 \leq v_{real} \leq 120 \ \frac{km}{h} \tag{2}$$

where $v_{display}$ is the speed displayed on the dashboard of the ego-vehicle, and v_{real} is the actual vehicle speed. Before its release, the vehicle speedometer is subject to an initial calibration, which depends strongly on the vehicle model and configuration. As long as the car is maintained according to its factory specifications, the speedometer should continue to work within its predefined range. Once a parameter in the system configuration is changed, the speedometer must be recalibrated. Consider for example when tires with a profile different from that mentioned in the factory specification are mounted on the vehicle [4]. The problem of the ego-vehicle speed estimation is an instance of a larger one, namely the problem of precise parameter estimation.

There are various approaches developed for the ego-vehicle precise parameter estimation in the automotive domain. These approaches use a combination of sensors to estimate as accurate as possible the motion of the ego-vehicle: laser range finder combined with monocular camera to estimate the ego-vehicle orientation and the scale, i.e. the length of the translation direction vector [6] and a combination of monocular and stereo cameras to estimate rotational and respectively translational movements of the ego-vehicle [7]. Other approaches use deep learning methods to process optical flow and depth estimation with a monocular camera in order to approximate the ego-vehicle speed [10].

These approaches present, however, various disadvantages. Laser range finders and cameras can be affected by unfavorable weather conditions. Algorithms relying on feature matching between consecutive frames usually use various mechanism to reject poor features from the second of two consecutive frames. One such mechanism is to apply optical flow backwards and reject those feature for which the distance between initial and computed position in the first frame is below a certain threshold [7]. However, such algorithms suffer, if poor weather conditions or significant illumination changes cause several consecutive camera frames to be unusable. Furthermore, optical flow can be problematic, if significant changes in illumination appear, e.g., too dark or too bright.

For the estimation of ego-vehicle speed displayed on the dashboard instrument, we propose a data-oriented approach. The approach builds upon the theoretical frameworks proposed in [3] and [2] and combines long-term and short-term estimation mechanisms for the accurate approximation of vehicle tire circumference. On one hand, the long-term estimation mechanism makes use of the characteristics defined in the vehicle configuration, which remain relatively constant over time. On the other hand, the short-term estimation mechanism uses GPS sensor measurements in order to derive a corrective value, which is then used to adjust the result of the long-term estimation procedure. We apply several filters in order to filter out poor or unreliable GPS data, which appears due to loss of signal in blocked areas or due to sudden acceleration or deceleration of the ego-vehicle.

The rest of the paper is structured as follows. Section III illustrates the overall approach of this paper, while in Section IV the realization of the presented concept is demonstrated on the case study of a speedometer model implemented in MATLAB/SIMULINK. In Section V, experimental validation of the proposed vehicle speed estimation approach is performed on real-world scenarios and results are discussed. Section VI concludes this paper and point out interesting future research directions.

II. RELATED WORK

There are several works which focus on the problem of ego-vehicle parameters estimation. Huang and Stachniss [6] present an approach for ego-motion using a monocular camera together with a laser range finder. The approach uses the camera images to estimate the five degrees of freedom relative orientation and a variant of the iterative closest point algorithm with one degree of freedom to estimate the scale. Nedevschi et al. [7] use video data to increase the accuracy of the ego-vehicle motion estimation. The video data is processed through procedures for feature detection and filtering, optical flow and epipolar geometry in order to obtain the essential matrix, from which the rotation and the translation of the ego-vehicle are computed.

Lee et al. [8] use a multi-camera system with minimal field-of-views for ego-motion estimation. The camera system is modelled as a generalized camera and the motion of the ego-vehicle is constrained to the Ackerman motion model. The method is compared to the ground truth provided by GPS and Inertial Navigation System (INS) sensors. Qimin et al. [9] developed a method for computing vehicle speed on the basis of sparse optical flow obtained from image sequences. The proposed method identifies distinct corners in camera images and maps the feature set of one frame on the consecutive frame. The vehicle speed is computed as the average of all speeds estimated by every matched corner. The time of execution for one iteration is 59 ms, while the mean error of speed estimation relative to the GPS measurement is $0.121\ \frac{m}{s}$.

Rill [10] uses the intuition that the magnitude of optical flow is positively correlated with the speed of the moving observer to develop a method for ego-speed estimation. The presented approach applies deep neural network based optical flow estimation and monocular depth prediction on camera images. The method is evaluated on input recordings from the KITTI benchmark [11] [12], reporting a root mean square error of less than $1\ \frac{m}{s}$.

III. DATA-DRIVEN MULTIRESOLUTIONAL LEARNING FOR ACCURATE PARAMETER ESTIMATION

Several data-oriented models proposed in various research works are relevant from a theoretical point of view for the problem of precise parameter estimation. In the field of human psychology and human memory research, Atkinson and Shiffrin [3] propose the dual-store model for the representation of human memory. According to this model, the human memory has a Sensory Register (SR) and two storage areas, the Short-Term Memory (STM) and the Long-Term Memory (LTM). Sensory information is first stored in the SR and, from there, transferred to the STM. The information stored in the STM decays and dissappears completely over time. Nevertheless, the information can be retained in the STM for a certain period of time via rehearsal mechanisms. Selected inputs from the LTM can also be transferred back to STM to serve as reference information for the recent inputs received from the SR. Losing et al. [2] propose the Self-Adjusting Memory (SAM) model for the k Nearest Neighbor (kNN) algorithm, which is partially based on the dual-store model in [3]. In the SAM architecture, current concepts stored in the STM and former concepts residing in the LTM are handled by dedicated models in accordance with the given situation.

An overview of our approach is depicted in Figure 1. Our concept is inspired by the dual-store model of the human memory, which comprises STM and LTM [3], and by the SAM architectural pattern [2]. The input datastream is processed and the situation reflected in the received data is evaluated. We are especially interested to determine whether any perturbations occur in the data and what is the magnitude of these perturbations. In case no disruptions are identified in the datastream or if these disruptions are smaller than a predefined threshold, we use long-term estimation mechanisms to approximate our parameters. We call this the *standard parameter value approximation*. The basis for our long-term estimation method are the system characteristics contained in the current system configuration. This is due to the fact that, in case of normal usage of the system, any changes to system characteristics are detectable over long periods of time, e.g., deterioration of vehicle tires.

However, in case of large disruptions in the datastream, we apply short-term estimation mechanisms in order to adjust the previously estimated standard value with a deviation error characteristic to the disruptive data. The basis for our short-term estimation approach are the input data received received by the system from its environment. Consider the example of a vehicle equipped with a GPS device. Disruptions in the GPS data may occur due to fluctuating GPS signal strength, which depends on the satellite geometry and on the road landscape.

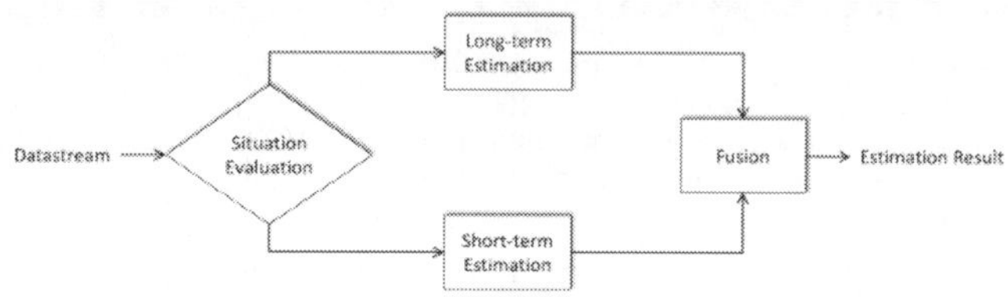

Figure 1. Overview of data-driven multiresolutiuonal learning.

In the current situation of the vehicle, old GPS data may not be relevant anymore. Therefore, recent GPS data must be taken into account in order to adjust the vehicle location displayed in the vehicle's navigation system.

Notice that the two categories of estimation mechanisms, short-term and long-term, work on differen time resolutions. As their names suggest, the short-term estimated values are updated more often than the long-term approximations. This is because system configurations change more slowly than current inputs from the system environment.

IV. Data-driven Vehicle Speed Estimation

In order to evaluate our concept, we build a case-study around an example system from the automotive domain. This section presents the system, which implements a vehicle speed estimation algorithm, together with the Euro NCAP requirements, as well as the preconditions and physical boundaries imposed on the system. The vehicle estimation algorithm has four major components: (A) estimation of the tire circumference, (B) plausibility check of the tire circumference, (C) computation and roundoff of the vehicle speed, and (D) smoothing of the vehicle speed curve (see Figure 2).

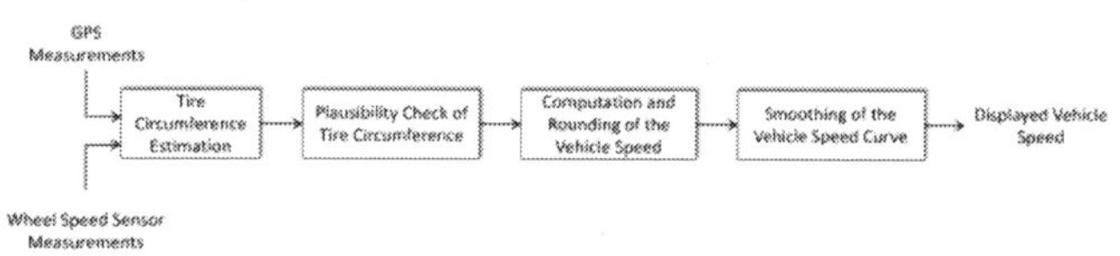

Figure 2. Overview of vehicle speed estimation algorithm.

A. System Requirements, Assumptions and Physical Boundaries

The proposed vehicle speed estimation algorithm must satisfy the NCAP requirement in (3):

$$0 \leq v_{display} - v_{real} \leq 5 \ \frac{km}{h} \tag{3}$$

where $v_{display}$ is the vehicle speed displayed on the dashboard of the car, and v_{real} is the actual vehicle speed. This requirement must be held under the assumption that the vehicle does not drive slower than 50 $\frac{km}{h}$ or faster than 120 $\frac{km}{h}$:

$$50 \leq v_{real} \leq 120 \ \frac{km}{h} \tag{4}$$

Notice that this requirement is stronger than the constraint imposed by the current european legal regulations [5].

The minimum and maximum values of the tire circumference are denoted TC_{min} and TC_{max}, and represent its lower and upper physical limits. Notice that these physical boundaries are specific for each tire profile. The vehicle speed estimation algorithm assumes the following boundaries for TC_{real}, the actual tire circumference:

$$TC_{min} = 2118 \ mm \ ; \ TC_{max} = 2293 \ mm$$

Based on the phyiscal boudaries of the tire circumference and on the maximum vehicle speed error of 5 $\frac{km}{h}$ allowed by the NCAP requirement, we can derive the lower and upper physical limit, n_{min} and n_{max}, for the wheel speed $n_{current}$ measured by the wheel speed sensor:

$$n_{min} = 6.056 \ \frac{1}{s} \ ; \ n_{max} = 15.738 \ \frac{1}{s}$$

B. Estimation of the Tire Circumference

The estimated tire circumference has two components: (A) a system-oriented approximation of the standard tire circumference on the basis of wheel speed measurements and (B) an environment-oriented estimation of the tire circumference error on the basis of selected GPS data. Since system characteristics are subject to rather slow changes over time, long-term estimation is used to approximate the standard tire circumference. On the other hand, input data coming from the environment is subject to decay and becomes useless in a comparably short period of time. Thus, short-term estimation is more appropriate for the estimation of the tire circumference error. The computation of the estimated tire circumference is shown in (5):

$$TC_{learned} = TC_{standard} + \Delta TC_{learned} \tag{5}$$

Approximation of the Standard Tire Circumference. The standard tire circumference is estimated on the basis of the currently measured wheel speed $n_{current}$, according to the approximation curve defined by (6):

$$TC_{standard} = a \cdot sin(n_{current} - \pi) + b \cdot (n_{current} - 10)^2 + c \tag{6}$$

where $a = -0,5152$, $b = 0,07646$, and $c = 2175$. The coefficients a, b and c used in (6) have been chosen so that the curve matches approximately the ground truth of the tire circumference measurements. The ground truth data has been computed from the vehicle speed measurements performed with an ADMA sensor at a test facility of our industry project partner.

Estimation of the Tire Circumference Error. The tire circumference error is estimated on the basis of GPS data. The received GPS data contains GPS measurements of the tire circumference as well as information about the quality of the received data. Usually, a strong GPS signal means also a high quality of the received GPS data. Consequently, the error contained in high quality GPS data is very small. In order for the received GPS data to be considered for further computations, the error of the GPS data e_{GPS} must be under a certain threshold e^{GPS}_{max}. For our concept, we considered $e^{GPS}_{max} = 0.15$, which causes a deviation of the estimated vehicle speed of at most $\pm 0.15 \ \frac{m}{s}$. The main procedure for the estimation of the tire circumference error is described by Algorithm 1 depicted in Figure 3.

Notice that the computations in Algorithm 1 are controlled by a boolean flag, denoted as $updateFlag$. The update of the tire circumference error is performed only when certain conditions are met. These conditions are:

1) *small GPS data error:* $e^{GPS}_{max} = 0.15 \ \frac{m}{s}$,

Algorithm 1: Estimation of the tire circumference error.

procedure $TCError(TC^{GPS}_{measured}, n_{current}, e_{GPS}, a_{long}, a_{lat}, a_{road})$
 $updateFlag \leftarrow UpdateFlag(e_{GPS}, a_{long}, a_{lat}, a_{road})$
 $\Delta TC_{init} \leftarrow \frac{2.5}{n_{current}} \cdot \frac{1000}{3.6}$
 $\Delta TC_{max} \leftarrow \frac{5}{n_{current}} \cdot \frac{1000}{3.6}$
 $\Delta TC_{learned} \leftarrow \Delta TC_{init}$
 if $updateFlag \neq false$ **then**
  $\Delta TC_{update} \leftarrow TCErrorUpdate(TC_{standard}, TC^{GPS}_{measured}, n_{current}, e_{GPS}, \Delta TC_{max})$
  $\Delta TC_{learned} \leftarrow (1 - w) \cdot \Delta TC_{learned} + w \cdot \Delta TC_{update}$
 end if
 return $\Delta TC_{learned}$
end procedure

Figure 3. Algorithm for the estimation of the tire circumference error.

2) *longitudinal acceleration limited by an upper bound:* $a^{long}_{max} = 0.001\ \frac{m}{s^2}$,
3) *small lateral acceleration to avoid skidding scenarios:* $a^{lat}_{max} = 0.0001\frac{m}{s^2}$, and
4) *small road gradient:* $\alpha^{road}_{max} = 12\%$.

The computation of the update flag is depicted in Algorithm 2 (see Figure 4).

Algorithm 2: Computation of the update flag.

procedure $UpdateFlag(e_{GPS}, a_{long}, a_{lat}, a_{road})$
 $gpsErrorFlag \leftarrow e_{GPS} \leq e^{GPS}_{max}$
 $roadSlopeFlag \leftarrow a_{road} \leq a^{road}_{max}$
 $longAccelFlag \leftarrow a_{long} \leq a^{long}_{max}$
 $latAccelFlag \leftarrow a_{lat} \leq a^{lat}_{max}$
 if $(gpsErrorFlag = false$ **or** $roadSlopeFlag = false$ **or**
  $longAccelFlag = false$ **or** $latAccelFlag = false)$
 then
  return $false$
 else
  return $true$
 end if
end procedure

Figure 4. Algorithm for the computation of the update flag.

Observe that in the first iteration of TCERROR procedure, the tire circumference error $\Delta TC_{learned}$ is initialised with an initial value ΔTC_{init}. Due to the NCAP requirement, the error $\Delta TC_{learned}$ has the upper bound ΔTC_{max}. Notice that the upper bound ΔTC_{max} necessarily depends on the maximum vehicle speed error permitted by the NCAP requirement.

In every subsequent iteration of the estimation algorithm TCERROR, the tire circumference error is updated on-the-fly based on current GPS measurements. Thus, the estimated tire circumference error is a function of previous estimations and updates based on current GPS data, as depicted in (7):

$$\Delta TC_{learned} = (1 - w) \cdot \Delta TC_{learned} + w \cdot \Delta TC_{update} \quad (7)$$

where $w = 0.1$ is an application parameter.

In order to comply with the NCAP requirements, the updates to the tire circumference error are computed exclusively with adequate GPS data. Such data carries a maximum error of $e^{GPS}_{max} = 0.15$ and can be used for further computations. Any other received GPS data, which bears a larger error than the defined maximum threshold, is discarded. It is therefore necessary to define a mechanism by which intervals of good GPS data can be identified and selected from the entire GPS data batch received by the vehicle sensors. The mechannism for the selection of the GPS data is illustrated visually in Figure 5. Based on the selected GPS data, Algorithm 3 computes the update of the tire circumference error (see Figure 6).

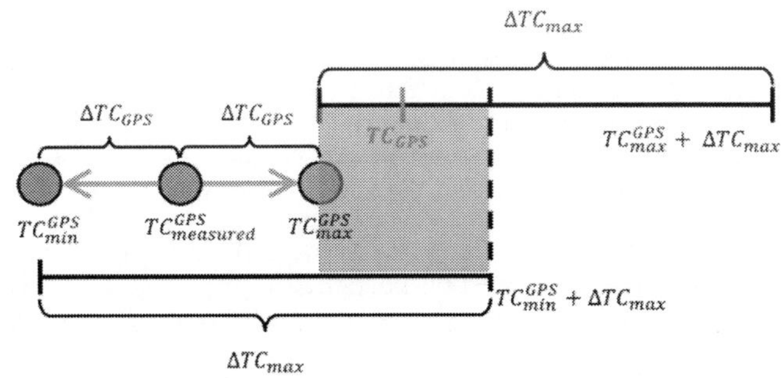

Figure 5. A visual intuition for the selection of adequate GPS data.

Algorithm 3: Computation of the tire circumference error update.

procedure $TCErrorUpdate(TC_{standatd}, TC^{GPS}_{measured}, n_{current}, e_{GPS}, \Delta TC_{max})$
 $\Delta TC_{GPS} \leftarrow \frac{e^{GPS}_{max} \cdot 1000}{n_{current}}$
 $TC^{GPS}_{max} \leftarrow TC^{GPS}_{measured} + \Delta TC_{GPS}$
 $TC^{GPS}_{min} \leftarrow TC^{GPS}_{measured} - \Delta TC_{GPS}$
 $TC_{GPS} \leftarrow \frac{TC^{GPS}_{max} + (TC^{GPS}_{min} + \Delta TC_{max})}{2}$
 $\Delta TC_{update} \leftarrow TC_{GPS} - TC_{standard}$
end procedure

Figure 6. Algorithm for the computation of the tire circumference error update.

The proposed algorithm takes further errors into consideration, e.g., errors due to the road gradient and rounding of the instrument display. We employ several mechanisms in order to compensate for these errors. Due to space restrictions, these mechanisms are not explained in this paper.

C. Plausibility Check of the Tire Circumference

For each tire profile, there are specific lower and upper limits, which constitute the physical boundaries of the real and of the estimated tire circumferences. Plausibility checks are necessary in order to eliminate any outliers.

However, before making any plausibility checks, we use a filter on the newly estimated tire circumference, in order to make sure that the difference between the new value and the old value estimated in the previous iteration does not exceed the threshold $P = 20\ mm$ in $3\ s$. An overshoot of the threshold P usually means that some of the data necessary for the estimation of the tire circumference has been missing, e.g., due to the vehicle not running. In this case, the old data is not useful anymore, and therefore must be discarded. The computation continues only with the newly estimated tire circumference. Afterwards, the plausibility checks filter out the physically implausible values, i.e., values situated outside the interval spanned by the predefined physical boundaries $[TC_{min}, TC_{max}]$, as shown in (8):

$$TC_{plausible} = max(TC_{min}, min(TC_{learned}, TC_{max})) \quad (8)$$

D. Computation and Roundoff of the Vehicle Speed

The instanteneous vehicle speed is then computed based on the tire circumference and current wheel speed measured by the wheel speed sensors of the vehicle, as shown (9).

$$v = \frac{3.6}{1000} \cdot n_{current} \cdot TC_{plausible} \quad (9)$$

The speedometer dial in every vehicle displays a range of natural numbers from zero to an upper limit, which varies by make and model of the car. The displayed speed $v_{display}$ is computed by rounding off the vehicle speed v, so that it matches the numbers on the speedometer range.

E. Smoothing of the Vehicle Speed Curve

A smoothing function is applied to the resulting curve of the vehicle speed, in order to avoid the pointer needle of the speedometer bouncing back and forth at every small change in the estimation of the vehicle speed.

V. EXPERIMENTS

We implemented the proposed vehicle speed estimation algorithm using MATLAB/SIMULINK and performed the evaluation on two driving scenarios. The data in both driving scenarios has been collected and provided by our industrial project partner, who collected the data using its own field test platform. The two scenarios are depicted in Figure 7 and in Figure 8 respectively, along with the algorithm evaluation. In both scenarios, the travelling time bears 1000 seconds, approximately 16.7 minutes. In each scenario, the first graph illustrates the evolution over time of three variables:

1) the 2D GPS speed measured with the GPS device of the test vehicle,
2) the actual vehicle speed, considered to be the ground truth and which is measured by ADMA sensors, and
3) the NCAP upper bound, which is the maximum speed allowed by the NCAP requirement.

The second graph shows the performance of our algorithm with respect to the maximum vehicle speed deviation permitted by the NCAP requirement.

The first scenario illustrates the ideal situation, specified also by the NCAP requirements and preconditions. The value range of the actual vehicle speed is situated between 50 $\frac{km}{h}$ and 130 $\frac{km}{h}$. The ADMA speed curve depicts a relatively smooth driving style, with clear-cut acceleration and decceleration segments and continuous periods of time with constant driving. It is fairly easy to see that in this scenario the vehicle speed deviation, $v_{display} - v_{real}$ is between cca 0.5 $\frac{km}{h}$ and cca 3.0 $\frac{km}{h}$, which satisfies the NCAP requirement specified in (3).

The second scenario depicts a more dynamic situation. The ADMA speed curve, with a value range between 0 $\frac{km}{h}$ and 180 $\frac{km}{h}$, illustrates a more sporty driving style, with abrupt speed-ups and sharp brakes, which alternate frequently. Notice that, after 100 s, the estimation of vehicle speed deviation

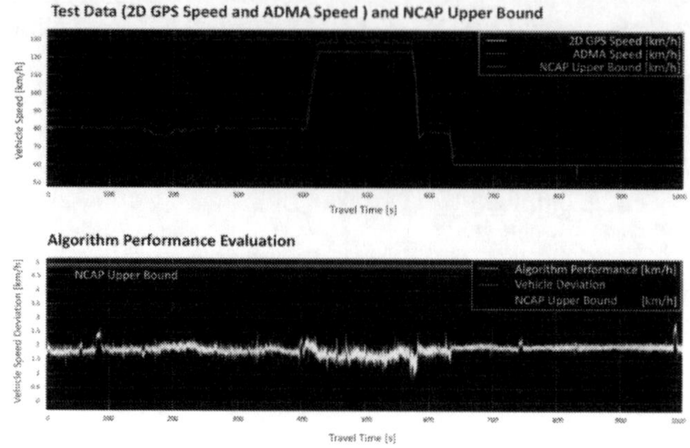

Figure 7. First scenario: smooth driving.

$v_{display} - v_{real}$ is stabilized between a minimum of cca 0.5 $\frac{km}{h}$ and a maximum of cca 3.5 $\frac{km}{h}$, thus satisfying the NCAP requirement.

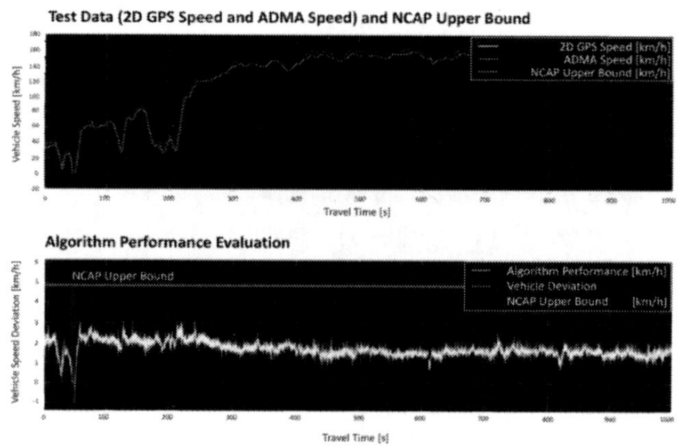

Figure 8. Second scenario: dynamic driving.

However, in this second scenario, the time period of the first 100 s is of particularly interest to us. Notice that the estimated vehicle speed deviation drops down to -1 $\frac{km}{h}$ around the middle of this time interval, meaning that the actual vehicle speed is underestimated. This occurrence can be attributed to the fact that, at that time, the ADMA speed decreases down to 0 $\frac{km}{h}$, i.e., the vehicle has stopped. It is obvious that no valid wheel speed measurements and GPS sensor data can be collected while the vehicle is stopped.

VI. SUMMARY AND CONCLUSIONS

We proposed an algorithm for the estimation of the ego-vehicle speed displayed on the dashboard instrument. Our approach is built upon the concepts of Short-Term Memory and Long-Termy Memory introduced by Atkinson and Shiffrin [3], which have been further developed in the Self-Adjusting Memory architectural pattern by Losing et al. [2]. We estimate the ego-vehicle speed by approximating its actual tire circumference.

In our approach, long-term estimation is used for the approximation of a standard tire circumference on the basis of current measurements of the wheel speed sensors. The wheel speed readings depend directly on the vehicle configuration, i.e., the profile of the tires mounted on the vehicle, which remains rather stable over time. An accurate approximation of the tire circumference is critical for a precise estimation of the displayed vehicle speed. Therefore, we use short-term estimation mechanisms to estimate a tire circumference error, with which the standard tire circumference is corrected. The short-term estimation method makes use of the sensor data collected with the ego-vehicle's GPS device, during the vehicle travel time. Not every received GPS data is used for the short-term estimation. Instead, we define a mechanism by which only the adequate data is selected and used for the estimation of the tire circumference error. We define several constraints, which specify in what sort of situations the short-term mechanism can be triggered. These criteria take into account the error of the GPS data, the vehicle's longitudinal and lateral acceleration and the road gradient. Through this approach, we are able to better control the process for the tire circumference approximation and, by extension, that of the vehicle speed estimation. Furthermore, our algorithm compensates for errors of the tire circumference estimation occurring due to the road gradient and the rounding off necessary for the speedometer dial. An experimental validation of the algorithm on two scenarios with real-world test data shows that the proposed approach performs well within the limits of the Euro NCAP requirements.

Nevertheless, there is potential for further optimization, which we intend to investigate in future research work. This optimization potential refers to the possible deviations, which may occur due to slippage, since slippage errors have a direct influence on the wheel speed measurements. For this, we need to perform an extensive analysis on a larger test data set. Moreover, it would be interesting to apply the presented vehicle speed estimation approach on test data gathered in more difficult driving conditions, e.g. patches of wet roadway alternating with dry road areas. Furthermore, we plan to extend our case study and investigate mechanisms for long-term estimation and short-term estimation, which can be used interchangeably in support of each other, i.e., use LTM to provide reference values for STM and STM to correct previously approximated values by LTM.

Since the speedometer is a critical vehicle instrument, experimental validation and testing are not enough to provide adequate confidence in the correct functioning of the vehicle speed estimation method. For this, we plan to use formal verification methods, since they are especially suitable to provide a mathematical proof that a system conforms to the legal and and the customer requirements. Furthermore, formal verification methods can be used to construct a solid argument for the system certification.

References

[1] M. Kwiatkowska, G. Norman, and D. Parker, "PRISM 4.0: Verification of Probabilistic Real-time Systems," in Proc. 23rd International Conference on Computer Aided Verification (CAV'11), ser. LNCS, G. Gopalakrishnan and S. Qadeer, Eds., vol. 6806. Springer, 2011, pp. 585–591.

[2] V. Losing, B. Hammer, and H. Wersing, "Self-Adjusting Memory: How to Deal with Diverse Drift Types," in Proceedings of the 26th International Joint Conference on Artificial Intelligence, IJCAI-17, 19-25 August 2017, Melbourne, Australia. IJCAI, Aug. 2017, pp. 4899–4903, Sierra, C. Ed., ISBN: 978-0-9992411-0-3, URL: https://www.ijcai.org/proceedings/2017/690 [accessed: 2020-01-07].

[3] R. C. Atkinson and R. M. Shiffrin, Human memory: A proposed system and its control processes. Academic Press, Jan. 1968, chapter 3, pp. 89–198, in Spence, K. W. and Spence, J. T. The Psychology of Learning and Motivation, ISBN: 0079-7421.

[4] W. Harris, "How Speedometers Work," 2007, URL: https://auto.howstuffworks.com/car-driving-safety/safety-regulatory-devices/speedometer.htm [accessed: 2020-01-09].

[5] "Richtlinie 75/443/EWG des Rates vom 26. Juni 1975 zur Angleichung der Rechtsvorschriften der Mitgliedstaaten über den Rückwärtsgang und das Geschwindigkeitsmeßgerät in Kraftfahrzeugen," 1975, URL: https://eur-lex.europa.eu/LexUriServ/LexUriServ.do?uri=CELEX:31975L0443:DE:HTML [accessed: 2020-01-06].

[6] K. Huang and C. Stachniss, "Joint Ego-motion Estimation Using a Laser Scanner and a Monocular Camera Through Relative Orientation Estimation and 1-DoF ICP," in 2018 IEEE/RSJ International Conference on Intelligent Robots and Systems (IROS), 1-5 October 2018, Madrid, Spain. IEEE, Oct. 2018, pp. 671–677, Maciejewski, A. A. Ed., ISBN: 978-1-5386-8095-7, ISSN: 2153-0858, URL: https://doi.org/10.1109/IROS.2018.8593965 [accessed: 2020-01-08].

[7] S. Nedevschi, C. Golban, and C. Mitran, "Improving accuracy for Ego vehicle motion estimation using epipolar geometry," in 2009 12th International IEEE Conference on Intelligent Transportation Systems, 4-7 October 2009, St. Louis, MO, USA. IEEE, Oct. 2009, pp. 1–7, ISBN: 978-1-4244-5519-5 ISSN: 2153-0017, URL: https://doi.org/10.1109/ITSC.2009.5309610 [accessed: 2020-01-08].

[8] G. H. Lee, F. Fraundorfer, and M. Pollefeys, "Motion Estimation for Self-Driving Cars with a Generalized Camera," in 2013 IEEE Conference on Computer Vision and Pattern Recognition, 23-28 June 2013, Portland, OR, USA. IEEE, Jun. 2013, pp. 2746–2753, Kellenberger, P. Ed., ISSN: 1063-6919, URL: https://doi.org/10.1109/CVPR.2013.354 [accessed: 2020-01-08].

[9] X. Qimin, L. Xu, W. Mingming, L. Bin, and S. Xianghui, "A methodology of vehicle speed estimation based on optical flow," in Proceedings of 2014 IEEE International Conference on Service Operations and Logistics, and Informatics, 8-10 October 2014, Qingdao, China. IEEE, Oct. 2014, pp. 33–37, ISBN: 978-1-4799-6058-3, URL: https://doi.org/10.1109/SOLI.2014.6960689 [accessed: 2020-01-09].

[10] R.-A. Rill, "Speed estimation evaluation on the kitti benchmark based on motion and monocular depth information," 2019.

[11] A. Geiger, P. Lenz, and R. Urtasun, "Are we ready for autonomous driving? the kitti vision benchmark suite," in Conference on Computer Vision and Pattern Recognition (CVPR), 2012.

[12] A. Geiger, P. Lenz, C. Stiller, and R. Urtasun, "Vision meets robotics: The kitti dataset," International Journal of Robotics Research (IJRR), 2013.

Adapting the CO_2-Compass Architecture to Further Optimize Data Generation Methods

Enhancing CO_2 Emission Forecasts by Minimizing the Area of Observation

Lucas Hüer, Hans-Jürgen Pfisterer
Faculty of Engineering & Computer Science
University of Applied Sciences Osnabrück
Osnabrück, Germany
Email: {l.hueer | j.pfisterer}@hs-osnabrueck.de

Helge Fischer, Sebastian Lawrenz
Institute for Software & Systems Engineering
Technische Universität Clausthal
Clausthal-Zellerfeld, Germany
Email: {helge.fischer | sebastian.lawrenz}@tu-clausthal.de

Oliver Thomas
Chair of Information Management & Information Systems
University of Osnabrück
Osnabrück, Germany
Email: oliver.thomas@uni-osnabrueck.de

***Abstract*—Climate change is one of the most important social issues of recent years. Every new scientific insights and political decisions make it clear that innovative ways of attacking the climate change are needed. Minimizing emissions are especially important in order to stop the greenhouse effect and thus a source for global warming. Therefore, the software of the CO_2-Compass was developed to provide a transparent overview of the electricity production and related CO_2 emissions. Containing the service of a 24 hour forecast of these data, the CO_2-Compass serves as a control tool to decide when electrical devices should be used from an ecological point of view. This paper strives to improve the existing architecture of the tool, by adding new sources of data collection and thus optimize the outcome of all offered services by the CO_2-Compass. Therefore, the main goal of this paper is to improve the existing architecture of the first monomythical prototype towards a flexible and expandable microservice based architecture.**

Keywords-CO_2 Emission Reduction; Software Engineering; Energy Production; Renewable Energies; Energy Transition; Data Warehouse; Microservices.

I. INTRODUCTION

In the wake of an undergoing energy transition, several parts of the German energy industry are continuously changing. This mainly implies a shift from centralized to decentralized energy production, as well as a shift from conventional towards renewable energy sources [1]. Moving towards an increased utilization of renewable energy sources has multiple advantages, such as security of supply due to unlimited sources or higher sustainability levels due to decreased CO_2 emissions [2] [3]. However, to better facilitate all advantages that go hand in hand with using renewable energies, it is necessary to align the electricity usage of electrical devices with a more resource-saving energy production [4] [5]. Thus, electrical devices can be used at times in which the regenerative part of created energy is high and CO_2 emissions are low. To determine the best time of a day for this scenario, the software tool "CO_2-Compass" was created [6]. By using this tool companies, as well as households can get a transparent overview of the electricity production and CO_2 emissions that go along with it. Further, a 24-hour-forecast will be provided to show the likely development of electricity production and belonging CO_2 emissions. This source of information supports a user's decision when to use energy-intensive hardware (like heat pumps, air conditioners, charging stations or production machines) by determining the point of time at which CO_2 emissions of the energy production are lowest. In a first version of the CO_2-Compass, data collection is limited to the aggregated information that is made available by the four major power grid operators in Germany (50Hertz, Amprion, TenneT, Transnet BW) [7]. Decentralized power supply information and detailed data broke down to local energy providers are not yet included. However, to have a reliable knowledge base about power generation and its CO_2 emissions, it is necessary to have as much local information as possible, which in turn would optimize the data in terms of relevance, reliability and accuracy. A growing share of renewables and a fluctuating, decentralized power production will require flexible and open interfaces in order to process the accruing data. In order to tackle this problem and further optimize the data generation of the CO_2-Compass, this paper is tackling the following research question:

What kind of changes can be made to the existing CO_2-Compass architecture to improve its data generation in terms of data quality while keeping it expandable?

To answer this question thoroughly, following structure will guide the reader through this article: Once a scientific and political background is given in Section 2, there will be a description of the current CO_2-Compass architecture and its limitations in Section 3. Those limitations will then serve as an explanation for the refactoring of the existing architecture. All changes that are necessary to optimize the data generation of the CO_2-Compass will then be described in Section 4, which is followed by an elaboration on the creation of timelines in terms of gathering data in Section 5. Once all changes are explained, a discussion and conclusion will complement this paper.

II. Scientific and Political Background

The 21st century has so far been largely shaped by scientific and political discussions and decisions relating to climate change [8]. Government representatives from most countries meet regularly and reach agreements on various actions to protect the environment and society from negative consequences of the climate change. One of the biggest factors that has been addressed in previous climate summits is the emission of greenhouse gases [9]. A main objective of the Paris Agreement is to limit global warming to 1.5°C [10].

In order to curb the emission of these gases and thus to combat the greenhouse effect that primarily leads to global warming, the global community is setting ever more ambitious goals. The German government has, for instance, decided to reduce greenhouse gas emissions by 40% between 1990 and 2020 [11]; goals for the following decades are even more ambitious. It is therefore necessary to develop innovative products and services that support companies and consumers in reducing CO_2 emissions. A promising field in which CO_2 emissions can be vastly minimized is the electrical power generation [12]. The saving potential can be seen when looking at the development of direct CO_2 emissions per kilowatt hour of electricity related to the German electricity mix. Since 1990 the direct CO_2 emissions per kilowatt hour of electricity (in g/kWh) was reduced from 764 g/kWh to 523 g/kWh in 2016. This is equivalent to a reduction of 31% [12]. This reduction is explained by Petra Icha as follows: "If the proportion of an energy source with a high CO_2 emission factor, such as brown or hard coal, falls in favor of an energy source with a lower CO_2 emission factor, such as a renewable energy sources […] the emission factor of the electricity mix also decreases" [12]. In other words, different energy sources are associated with different levels of CO_2 emissions. Therefore, improved transparency in terms of the energy mix and its forecasted development over the next hours is needed, to base decisions on electricity usage of electrical devices on the decrease of CO_2 emissions. Based on our knowledge, there are some associations that transparently show the electricity mix and the associated CO_2 emissions. Good examples of this are Agora Energiewende, electricityMap or KlimAktiv Consulting. However, there are some drawbacks when using these services and thus the CO2-Compass was developed in order to offer new solutions in the field. The CO_2-Compass has two major advantages over potential competitors: On the one hand, there is the possibility of displaying the CO_2 emissions per individual transmission network provider, which leads to more relevant information for individual households and companies. On the other hand, there is a REST interface with which the software can be coupled to any hardware in the form of devices and machines. However, in order to add new functions, interfaces and solutions or to optimize all existing ones, the CO_2-Compass is under continuous improvement. One of these improvements is the change of its architecture to increase the data quality.

III. Existing Architecture of the CO2-Compass and it's Limitations

Initially, the CO_2-Compass software was developed on basis of the SCRUM method. By setting up, processing and completing functional and non-functional system requirements, the software was created incrementally. The system requirements were based on an interview with an expert in the field of electrical engineering. However, to optimize the CO_2-Compass, further software-development methods were used. The decision to use as an agile, user centred approach aimed to generate a first prototype.

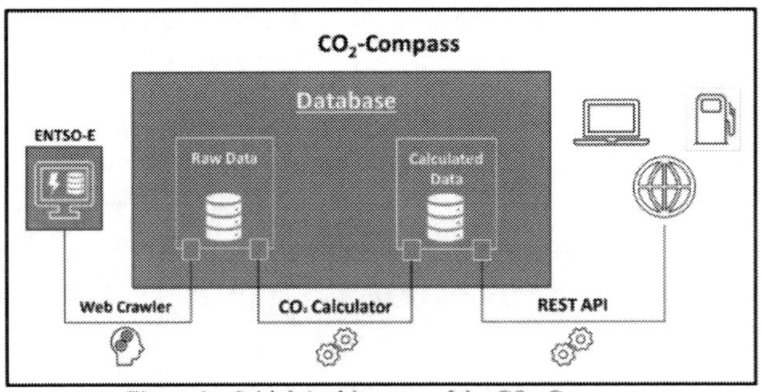

Figure 1 – Initial Architecture of the CO_2-Compass

The initial architecture of the CO_2-Compass consists of three main system-parts (see Figure 1): The Crawler, the CO_2-Calculator and the REST API. Within a first step, the raw data from the European Network of Transmission System Operators for Electricity (ENTSO-E) is collected by a self-developed crawler at five-minute intervals, before being stored in a separate database. The electricity production data (in MW) for every high-voltage power grid operator in Germany (50Hertz, Amprion, TenneT, Transnet BW) and for Germany as a whole are now stored in this database. There are currently 18 different types of energy sources for producing electricity. After the crawler updates and collects the raw data from the transmission networks, the specific CO_2 values for the associated production figures are calculated by the CO_2-Calculator. These values are also stored in the database and can thus be assigned to the network operator and the type of production. This calculation takes place for each individual provider in five-minute intervals and provides values every 15 minutes. Furthermore, the CO_2-Calculator creates a CO_2 forecast for each production type for the next 24 hours every day at midnight, which is also stored in the internal database. An integrated REST API enables public access to the generated data and the forecast values. This interface can be used in a variety of ways to couple the emission information with electrical devices. One example is the connection of the CO_2-Compass to intelligent charging stations, which continuously query the current electricity mix (including the associated emission values). In combination with the predicted values from the forecast, charging stations can thus be switched in such a way that they only start charging when there is a low-emission electricity mix. However, a fast-charging option instead of the eco-friendly charging is still possible and customers can use an approach which suits them best.

The current implementation of the CO_2-Compass is based and limited on an input interface which collects data from ENTSO-E. Information about power generation and CO_2 emissions are published through their transparency platform at the abstract level of control areas. They hereby fulfill an EU Regulation, where data must be published by control areas. By definition, these control areas are "a coherent part of the interconnected system, operated by a single system operator" [13]. These areas usually reflect the high-voltage grid of a whole country (e.g., in France or Portugal) or supra-regional network operators (e.g., in Germany the four control areas of the in Section 1 mentioned transmission system operators). Since TenneT's geographical coverage, to name an example, ranges from the Danish border to the Austrian border (see Figure 2 and [7]), a precise indication of the CO_2 emissions of locally consumed power is hardly possible.

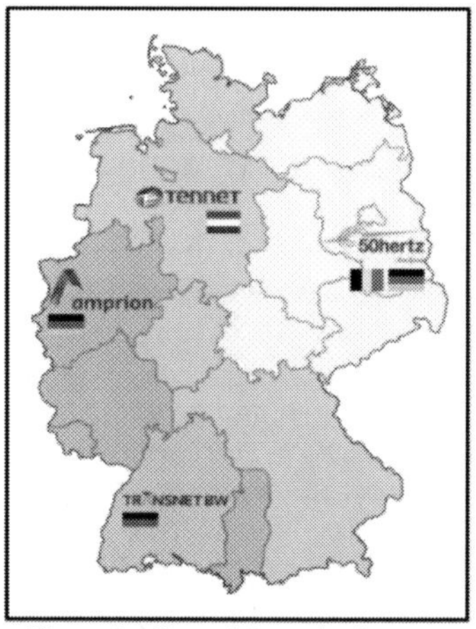

Figure 2 – Control Areas in Germany

One reason for this is the so called "copper plate illusion" (translated from the German term: Illusion einer Kupferplatte), which describes the problem of assuming that electricity producers and consumers act without restrictions, and can thus generate and consume electricity as they please without transmission bottlenecks or energy loss [14] [15]. However, for a lossless transmission of electricity, the power grid would have to be a superconducting (copper) plate - hence the name - which is not the case. Therefore, an extension of the input interfaces in order to have more specific, locally relevant data is needed. Those changes and their relevance will be presented and explained in the coming sections.

IV. Proposed Architecture

The actual state of the architecture (see Figure 1) was explained in the previous section. An agile procedure was chosen to prove the functionality of the CO_2-Compass at short term. However, after a successful establishment of the prototype, the next step will be a change in the architecture to a more modular system, within the goal of "low coupling, high cohesion". This paradigm means that modules or services inside the software architecture should be as self-contained and independent as possible, and thus depending as less as possible on other components [16]. Based on this, following objectives for the architecture have been defined:

1. Modular design and expandable splitting of the monolith and change the architecture to micro-services [17]
2. A clear division of components into layers to define security and sovereignty of data
3. Data-driven design for analytic services

The proposed architecture is shown in Figure 3 consisting of separated layers. On the left hand side there are various data sources, such as IoT-Devices and (smart) meters to measure the current power production and calculate related CO_2 emissions at specific points. In addition to the ENTSO-E database and other sources of forecast (such as local weather and solar radiation data) should be imported by a (web)-crawler. Based on this information local power generation which is not metered online (e.g., solar panels on rooftops) can be forecasted and taken into account. For all own and third parties' generators in a local grid with measuring devices, the available data should be transferred via a clear defined interface into the databases. Now, based on these extended data collection, additional substitute values can be generated and processed together with metered raw data in the CO_2-Calculator. Data integration into the data warehouse takes place in the **Data Integration Layer.** This layer manages the incoming data flows, filters and cleans it (if necessary) and transfers it into a data warehouse. Services, like a broker or the web crawler, receive and structure the data beforehand. The following **Data Warehouse Layer** stores and manages the data for all services and handles incoming raw data. The raw data are divided into at least two

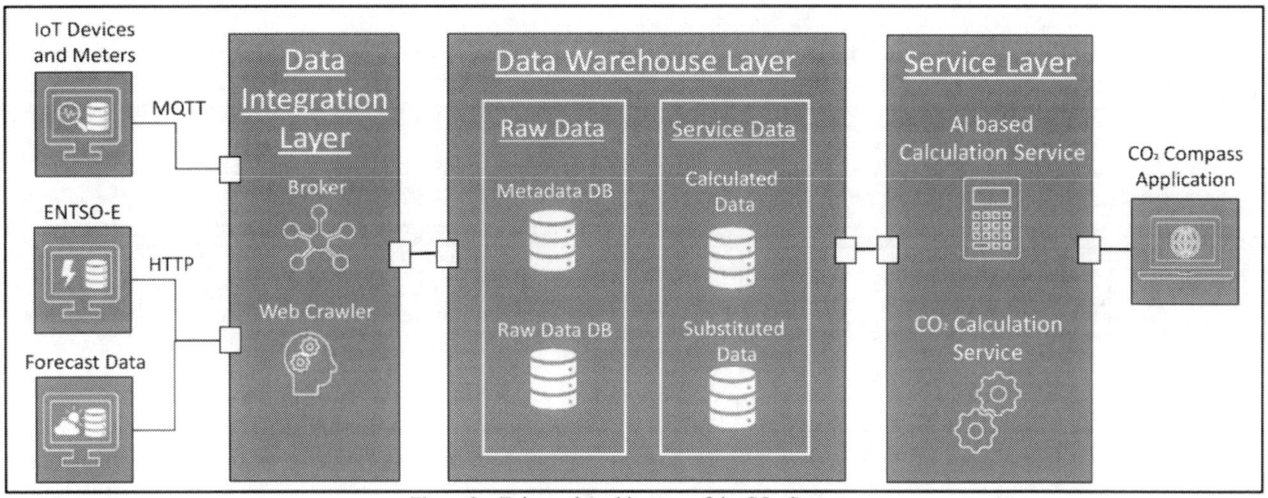

Figure 3 – Enhanced Architecture of the CO_2-Compass

different databases. The first one is the *Metadata DB*, which contains meta data and information about the data itself, such as the origin of this data. The *Raw Data DB* contains the values themselves (or based on the DIKW-Pyramide so called data [18]) that means for example the measured electric power (*12.5* megawatts per hour at *2019-05-08 12:35:00*).

However, even if the *Metadata DB* and the *Raw Data DB* are independent at first sight, they have a close relation. This comes out of the fact that every column with specific values in the Raw Data DB has a meta description in the Metadata DB (see Table 1).

TABLE I. SMALL EXTRACT FROM TWO RAW DATA COLUMNS

Power Volumes	Timestamp
12.5	2019-05-08 12:35:00
15.5	2019-05-08 12:37:00
24.4	2019-05-08 12:39:00

The associated metadata in the *Metadata DB* contains, for example, the link to the corresponding columns, the *unit* (here megawatts per hour and datetime in the format YYYY-MM-DD HH-MM-SS), information about the sensor (time interval between two measuring points [here 2 Minutes]) and the *description* of the data source (e.g., metering device of a wind park).

Moreover, as shown in Figure 3 the service data are separated from the raw data. The service data (here shown as *Calculated Data* and *Substituted Data*) are the data sources which belong to a specific service inside the Service Layer. This separation ensures to have a clear separation on the one hand and on the other hand to improve the data access depending on the intended use. This ensures that the generated data (which might be wrong when the service or the AI fails) does not get mixed up with the raw data.

The **Service Layer** contains the modules and services for the application of the CO_2-Compass itself. One service for example calculates the CO_2 component of the current power mix (*CO_2-Calculation Service)* and proposes services to generate missing data (indicated here as *AI based Calculation Services*) to increase the accuracy (see also Section 5). Via a REST Interface the user can then interact with the frontend of the *CO_2-Compass Application*.

In summary, it can be stated that a clearly separated but extendable architecture was introduced, which allows to extend the use cases of the CO_2-Compass and to further develop mechanism to control and reduce the CO_2 emissions. By introducing different layers, a high level of data security and a clean separation of incoming data is made possible. Thus, it can be differentiated easily between public non-critical data sources like ENTSO-E and private data sources like smart meters. Furthermore, the *Data Integration Layer* will be designed similarly dynamic and expandable as the *Service Layer*. This enables an uncomplicated extension of the data warehouse with further data sources.

V. CREATION OF TIMELINES

To fulfill the requirements of more detailed information at local level, more timelines have to be implemented. Local data, as well as artificial data will give the necessary added value to have an in-depth view on a distinct power grid (hereafter simplified called "distribution grid"). The local data may be generated by measuring the power production like windmills or Combined Heat and Powerplants (CHPs) in the distribution grid. These metering devices have to be connected "online" and submit the data continuously. Missing values (see crosshatched bars in Figure 4) can be substituted by replacement values and discrepancies to the defined time patterns (e.g., hourly values instead of expected 15 minutes) may be aligned immediately in the service layer.

Estimating and generating artificial data opens the opportunity to gain a holistic view as well as compensate poor data quality from certain metering devices or other input sources. If not every power production (especially the small ones) or battery storages in cars or households are metered online a precise allocation of CO_2 emissions is hardly possible. Even, for example, if a field of solar panels is equipped with metering devices, but poorly connected online, it may make sense to calculate artificial data and short-term prognoses based on solar radiation forecasts. It would also open opportunities to simplify the technical requirements and perform a cost-benefit consideration concerning metering in the context of an organically growing distribution grid driven by the energy transition ('Energiewende').

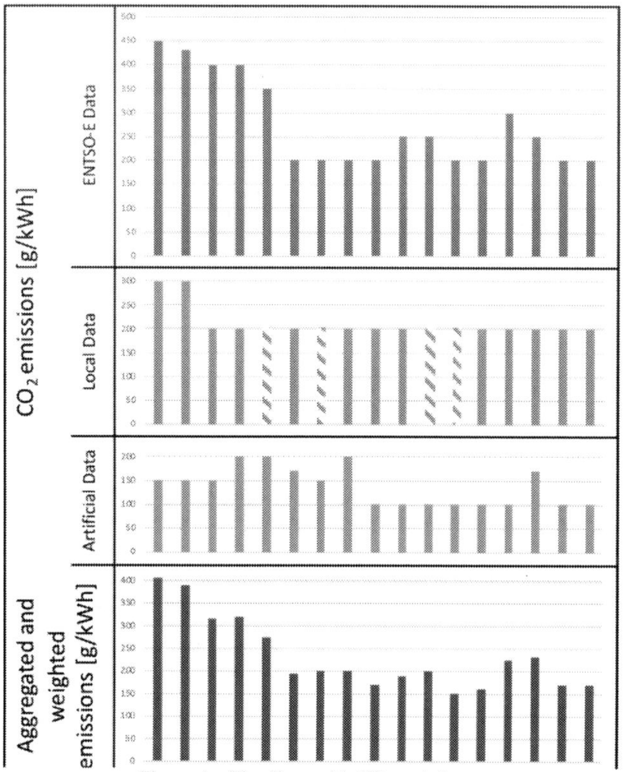

Figure 4 – Timelines with CO_2 emissions

An AI based calculation service (see Figure 5) can be used to generate the artificial data. It will base on AI methods like the recurrent network algorithm Long Short-Term Memory (LSTM) [19] and considers former results, non-online metered devices which are submitted with delay, as well as relevant input variables (e.g., solar radiation, wind, energy prices or time of day) in order to train a neuronal network.

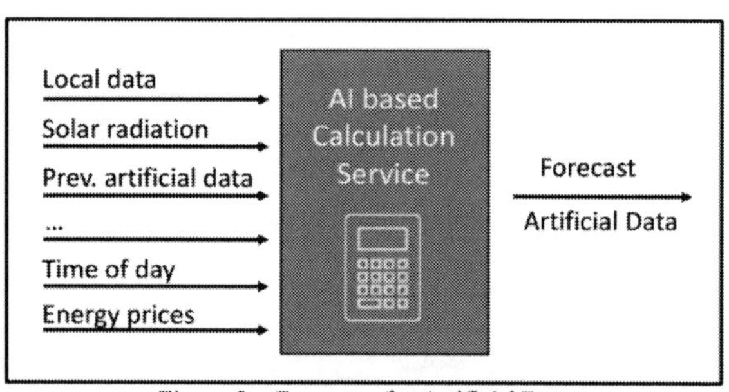

Figure 5 – Generator for Artificial Data

The output will be an estimation of produced power volumes and their dedicated CO_2 emissions reflecting the characteristics of grid topologies and individual influencing factors in the local energy mix. Finally, the three data timelines containing specific CO_2 emissions have to be weighted with allocated power volumes at the connection from the upstream grid, metered local power generators and estimated miscellaneous devices. As a result, this aggregation will now give a more precise, average CO_2 emissions factor for the distribution grid in comparison to the rough proxy based on the ENTSO-E data.

VI. CONCLUSION

Scientific warnings, as well as political decisions with regard to global problems arising from the climate change call for innovative solutions to minimize CO_2 emissions. One of these solutions was developed in 2019 and is since being continuously improved to optimize its functions: the so-called CO_2-Compass.

Initially, the architecture of the CO_2-Compass was focused on basic data collection in order to transparently present all CO_2 emissions from the power mix based only on the data of ENTSO-E and thus from the four big power grid operators in Germany: 50Hertz, Amprion, TenneT, and Transnet BW. However, as explained in Sections 3 and 4, the data quality can be improved significantly when additionally taking local data sources, as well as artificial data sources into account. While local data can be gained out of decentral energy sources, such as solar panels or wind parks, the generation of artificial data is based on calculations of artificial intelligence algorithms. The artificial data thus opens the opportunity to gain a holistic view by closing gaps in which no local data collection is possible due to pure connection for instance. These new data sources improve the total data quality in terms of accuracy and completeness and thus enable the possibility to generate more precise information.

In total, a new data-driven architecture with a modular design has been developed, which can still be extended in case of future adaptions and include more and new data sources. Via a new separation into three layers based on microservices, a high level of data security and a clean separation of incoming data is made possible. First, the Data Integration Layer manages all incoming data flows, filters and cleans it (if necessary) before transferring it into a data warehouse. This is where the second layer, the Data Warehouse Layer, stores and manages all relevant data in different databases. In the final Service Layer, all transferred and stored data is then used for creating solutions for different customers.

Future research will elaborate even further on the CO_2-Compass, its optimization potential and especially the testing in different environments. On the one hand, it is planned that the software will then act as part of a product-service system, by creating and utilizing interfaces with different kinds of electrical devices, such as charging stations or heat-pumps.

On the other hand, there will be additional research related to trigger IoT devices and to control conventional power generators via results of the CO_2-Compass with the aim of minimizing the CO_2 emissions to meet individual emission reduction paths.

ACKNOWLEDGMENT

This research was conducted in the scope of the research project SmartHybrid – Electrical Engineering (ID: ZW 685003732), which is partly funded by the European Regional Development Fund (ERDF) and the State of Lower Saxony (Investitions- und Förderbank Niedersachsen – NBank). We would like to thank them for their support.

REFERENCES

[1] M. Guidolin and R. Guseo, "The German energy transition: Modeling competition and substitution between nuclear power and Renewable Energy Technologies.," *Renewable and Sustainable Energy Reviews*, no. 60, pp. 1498–1504, 2016.

[2] G. Resch, A. Held, T. Faber et al., "Potentials and prospects for renewable energies at global scale.," *Energy policy*, vol. 36, no. 11, pp. 4048–4056, 2008.

[3] S. Shafiei and R. A. Salim, "Non-renewable and renewable energy consumption and CO2 emissions in OECD countries: A comparative analysis.," *Energy policy*, vol. 66, pp. 547–556, 2014.

[4] P. Finn, C. Fitzpatrick, D. Connolly et al., "Facilitation of renewableelectricity using price based appliance control in Ireland's electricity market," *Energy*, vol. 36, no. 5, 2952_2960, 2011.

[5] A. Pina, C. Silva, and P. Ferrão, "The impact of demand side management strategies in the penetration of renewable electricity," *Energy*, vol. 41, no. 1, pp. 128–137, 2012.

[6] L. Hüer, N. Stadie, S. Hagen et al., "Der CO2-Kompass: Konzeption und Entwicklung eines Tools zur emissionsarmen Stromnutzung," *INFORMATIK 2019: 50 Jahre Gesellschaft für Informatik-Informatik für Gesellschaft*, 2019.

[7] K. Heuck, K. D. Dettmann, and D. Schulz, eds., *Überblick über die geschichtliche Entwicklung der elektrischen Energieversorgung*, Springer Vieweg, Wiesbaden, 2013.

[8] G. P. Brasseur, D. Jacob, and S. Schuck-Zöller, *Klimawandel in Deutschland: Entwicklung, Folgen, Risiken und Perspektiven.*, Springer, 2017.

[9] M. Prys-Hansen, M. Lellmann, and M. Röseler, "Die Bedeutung der Klimafinanzierung für den Pariser Klimagipfel 2015," 2015.

[10] J. Rogelj, M. den Elzen, N. Höhne et al., "Paris Agreement climate proposals need a boost to keep warming well below 2 °C," *Nature*, vol. 534, no. 7609, pp. 631–639, 2016.

[11] B. Schlomann and W. Eichhammer, eds., *Energieverbrauch und CO2-Emissionen industrieller Prozesstechnologien: Einsparpotenziale, Hemmnisse und Instrumente.*, Fraunhofer-Verlag, 2013.

[12] P. Icha, "Entwicklung der spezifischen Kohlendioxid-Emissionen des deutschen Strommix in den Jahren 1990 - 2018," *Umweltbundesamt*, 2019.

[13] European Parliament and Council, *Commission Regulation (EU) No 543/2013 of 14 June 2013 on submission and publication of data in electricity markets and amending Annex I to Regulation (EC) No 714/2009*, 2013.

[14] M. Kahles, "Überprüfung der einheitlichen deutschen Stromgebotszone nach der Elektrizitätsbinnenmarkt-Verordnung," *Würzburger Berichte zum Umweltenergierecht*, no. 44, 2019.

[15] J. Aengenvoort and H. Sämisch, "Die Illusion einer Kupferplatte," https://www.next-kraftwerke.de/energie-blog/kupferplatte-stromnetz.

[16] S. Newman, "Building microservices: designing fine-grained systems," *O'Reilly Media Inc.*, 2015.

[17] S. Newman, "Monolith to Microservices: Evolutionary Patterns to Transform Your Monolith," *O'Reilly Media*, 2019.

[18] J. Rowley, "The wisdom hierarchy: Representations of the DIKW hierarchy.," *Journal of Information Science*, vol. 33, no. 2, pp. 163–180, 2007.

[19] S. Hochreiter and J. Schmidhuber, "Long short-term memory," *Neural Computation (Journal)*, vol. 9, no. 8, pp. 1735–1780, 1997.

An Approach for Configuration of the Industry 4.0 Technologies on Production Systems

Daning Wang, Christoph Knieke, Helge Fischer, Andreas Rausch
Technische Universität Clausthal, Institute for Software and Systems Engineering
Arnold-Sommerfeld-Straße 1, 38678 Clausthal-Zellerfeld, Germany
Email: {daning.wang|christoph.knieke|helge.fischer|andreas.rausch}@tu-clausthal.de

Abstract—**From embedded systems to intelligent embedded systems and Cyber-physical Systems (CPSs), the production system is always evolved with the challenge of rapid technology change. But the redesign and development of a complex production system is considered a hard task and with high risk. This paper provides an approach for the managed evolution of a complex production system, which is understood as a CPS and presents a unified view of computing systems that interact strongly with their physical environment. This approach is used to guarantee the consistency between the system evolution requirements and system implementation during the evolution of this production system, which is driven by the using of Industry 4.0 (I4.0) technologies. Furthermore, the cost of implementation can be optimized with this approach. At the end of this paper, two cases are used to evaluate this approach to ascertain the suitability for the managed evolution of production systems.**

Keywords–Architecture Evolution; Industry 4.0; Configuration of Components; Cyber-physical System; Production System.

I. Introduction

The digital manufacturing and smart factory are two important application areas of I4.0 technologies, which are synonymous with highly flexible production. I4.0 technologies enable companies to offer highly individualized products by linking the internet to conventional processes and services, and to actively involve their customers very early in the development process [1]. The CPS plays an important role in the areas of digital manufacturing and smart manufacturing, where it combines the physical part with the cyber part in a holistic way. The two parts have to flexibly and dependably adapt to each other to adapt to the changing system environment.

A production system is a classical CPS, which consists of the physical part like assembly stations, warehouses, transport belts, etc. and the cyber part like the control programs and the software protocols, etc. These are connected together as an integrated complex production system. In general, a production system is not defined perfectly at the beginning and should permanently be operated in order to raise the productivity or meet changing requirements [2].

In this paper, an approach is introduced to generate a set of configuration plans for the implementation of the evolved production system according to the introduction of the I4.0 technologies on the ongoing production system. In order to describe this managed evolution of the production system, the ongoing production system is modeled with a component oriented modeling language, where the components in this production system are connected together as an integrated model and input model for the approach. This model is equivalently transformed to a graph representation, which keeps the system structure and properties of the components in the model [3]. This graph generates a set of different graphs by using of graph-based algorithms, where each generated graph represents a configuration plan of the new production system. By applying user defined combination rules, the configuration plans, which can not meet the requirements of the new production system, are detected and canceled. The rest of the generated configuration plans meet the defined combination rules and requirements in the new production system. The ones that are cost-optimal will then be simulated and implemented as a new production system. This implemented configuration plan can be continually evaluated into the second iteration of system evolution.

The paper is organized as follows: Section II gives an overview on the related work in the field of production system evolution. The system requirements, restructure of the input models, and the implementation of this approach are introduced in Section III. Two application cases are introduced in Section IV to evaluate the efficiency of the approach. Finally, Section V concludes.

II. Related Work

I4.0 is the short name for the fourth industrial evolution. The technologies of I4.0 can improve the quality and competitiveness of products, but there are few opportunities for the Small and Medium-size Enterprises (SMEs) to participate and take advantages of this trend. One major challenge is the lack of IT specialists to develop technical innovations. For example, recent studies in Germany [4] [5] show that three-quarters of the SMEs are unable to find the proper experts to bring IT innovations and the digital transformation forward. Another associated issue is also the difficulty to gather specific information which they need to adopt I4.0 technologies and solutions.

An information portal provides access to the research results developed by Stechert and Franke [6], where the basic approaches for digitization were revealed. These approaches were used to help the digitization of the product development, which was driven by the functional areas of the I4.0 technologies. However, the applications of concrete I4.0 technologies were not introduced in this study.

In the project "Intro 4.0" [7], the specific I4.0 solutions were developed and introduced to the participating industrial enterprises. The findings of the implementation of these solutions were used to derive the recommendations of these I4.0 solutions to more industrial partners. However, a comparison of the alternative I4.0 solutions was not considered.

In the work of Simko et al. [8], a CPS specific modeling language (CyPhyML) was developed and introduced to model the structure and behaviour of physical and cyber components in a CPS. The CyPhyML supported not only the non-causal modeling, but also the causal modeling in a hierarchical composition. The authors formalized the CyPhyML model with a tuple structure, which comprises sets of components by different types, sets of ports, sets of containment functions for design elements and component assemblies, and sets of flows by different types. An important advantage of the CyPhyML was that the structural and behavioural specifications of a CPS can be written in one model, whereby both can be used for deductive reasoning.

Blochwitz et al. [9] developed a standardized interface named Functional Mock-up Interface (FMI) and introduced it in their work. This FMI is based on the framework of the MODELISAR project and was used for the coupling of various simulation modules in MODELISAR. That made it possible to integrate the different simulation modules together with the common interfaces. In the work of Blochwitz et al., a master simulation is introduced to couple the appropriate different modules together. But the data exchange between the different modules is not supported.

To summarize, none of the approaches provides a suitable configuration plan for implementation by correlating of the concrete I4.0 technologies and solutions during the evolution of production system. Thus, in this paper we introduce an approach which generates the configuration plan of a production system integrating the corresponding I4.0 technologies and solutions. That enables the evaluation of the proposed integration before to implement a new production system.

III. Approach

The approach has to be realized within the scope of a suitable environment and a clear implementation process, which will be introduced in this section. At first, the system requirements of this application are briefly explained. Subsequently, the restructuring of the input models for this application is introduced. Then, the implementation of this approach is introduced by using a class diagram. The necessary mathematical basics and fundamentals of this approach were already introduced and exampled in a previous paper [10].

A. System requirements

Our application is named "Solution generation system for the managed evolution of a production system". The application contains a Graphical User Interface (GUI) and a part called "Generating". The system environment consists of an *industry 4.0 technologies expert*, and a *production system planner*. The expert offers a set of existing I4.0 technologies for the managed evolution of the production system by using the GUI after his professional analysis on the ongoing production system. The production system designer models the ongoing production system and gives this model as an input model into the application by using the GUI. Meanwhile, he/she has to define the configuration rules, which describe the allowed configurations between the components in this production system. By using this application, the production system designer gets a set of alternative models as the solutions of the managed evolution of this production system, which is visualized by the GUI. The algorithms and functions of the approach are implemented in the "Generating" part.

B. Restructure of the input models

In practice, a production system is typically described and analyzed by using different models, where each model focuses on a fixed set of concerns on the system. That enables the system planners and engineers to understand a production system from different disciplines. The input model describing the ongoing production system will be reformed with a key-value data structure in a pair of documents, which serves as the basis for the later data processing. One document describes every component in the production system, and the other one represents the connection relationships between the components. In addition, the I4.0 technologies offered by the expert have to be described with the same data structure as the components in the production system. The configuration rules are reformed to a two tuple structure, which represents the configuration relationships from one object to another object. Besides, the targeted production system models have the same representation data structure as the ongoing production system.

C. Implementation

A class diagram is used to describe the system structure reflecting the functional requirements of the application and represents the organization and arrangement of interrelated components in a system. The class diagram in Figure 1 shows the system structure of this application, which is implemented by the object oriented programming language Java. The class `home` implements the graphical user interface for the I4.0 technologies expert and the production system designer. It provides the generic organizing and structuring of this application and the application starts with the main function in this class. Class `Algorithms` is an algorithms library comprising all of the algorithms in this application like the algorithms for path morphism, model transformation to graph structure, etc., which are called by the class `home` to implement the functional requirements in this application. Class `SystemRules` provides the combination rules for the class `Algorithms` and exchanges the information with the GUI. The transformed input model is stored in classes `node`, `ibdNode`, and `graph` providing the graph structure to keep the descriptions of the components and connection relationships in the production system.

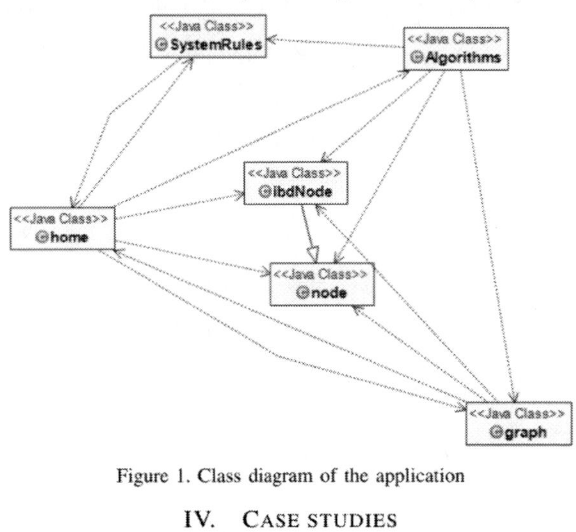

Figure 1. Class diagram of the application

IV. Case studies

In this section, two application cases are introduced to evaluate the efficiency of the approach. On the one hand, the development risks during the managed evolution of a production system should be reduced by using this approach. On the other hand, the reconstruction costs of the implementation for the targeted production system should be optimized. Therefore, the evaluation can be divided into two parts: the development risks evaluation and the economic evaluation. One case in this section is a laboratory model of a conveyor system with *Automated Storage and Retrieval System* (ASRS). The other one is part of a project named: *Methods and tools for the synergetic conception and evaluation of Industry 4.0 solutions*, in short "Synus".

A. *Case 1: Conveyor System with ASRS*

This laboratory model of a conveyor system with ASRS is defined as an ongoing production system and modeled with Internal Block Diagram (IBD), which provides the internal view of a system block and represents the assembly of all blocks within the main system block. The composite blocks are connected to each other through ports/interfaces and connectors. In this case, the mechanical part in this system comprises four conveyor belts in a cycle form, a buffer belt, a RFID read/write sensor, a photoelectric sensor, a warehouse and a gripper robot. The automated tasks in this system are controlled through two industrial programmable logic controllers (PLC) of Siemens. The mechanical part and the automated part are connect to each other over the Ethernet to ensure the safety and reliability of the connection. A computer is used as a human-machine-interface (HMI) to exchange the information between workers and PLCs. In this conveyor system, wares like machine parts should be transported with the conveyor system from warehouse to the hall for the painting and dry processes by using the gripper robot, conveyor belts and the buffer-belt in accordance with the production plan. One worker (the Worker 2 in Figure 2) defines the color information of the ware by using the computer and the RFID read/write sensor, when any ware arrives at the RFID sensor. The wares will continue to be transported to a painting and dry hall. After the painting and dry processes, the wares will be transported back to the warehouse by using the buffer belt and conveyor belts and wait for the following manufacturing processes. The storage of painted wares must follow certain rules and standards, e.g., the wares with different types, sizes, materials or paint colors can be divided into different groups and stored in the designated location or floor. For this reason, a worker (the Worker 1 in Figure 2) stands by the buffer belt and sorts the wares by a predefined sorting order. This is a manual task.

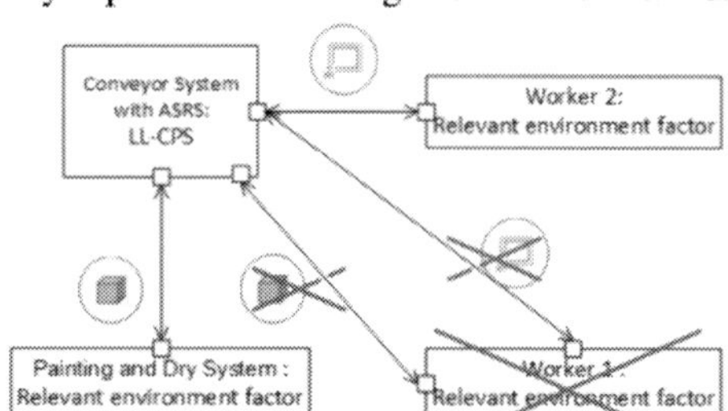

Figure 2. Comparison of the system environments between the ongoing system and the targeted system

From the perspective of production efficiency, this ongoing system is not perfect, because the manual work of Worker 1 in this ongoing system could cause an increase in production time. An automated machine definitely would have higher production efficiency. Furthermore, the worker who stands by the buffer belt repeatedly performs the same task (sorting the wares), which increases the risk of making mistakes. In many factories, this is a main reason for the poor product quality.

Hence, a new system as a targeted system is clearly defined. By using the approach, a set of solutions are generated. Therein two solutions are implemented and used to evaluate the efficiency of the approach. The first solution is named "solution 1". There is no worker (Worker 1 in Figure 2) standing by the buffer belt to sort the wares that come back from the painting hall in solution 1. Instead of the worker, a new RFID read sensor is procured and installed on the conveyor belt (in Figure 3). It is used to read the color information from the wares. Simultaneously, this new sensor will also replace the account work of the wares of the photoelectric sensor (`PH: Sensor` in Figure 3). Not only the physical components, but also the software code in the control system and information system has to be changed to adapt to the reconstruction in the system environment and mechanical system.

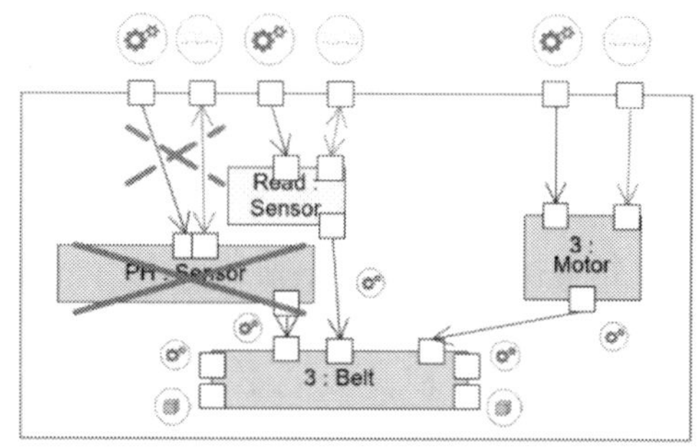

Figure 3. Comparison of the mechanical components between the ongoing system and solution 1

Figure 4 shows the changes of the software code in the control system of the targeted system compared with the ongoing system. In this figure, symbol "-" marks the deleted code parts during the managed evolution of this ongoing system. The symbol "+" marks the new added code parts and the "△" labels the code parts that changed the executing place.

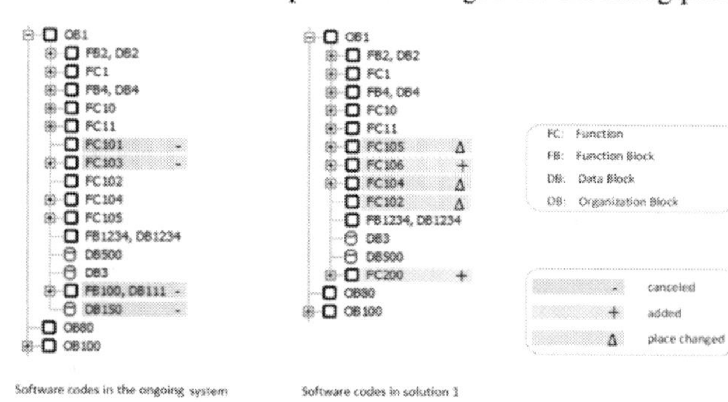

Figure 4. Comparison of software code in the PLC control system between the ongoing system and solution 1

The second solution is solution 2, where the system environments have the same changes as the solution 1 (see Figure 2). But the components in mechanical system have no changes compared with the ongoing system. In order to reach the requirement in the targeted system, the existing RFID read/write sensor is used to write the color information into the ware, when the ware reaches it for the first time, and it is reused to read the color information from the ware, when the ware reaches it again. In this situation, the other mechanical components and software code have to be adapted by using the controllers to reach this task. Accordingly, all four conveyor belts have to continually transport the wares in a cycle after the painting color process to enable the wares to reach the existing RFID read/write sensor again. Meanwhile, the gripper and the photoelectric sensor are blocked to let the ware run in a cycle and activates again, when the read/write sensor obtains the full information of all wares.

In this case, the matching of functions is identified as the most import risk factor for the development risk evaluation of the managed evolution of production systems. The functional requirements are specified with the following points: (1) There is no worker standing by the buffer belt to sort the wares. (2) The color information is read by using the RFID sensor. (3) The wares are retrieved through the gripper robot with the sort information in the predefined floor in the warehouse. In order to evaluate these two solutions, we have implemented these two configuration plans as two production systems and evaluate their development risks with the specified functional requirements. The solution 1 and 2 satisfied all of the functional requirements.

For the evaluation of the economic efficiency, the direct costs are defined as the exclusive costs in the total reconstruction. That means, the indirect costs, the non-construction related costs, the time dependent costs, the software code rewriting costs, e.g., are not included in the total reconstruction costs. The reconstruction costs for different components are specified by characters. The addition of a new hardware component is among the most expensive in all of the reconstruction actions. The modifications of hardware and software components incur more costs than their deletions. After the evaluation, the solution 2 is confirmed as the optimal solution in the set of all solutions, which were generated by using the approach.

B. Case 2: Project Synus

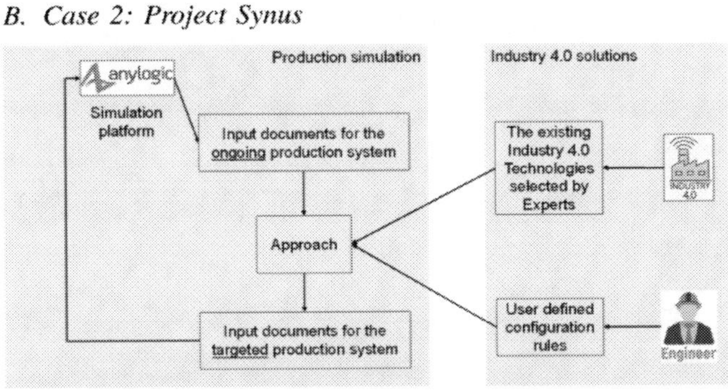

Figure 5. System architecture in project Synus

Figure 5 shows a concept for the system architecture in project "Synus" [11]. The evaluating factors like production time, energy consumption and processing costs are extracted for the evaluation of the ongoing production system. During the analysis of the result of the evaluation by the experts, some current I4.0 technologies are proposed to improve the production performance of the ongoing production system. The application of these technologies drives the evolution of this ongoing system. The ongoing system is simulated by using a simulation software "AnyLogic" [12]. Our approach generates a set of configurations of the components in the targeted status of this production system, which have to meet the configuration rules defined by system engineer. One of these configurations will then be simulated and implemented as a new production system.

V. Conclusion and Further Work

We introduced an approach to generate a set of configuration plans as the solutions for the implementation for the evolved production system according to the using of the I4.0 technologies on an ongoing production system. The approach was implemented within the scope of a Java environment and a clear implementation process.

We conducted two case studies to evaluate the approach focusing on the development risks evaluation and the economic evaluation. The case studies could show the applicability, efficiency, and suitability of the approach in example product systems. Moreover, development risks could be minimized by providing appropriate solutions for configuration plans. Furthermore cost estimations have turned out to be beneficial to optimize the overall costs by selecting an economic solution.

The underlying concept of managed evolution of production systems is currently being formalized including the formal descriptions and transformations. The results will be published in a future work.

Acknowledgement

This paper evolved of the research project "Synus" (Methods and tools for the synergetic conception and evaluation of Industry 4.0 solutions) which is funded by the European Regional Development Fund (EFRE — ZW 6-85012454) and managed by the Project Management Agency NBank.

References

[1] MCKINSEY DIGITAL, "Industry 4.0: How to navigate digitization of the manufacturing sector." [Online]. Available: https://www.mckinsey.de/files/mck_industry_40_report.pdf

[2] H. Giese, B. Rumpe, B. Schätz, and J. Sztipanovits, "Science and engineering of cyber-physical systems (dagstuhl seminar 11441)," Dagstuhl Reports, vol. 1, no. 11, 2012.

[3] H. Grönniger, J. O. Ringert, and B. Rumpe, "System Model-Based Definition of Modeling Language Semantics," Formal techniques for distributed systems, 2009, pp. 152–166.

[4] Institut der deutschen Wirtschaft Köln e.V. and VDI Verein Deutscher Ingenieure e.V., "Ingenieurmonitor 2019/I - Der regionale Arbeitsmarkt in den Ingenieurberufen." Institut der deutschen Wirtschaft Köln e.V., 2019. [Online]. Available: https://www.vdi.de/

[5] DZ BANK AG, "Mittelstand im Mittelpunkt - Ausgabe Frühjahr 2017." DZ BANK AG, Frankfurt am Main, 2017. [Online]. Available: https://www.dzbank.de/

[6] C. Stechert and H.-J. Franke, "Requirements Models for Modular Products," ICORD 09: Proc. of the 2nd International Conference on Research into Design, Bangalore, India, 2009.

[7] J. Schmitt, D. Inkermann, C. Stechert, A. Raatz, and T. Vietor, "Requirement Oriented Reconfiguration of Parallel Robotic Systems," Robotic Systems-Applications, Control and Programming, 2012.

[8] G. Simko, D. Lindecker, T. Levendovszky, S. Neema, and J. Sztipanovits, "Specification of Cyber-Physical Components with Formal Semantics – Integration and Composition," Specification of cyber-physical components with formal semantics - Integration and composition, vol. 8107 LNCS, 2013, pp. 471–487.

[9] T. Blochwitz et al., "Functional Mockup Interface 2.0: The Standard for Tool independent Exchange of Simulation Models," in Proc. of the 9th International MODELICA Conference, no. 076, 2012, pp. 173–184.

[10] D. Wang, C. Knieke, and A. Rausch, "Data-driven Component Configuration in Production Systems," in Proc. of the ADAPTIVE 2019: The Eleventh International Conference on Adaptive and Self-Adaptive Systems and Applications. IARIA, 2019, pp. 44–47.

[11] [Online]. Available: https://isse.tu-clausthal.de/en/research/current-projects/synus/

[12] [Online]. Available: https://www.anylogic.com

International Academy, Research, and Industry Association (IARIA)
412 Derby Way
Wilmington, DE 19810

ISBN 978-1-7138-1208-1

CURRAN ASSOCIATES INC.
proceedings.com

Eighth International Conference on Information, Process, and Knowledge Management (eKNOW 2016)

Held at DigitalWorld 2016

Venice, Italy
24 - 28 April 2016

IARIA